MW01097556

The Professional Chef's® Book of CHARCUTERIE

The Professional Chef's® Book of CHARCUTERIE

PATES, TERRINES, TIMBALES, GALANTINES, SAUSAGES, AND OTHER CULINARY DELIGHTS

T.G. MUELLER

VAN NOSTRAND REINHOLD
New York

Library of Congress Catalog Card Number 86-30768
ISBN 0-442-26425-9

Printed in the United States of America
Designed by Sharon DuGoff Egana
Illustrated by Michael Grejniec

Van Nostrand Reinhold
115 Fifth Avenue
New York, New York 10003

Van Nostrand Reinhold (International) Limited
11 New Fetter Lane
London EC4P 4EE, England

Van Nostrand Reinhold
480 La Trobe Street
Melbourne, Victoria 3000, Australia

Macmillan of Canada
Division of Canada Publishing Corporation
164 Commander Boulevard
Agincourt, Ontario M1S 3C7, Canada

2 4 6 8 10 12 14 16 15 13 11 9 7 5 3

Library of Congress Cataloging-in-Publication Data
Mueller, T. G., 1952–
The professional chef's book of charcuterie.

Includes index.
1. Cookery (Pork) 2. Cookery, French. I. Title.
II. Title: Charcuterie.
TX749.M92 1987 641.6'6 86-30768
ISBN 0-442-26425-9

Thank you . . .

A special thanks to
my family, friends, and acquaintances
who contributed to
the making of this book.

Contents

Introduction

Charcuterie has come a long way since medieval France, when the term defined the products of the pork butcher's shop. Derived from the words *chair cuit,* charcuterie translated to cooked meat.

In the Middle Ages, strict separation between fisheries, slaughterhouses, butchers, and prepared-meat shops was enforced in order to control disease. Not until the sixteenth century did charcutiers, as these cooks were called, legally obtain the right to butcher their own pigs and sell both raw and cooked pork products. Charcutiers were permitted to sell salted herrings and a few other fish only during Lent, when meat products were forbidden. As legal restrictions eased and as other meats became more abundant and available, charcutiers included them in their repertoire. As time went on fish and vegetable preparations also showed up in their shops.

This book takes the meaning of charcuterie and extends it to our times. Charcuterie no longer is limited to the preparation of only certain food items, but instead the word is used in a broader sense to represent a method of cooking and a manner of serving food.

Charcuterie has come a long way. International and ethnic influences have broadened the scope of charcuterie so that today it comprises a vast variety of foods. Savory pies and filled pastries come in all shapes and sizes. Sausages can be made of fruits, fish, or vegetables. Meats, as well as fish and vegetables, are stuffed and poached to become galantines or are roasted into ballotines. There are cheese rillettes and dessert timbales. The gastronomic possibilities are limitless.

British, French, German, Italian, and Scandinavian settlers introduced pâtés and other charcuterie to this country. Italian families welcomed the arrival of spring by preparing *pizza rustica,* a traditional Easter pâté of cheese and sausage. The British brought with them deep-dish pies filled with leftover meats and vegetables sealed in pastry. The Scandinavians baked loaves of cooked meats in sour cream crusts and made rye pasties called *kalakukko,* or "fish fowl." These pasties resembled the shape of a bird, were stuffed with fish and pork, weighed up to eleven pounds, and could take five hours to bake. Variations of the Scandinavian and of the Cornish pasty remain popular lunchtime foods. Today Japanese culinary style exerts a new growing influence on charcuterie.

Immigrants of all times created new recipes by adapting their native charcuterie to ingredients available in the different regions of the New World. The European terrine evolved into the first early American meat loaf, initially made of game and later of pork, liver, and beef. The English-inspired iron kettles of pot pies that were slowly cooked in the fire's embers remain a favorite today among the Pennsylvania Dutch.

Smithfield hams from Virginia, beef and pork sausages from Pennsylvania, shellfish boudins of scallops, shrimp, and lobster, and vegetable terrines studded with colorful arrangements of garden vegetables all exemplify contemporary charcuterie.

In fact, charcuterie is one of the most adaptable of cooking methods. It lends itself to an improvisational approach to cooking. There is nothing exacting, rigid, or complicated about it. Once familiar with the fundamentals, you can invent your own specialties, using ingredients on hand or whatever is freshest and in season at the market. This book is designed to instruct you in the fundamentals and to aid you in experimentation.

Making your own charcuterie allows you to control the cost, assure high quality, and serve dishes quite out of the ordinary. You can transform leftover chicken gumbo into elegant yet inexpensive mousselines and fillings or turn an extra bit of smoked trout into delicious timbales within half an hour. Small pastry crescents or horns can be filled with chicken, spinach, ham, or cheese. For an unusual hors d'oeuvre, make Pâtésticks by wrapping a filling in a rectangle of dough, rolling it up like a breadstick, and swirling it in sesame seeds.

An extravagant and costly terrine consists of veal, sweetbreads, and morels, but an equally exquisite terrine can be prepared for a fraction of the cost. Substitute chicken or turkey farce for the veal, use diced meats instead of sweetbreads, and add sautéed mushrooms for morels. There are no rules to cooking charcuterie; the only imperative is fresh ingredients of high quality.

Charcuterie may be served morning, noon, and night—with cocktails, as appetizers, or as a main course, a side dish, a snack, or a dessert. They are good accompaniments to a hearty soup with a crusty loaf of bread in winter or to a light, crisp salad in summer. Although usually eaten slightly chilled, many of these dishes are equally delicious hot.

The first chapter of this book, *Fundamentals of Charcuterie,* illustrates and explains the hows and whys of making charcuterie. It describes the basic ingredients and gives step-by-step instructions for preparing a farce or a mousseline, stocks, aspics, chaud-froid, and doughs and pastry. Both classic and quick methods are given.

Each chapter of recipes opens with tips on preparing the charcuterie, followed by descriptions of general procedures. For example, Chapter 2, *Pâtés, Terrines, and Savory Pies,* demonstrates assembling a pâté, and Chapter 4, *Galantines, Ballotines, and Stuffed Meats,* illustrates how to bone poultry for a galantine or ballotine.

How food looks is as much a part of dining as how it tastes. It should excite both the eyes and the palate; its presentation should seduce and its taste satisfy. This book emphasizes the aesthetics of cooking. A cook, like a painter or a sculptor, learns to combine different colors, shapes, and textures of foods to create exciting new meals. Most recipes offer ideas for garnishing and presenting the final dish, along with suggestions for condiments, sauces, or dressings to accent their flavor. Chapter 6, *Condiments and Accompaniments,* contains recipes for many of the accompaniments recommended.

This cookbook presents the enormous versatility and convenience of charcuterie, and demystifies its presentation. *The Professional Chef's Book of Charcuterie* is designed to nurture the accomplished cook and to inspire the professional or gourmet to experiment with new ways of preparing and serving pâtés, terrines, timbales, and other fine charcuterie. Be bold and your creativity will emerge.

CHAPTER ONE

Fundamentals of Charcuterie

The fundamentals covered in this chapter are easy to learn and readily accessible for future reference. As with most of the recipes in this book, you can vary and recombine ingredients and cooking methods to make new dishes.

DOUGHS AND PASTRIES

Encase a terrine in pastry and you have a pâté. The choice of dough depends upon the texture desired and upon the delicacy of the filling. You can achieve different textures and flavors by changing the seasonings.

Classic Brioche Dough

Brioche forms a rich, tasty crust for pâtés and sausages. Prebaked individual or large brioches can be hollowed out and stuffed with savory or sweet fillings.

YIELD: about 2½ pounds

1 tablespoon (envelope) active dry yeast
2 teaspoons warm water
1½ teaspoons salt
2 tablespoons honey or sugar (3 tablespoons for a dessert pâté)
1½ tablespoons warm milk
3¾ cups all-purpose flour
6 eggs
¾ pound unsalted butter, melted but not hot

Dissolve the yeast in the warm water. In a mixing bowl, dissolve the salt and honey in the warm milk. Add the flour to the milk mixture, then add the dissolved yeast and water. Mix. Add 4 eggs at once and continue to beat until the dough feels firm and smooth. Mix the 2 remaining eggs with the melted butter. Add to the dough and beat for 10 to 20 minutes, until the dough is no longer sticky.

Place the dough in a large bowl, and cover with a damp cloth. Let it rise, undisturbed, at room temperature for 2 to 2½ hours. When the dough has risen to twice its size, punch it down and stretch it a couple of times. Let the dough rise in the refrigerator for another 2 or 3 hours, until doubled in volume. Punch the dough down again, cover it tightly, and refrigerate for 12 hours or overnight.

On a floured surface, roll out the brioche dough as required by the recipe. Once formed and filled with stuffing, let the dough rise for 1 to 1½ hours before baking.

Note: You can freeze brioche dough for 1 month by wrapping it tightly in plastic wrap and then aluminum foil. To use the dough, let it thaw for 24 hours in the refrigerator before rolling it out.

Quick Brioche Dough

YIELD: about 2 pounds

1 teaspoon honey or sugar (2 teaspoons for a dessert crust)
½ cup warm milk
2 tablespoons (envelopes) active dry yeast
4 cups all-purpose flour
½ teaspoon salt
1 cup unsalted butter, melted but not hot
4 eggs, lightly beaten

Dissolve the honey in the milk and stir in the yeast. Let stand for 5 to 10 minutes, until the surface is frothy.

Combine the flour and salt in a mixing bowl. Mix the butter and eggs together and add to the yeast mixture. Pour the yeast-butter mixture into the flour and beat until a dough forms. Knead the dough on a floured surface until it feels firm and smooth. Place the ball of dough in a large bowl and cover with a damp cloth. Let the dough rise, undisturbed, in a warm place for 30 minutes.

Lightly knead the risen dough on a floured surface and roll out or form the brioche to the size you need. Once formed and filled, let the dough rise for 15 minutes before baking.

White Yeast Dough

Bread dough forms a soft but sturdy crust.

YIELD: about 3¾ pounds

1 tablespoon (envelope) active dry yeast
3¾ cups warm water
½ teaspoon plus 1 tablespoon honey or sugar
7 to 8 cups all-purpose flour
3 tablespoons vegetable oil
1½ teaspoons salt

In a large mixing bowl, dissolve the yeast in ¼ cup of the warm water and stir in the ½ teaspoon honey. Let the mixture stand in a warm place for about 10 minutes, until the yeast is frothy. Add the remaining warm water and mix in 4 cups of the flour, 1 cup at a time. Cover the bowl and let the mixture rise in a warm place for 1 to 2 hours, until it forms a high, bubbly sponge.

Mix 1 tablespoon honey, the oil, and salt into the sponge. Add 2 cups flour and work into a dough. Scrape the sponge onto a heavily floured surface, and knead in the remaining flour or more as you need. Knead the dough for 10 minutes more. It will feel firm and elastic.

Place the ball of dough in a lightly greased bowl and turn to coat on all sides. Cover with a damp cloth and let it rise in a warm place, until doubled in volume, for 45 minutes to 1½ hours. Punch down the dough and knead it for 1 or 2 minutes to release any gas bubbles.

At this point, you can freeze the dough by wrapping it airtight in plastic. Thaw at room temperature, shape, and complete the rise.

Roll out or form the dough as required by the recipe. Allow the dough to rise for 10 minutes before baking.

Variations

For a softer crumb, substitute warm milk for the 3½ cups warm water.

Whole-Wheat Yeast Dough

The vitamin C tablet and gluten flour produce a better-rising dough. The soy flour and nonfat dry milk give the bread a soft, moist crumb.

YIELD: about 3¾ pounds

1 50-milligram vitamin C tablet, crushed (optional)
3¼ cups warm water
½ teaspoon plus 1 tablespoon honey or sugar
1 tablespoon (envelope) active dry yeast
¾ to 1 cup nonfat dry milk
5½ to 7 cups whole-wheat flour
¾ cup soy flour
¾ cup gluten flour
1 tablespoon salt
2 tablespoons vegetable oil

In a large bowl, combine the crushed vitamin C tablet with ¼ cup of the warm water. Stir in the ½ teaspoon honey and the yeast. Let the mixture stand in a warm place for about 10 minutes, until the yeast is frothy. Add the remaining warm water and the nonfat dry milk. Mix in 4 cups of the whole-wheat flour and cover the bowl. Let the mixture rise for 1½ to 2 hours, until a bubbly sponge forms.

Mix 1 tablespoon honey, the soy and gluten flours, salt, and oil into the sponge. Scrape the sponge onto a heavily floured surface and knead in the remaining whole-wheat flour or more as needed. When the dough forms, knead it for 10 minutes more. The dough will feel firm and elastic, dry on the outside, and slightly moist on the inside.

Place the ball of dough in a lightly greased bowl and turn to coat on all sides. Cover with a damp cloth and let it rise for 1½ to 2 hours, until doubled in volume.

Punch down the dough and knead it for a minute more to release any gas bubbles.

At this point you can freeze the dough by wrapping it airtight in plastic. Thaw at room temperature, shape, and complete the rise.

Roll out or form the dough as required by the recipe. Allow the dough to rise for 10 minutes before baking.

Variations:
To use whole milk, eliminate the nonfat dry milk and substitute warm whole milk for 3 cups warm water.

Rye Dough (Scandinavian Limpa)

Limpa makes a sturdy crust for meat and fish pasties. This recipe, which makes enough for 12 to 14 pasties, can be doubled.

YIELD: about 1¼ pounds

¼ cup hot tap water
½ cup beer or ale, heated to lukewarm
1 tablespoon honey or sugar
1 tablespoon unsalted butter, melted but not hot
1 teaspoon salt
½ tablespoon (½ envelope) active dry yeast
¼ cup warm water
½ teaspoon cardamom
1½ to 1¾ cups all-purpose flour
1¼ cups rye flour

Combine the hot water, beer, honey, butter, and salt in a mixing bowl and cool to lukewarm. Dissolve the yeast in the ¼ cup warm water, then add it to the first mixture. Gradually mix in 1½ cups of all-purpose flour and the cardamom. Knead well to develop the gluten. Slowly add the rye flour to make a soft dough. If necessary, add the remaining all-purpose flour. On a lightly floured surface, knead the dough for 10 minutes, adding more flour if the dough is too sticky. (It should remain slightly sticky.)

Place the ball of dough in a greased bowl and turn to coat on all sides. Cover with a damp cloth, and let it rise in a warm place for about 1 hour, or until doubled in volume. Punch down the dough and knead for 2 minutes more.

Roll out or form the dough as required by the recipe. Allow the dough to rise again for about 45 minutes before baking.

Pizza Dough

This dough provides a soft but firm crust.

YIELD: about 1½ pounds

1 tablespoon (envelope) active dry yeast
½ cup warm water
3 cups semolina or unbleached white flour
1 teaspoon salt
1 tablespoon olive or vegetable oil

Dissolve the yeast in the warm water. Combine the flour and salt in a mixing bowl, forming a well in the center. Slowly mix in the dissolved yeast and the oil. Continue mixing until the dough forms a ball. Remove the dough and knead it for 5 to 10 minutes.

Place the dough in a lightly greased bowl and cover with a damp cloth. Let it rise for about 3 hours, until doubled in volume. The dough will keep another 2 hours if necessary.

Punch the dough down and roll it out on a lightly floured surface.

Note: To freeze, roll the dough out and wrap tightly in plastic. It will keep for up to 3 months.

Whole-Wheat Pizza Dough

YIELD: about 2½ pounds

1 tablespoon (envelope) active dry yeast
½ cup warm water
¼ teaspoon honey or sugar
4 to 5 cups whole-wheat flour
½ teaspoon salt
1 tablespoon olive or vegetable oil
1 to 1½ cups water

Dissolve the yeast in ½ cup warm water, add the honey, and let stand for about 10 minutes, until surface is frothy. Combine the flour and salt in a mixing bowl, forming a well in the center. Mix in the dissolved yeast, oil, and 1 cup water. Continue mixing until the dough forms a ball, adding more water if needed. Remove the dough and knead for 8 to 10 minutes.

Place the dough in a lightly greased bowl and cover with a damp cloth. Let it rise for about 1 hour, until doubled in volume. Punch the dough down and roll it out on a lightly floured surface.

Note: To freeze, roll the dough out and wrap tightly in plastic. It will keep for up to 3 months.

Potato Gnocchi Dough

YIELD: about 2½ pounds

2 pounds potatoes (about 3 large)
1½ to 2 cups whole-wheat, semolina, or unbleached white flour
1 egg, lightly beaten

Steam or boil the potatoes until tender, then drain. When cool enough to handle, peel the potatoes, and shred them using a grater, a food mill, or a potato ricer.

Combine the shredded potatoes and egg. Add about 1½ cups flour and knead. Add the remaining flour as needed. Depending on the moisture content, some potatoes require more or less flour. The mixture is ready when it is soft but still slightly sticky.

Variations
You can make the dough without an egg by adding 2 tablespoons of water to the shredded potatoes instead.

Sweet-Potato Gnocchi Dough

This dough goes well with sweet fillings.

YIELD: about 2½ pounds

2 pounds sweet potatoes or yams
1½ to 2 cups whole-wheat, semolina, or unbleached white flour
1 teaspoon vanilla extract
1 teaspoon cinnamon
½ teaspoon nutmeg
1 egg

Follow the instructions for Potato Gnocchi Dough, adding the flavorings to the egg before combining it with the potatoes.

Pâté Pastry

Pâté dough makes a strong, all-purpose crust for soft or firm fillings. This recipe makes enough to line an 8-cup mold.

YIELD: about 1½ pounds

3½ cups all-purpose flour
1 teaspoon salt
¾ cup lard, broken into small pieces
¾ cup warm water
1 egg yolk

Combine the flour and salt in a bowl. Cut in the pieces of lard and mix until the flour becomes coarse, like meal. Blend ½ cup warm water with the egg yolk, and gradually add it to the flour mixture. Add the remaining water as needed. Remove the dough when it forms a ball. Do not overwork the dough. Cover with a damp cloth or plastic and let it rest for 4 to 5 hours. Roll out the dough on a lightly floured surface.

Note: Sealed in plastic wrap, this dough keeps for about 3 days, refrigerated, or 3 months if frozen. To use, defrost overnight in the refrigerator. If the dough is difficult to roll out, allow it to come to room temperature, then roll.

Hot-Water Crust

This dough makes a strong, dense crust for sealing in juices. The recipe can be halved, doubled, or multiplied up to ten times without changing the proportions.

YIELD: about 1½ pounds

⅞ cup water
¾ cup lard or unsalted butter
4 cups all-purpose flour
1 teaspoon salt
2½ teaspoons confectioners' sugar (optional)

Bring the water and lard to a boil. Meanwhile, mix the flour, salt, and sugar (if dough is to be used as a dessert crust) in a bowl, forming a well in the center. Slowly, pour the boiling water and lard into the well. Mix quickly and thoroughly until a smooth dough forms. Cover and let stand for about 30 minutes. While the dough is still warm and firm but malleable, roll it out on a lightly floured surface or shape it with your hands.

Short-Crust Pastry

This pastry provides a flaky crust for dessert, vegetable, or seafood preparations. The recipe can be doubled or tripled.

YIELD: about 1 pound

2½ cups all-purpose or pastry flour
½ teaspoon salt
¾ cup cold unsalted butter, broken into small pieces
1 egg, lightly beaten
Cold water as needed

Combine the flour and salt in a bowl. Cut in the pieces of butter, and mix until the flour becomes coarse, like meal. Add the egg to the mixture and beat until completely absorbed by the flour. A spoonful at a time, add cold water until the dough forms a ball. Then knead the dough lightly. Wrap it in plastic and refrigerate for at least 1 hour before rolling it out.

Securely wrapped in plastic, this dough keeps for 3 days, refrigerated, or 3 months if frozen. To use, defrost overnight in the refrigerator. If the dough is difficult to roll out, allow it to come to room temperature, then roll.

Rustic Piecrust

This recipe makes a strong, peppery crust for the Rustic Pie, or *pizza rustica* as it is called in Italian. The recipe can be doubled or tripled as needed.

YIELD: about 2 pounds

4 cups all-purpose or pastry flour
1⅓ teaspoons baking powder
1 teaspoon salt
2 teaspoons black pepper
6 tablespoons lard, broken into small pieces
2 eggs
1 cup (or more) cold water

Combine the flour, baking powder, salt, and black pepper in a bowl. Cut in the pieces of lard and mix until the flour becomes coarse, like meal. Blend the egg with 2 tablespoons cold water and add to the flour mixture. Add more cold water as needed, until the dough forms a ball.

Wrap the dough in plastic and refrigerate for at least 1 hour. Roll out the dough on a lightly floured surface.

Note: Securely wrapped in plastic, this dough keeps for 3 days, refrigerated, or 3 months if frozen. To use, defrost overnight in the refrigerator. If the dough is difficult to roll out, allow it to come to room temperature, then roll.

Sour-Cream Crust

This recipe makes a flavorful crust for savory pies, pâtés, and filled pastries.

YIELD: about 1¼ pounds

2¼ cups all-purpose or pastry flour
½ teaspoon salt
¾ cup cold unsalted butter, broken into small pieces
1 egg
½ cup sour cream
1 teaspoon honey or sugar (optional)

Combine the flour and salt in a bowl. Cut in the pieces of butter and mix until the flour becomes coarse, like meal. Lightly beat together the egg, sour cream, and honey (if used as a dessert crust), and mix it into the flour quickly until the dough forms a ball.

Wrap the dough in plastic and refrigerate for at least 1 hour before rolling out.

Note: Securely wrapped in plastic, this dough keeps for 3 days, refrigerated, or 3 months if frozen. To use, defrost overnight in the refrigerator. If the dough is difficult to roll out, allow it to come to room temperature, then roll.

Classic Puff Pastry

Puff pastry has many flaky layers. It makes a delicate crust for mousselines, for precooked fillings, or for decorative lids.

YIELD: about 2 pounds

3/4 teaspoon salt
1 cup less 1 tablespoon water
1 tablespoon vinegar or lemon juice
3 3/4 cups all-purpose flour
1/4 cup unsalted butter, softened
1 egg white
2 1/4 cups cold unsalted butter

Dissolve the salt in the water and vinegar. Beat the flour and 1/4 cup butter together and add the egg white. Mix in the liquid. Knead the dough about thirty times, or until a soft, smooth ball forms. Make two crosswise cuts, about 1/2 inch deep, on top of the dough ball and refrigerate, covered, for 2 hours or freeze for 30 to 40 minutes, until slightly hardened.

On a lightly floured surface, roll the dough into a 14-inch square. Flatten the 2 1/4 cups butter into a 6-inch square with rounded corners. Place the butter in the center of the dough and fold the sides of the dough over the butter (fig. 1-1). The butter should be completely encased in dough.

Arrange the dough so that the line of the last fold is perpendicular to you. Do not roll across this fold, only with it. Roll the dough into a rectangle a little more than 1/4 inch thick. Fold the dough into thirds (fig. 1-2) and give it a quarter turn, always keeping the last fold perpendicular to you. If butter breaks through the dough, heavily flour the break and continue rolling gently. Roll the dough out a second time, fold it again, and refrigerate, covered, for 1 hour.

Roll and fold the dough two more times and refrigerate for another hour.

When ready to use the refrigerated dough, roll and fold it two more times, making a total of six times, and refrigerate it 1 hour before rolling it into the shape and size required.

Note: Securely wrapped in plastic, the dough keeps for 3 to 4 days, refrigerated, or 3 months if frozen. Defrost the dough 24 hours prior to using.

1-1. Encase the butter in the dough.

1-2. Fold the dough in thirds and roll.

Quick Puff Pastry

This dough does not rise as high as Classic Puff Pastry and has fewer layers. However, the pastry is flaky and light and takes one-fifth the time to make. You can double or triple this recipe as needed.

YIELD: about 1 pound

2 cups all-purpose flour
1/4 teaspoon salt
1 cup cold unsalted butter, cut into tiny pieces
2/3 cup cold water

Combine the flour and salt in a mixing bowl. Add the butter, and toss to separate the pieces and to coat them in flour. Pour in the cold water all at once and mix quickly. Do not overwork the dough; it must remain lumpy. Knead it ten times on a lightly floured surface and form a ball. Shape the dough into a flattened rectangle.

Roll the dough into a rectangle, about 6 by 15 inches. Roll away from and toward yourself, not sideways, and try to keep the dough uniformly thick. Fold the dough into thirds and give it a quarter turn, always keeping the last fold perpendicular to you. If butter breaks through the dough, heavily flour the break and continue rolling gently. Roll the dough out and fold it two more times, for a total of three times. If the dough becomes difficult to roll, wrap it in plastic, refrigerate for 10 minutes, then continue. If the dough is streaky, roll and fold it a fourth time.

Refrigerate the dough for 1 hour before rolling it into the shape and size required.

Note: Securely wrapped in plastic, the dough keeps for 3 days, refrigerated, or 3 months if frozen. Defrost in the refrigerator 24 hours before using.

PASTRY VARIATIONS

Goose or Venison Pastry

Substitute half of the liquid called for in a recipe with goose or venison stock. Proceed as in the original recipe. Goose has a light flavor, while that of venison is sturdier and more aggressive.

Spice or Herb Pastry

For every pound of dough a recipe yields, add ½ to ¾ teaspoon of ground or chopped herbs or spices. Combine the herbs or spices with the flour, and proceed as in the original recipe.

For instance, juniper accents venison. Add nutmeg with poultry, fish, or vegetables. Cinnamon or allspice flavors sweets, and parsley, basil, or oregano tastes good with savory preparations. Try adding a sprinkling of cracked herb seeds such as dill or coriander.

Pastry Flavored with Spirits

Substitute 1 tablespoon of liquor for 1 tablespoon of water (per ½ cup) called for in a recipe and proceed as in the original recipe.

Cognac or sherry goes well in a crust for a savory meat pâté, while fruit liqueurs accent the sweet flavor of a dessert pastry.

Pastry Flavored with Juice

Replace half of the water called for in a recipe with a fruit or vegetable juice, or substitute 2 tablespoons of frozen juice concentrate for 2 tablespoons of water and proceed as in the original recipe.

Vegetable juices such as beet or carrot add color and flavor to a crust. Fruit juices go well with dessert fillings. When sweet juices are added to a recipe, watch the crust so that it doesn't overbrown. Either lower the heat or cover the crust with foil if it begins to darken.

Cheese Pastry

For every pound of dough a recipe yields, add 1 cup finely shredded or grated cheese. Combine the cheese with the flour and proceed as in the original recipe.

Cheddar, blue, and Parmesan cheeses work well with most doughs. Parmesan is especially suited to the light, flaky quality of puff pastry. Emmenthaler, Gruyère, and mozzarella also make tasty variations, but they should not be added to puff pastry because of the way they melt.

Bacon or Ham Pastry

For every pound of dough a recipe yields, add ½ cup cooked and finely diced bacon (well drained) or lean ham. Combine the meat with the flour and proceed as in the original recipe. This variation works well with all the recipes except puff pastry.

Vegetable Pastry

For every pound of dough a recipe yields, add ½ cup cooked, drained, and finely minced vegetables. Combine the vegetables with the flour and proceed as in the original recipe.

A mushroom duxelle offers a flavorful addition to any crust used with a savory filling. You can use other vegetables such as cauliflower, zucchini, or carrots by preparing them as you would a mushroom duxelle.

This variation works well with all the recipes except puff pastry.

Nut or Seed Pastry

For every pound of dough a recipe yields, add ¼ to ½ cup ground nuts or seeds. Combine the nuts or seeds with the flour and proceed as in the original recipe. You may need to add more water.

You can use sunflower or pumpkin seeds, almonds, pecans, hazelnuts, walnuts, macadamia nuts, or any other combination.

This variation works well with all the recipes except puff pastry.

Fruit Pastry

For every pound of dough a recipe yields, add ¼ cup finely minced dried fruit. Combine the fruit with the flour and proceed as in the original recipe.

This variation works well with all the recipes except puff pastry.

FARCES AND MOUSSELINES

A farce (forcemeat) or stuffing is the basic mixture of which charcuterie—pâtés, terrines, galantines, and sausages—is made. An interestingly textured and finely seasoned farce distinguishes a superb pâté or terrine from what might otherwise be considered a rather pedestrian meat loaf. These mixtures consist of finely chopped or ground meat, fish, vegetables, or fruit, seasoned and sometimes bound with a panada of bread, flour, potato, or rice. A mousseline is a forcemeat pureed to a smooth consistency and usually enriched with egg and cream.

You can make a succulent farce by juxtaposing smooth and coarse textures. For instance, bind a hand-chopped stuffing with a silky mousseline. Add cubes or strips of tender meat (or fish, fruit, or vegetables), pistachio nuts, pitted olives, whole green and red peppercorns, or julienned basil leaves for color, contrast, and flavor. Once generously seasoned, splash the ingredients with sherry, brandy, or liqueur. You can enhance the flavor of most farces by refrigerating them for a couple hours before cooking. This gives the flavor a chance to develop.

SALTPETER (SODIUM NITRATE)

Saltpeter should not be used in the preparation of pâtés or home-cured sausages and meats. Sodium nitrates and nitrites prevent the growth of *Clostridium botulinum* (a bacteria that causes botulism food poisoning), but in some foods the amount of sodium nitrate added may be too little to prevent bacterial growth. Commercially, saltpeter is used in the curing of ham, bacon, frankfurters, luncheon meats, and smoked fish to preserve their characteristic pink color and to contribute to their taste. Saltpeter is toxic at levels only moderately higher than the approved levels, and many fatalities have resulted from accidental overdoses.

Most ingested nitrate passes through the body unchanged, but some fraction may be converted to nitrite. Nitrites are highly reactive substances that can combine with chemicals in the body to form nitrosamines. Nitrosamines are potent carcinogens, teratogens (causing fetal malformation), and poisons.

To help preserve the pink or rosy color of the meat, you can add crystalline ascorbic acid to the farce in the proportion of 1/8 teaspoon for each 2 1/2 pounds of meat.

FUNDAMENTALS OF MAKING MEAT FARCE

You can choose from three methods of making a meat farce. One method is to use a food grinder. This works quickly and well for all but the coarsest of mixtures. You must hand-chop to make those rougher textured farces. And although a smooth farce can be obtained using either the food grinder or the hand-chopping method in conjunction with a drum sieve, the food processor takes less time and makes it equally smooth.

USING A FOOD GRINDER

Remove all connective membranes, tendons, nerve tissue, skin, and fat from the meat. Cut the trimmed meat and the fresh fat into thin strips.

Place the strips of meat and fat in a shallow bowl or pan. Season, then toss to distribute the ingredients.

Pass the ingredients through a food grinder. You can achieve a coarse or fine-textured farce by varying the size of the grinding disk. For a smoother-textured farce, pass the ingredients through the food grinder a second time using a smaller size disk. Chill.

Thoroughly blend together the ground meat, fat, and spices.

For a smooth meat farce, push the mixture through a drum sieve a little at a time, using a scraper (fig. 1-3), or puree it until smooth in a food processor with a metal blade. Test the seasonings and correct if necessary. Chill again.

USING A FOOD PROCESSOR

To prepare a meat farce or mousseline with a food processor, begin by cutting the meat and fat into 1-inch pieces. Add the seasonings. Using the metal blade, grind a small amount at a time. Process by frequently turning the machine on and off and scraping the mixture from the sides of the bowl until you achieve the desired consistency. The entire process takes only minutes.

CHOPPING BY HAND

Purists insist that only by hand chopping the ingredients will you produce a fine-quality farce. This method best conserves the natural juices of the meat or fish and does not crush or bruise the fibrous structures. The flavor-

1-3. For a smooth meat farce, push the farce through a drum sieve with a scraper.

1-4. Dice the meat using two knives.

ful juice remains trapped inside each morsel, resulting in a moist, savory filling.

Remove all connective membranes, tendons, nerve tissue, and skin. Cut the trimmed meat (or fish) and fat into thin strips. Dice the strips into tiny cubes (fig. 1-4), then combine the diced ingredients.

Chop the meat (or fish) and fat into still smaller pieces until they begin to adhere together. Holding two chef's knives of equal size and weight (one in each hand if you can), rhythmically alternate chopping with each knife, raising it slightly above the cutting surface. If you do not have two knives of equal size and weight, chop with one. Continue until you obtain the desired texture.

For a smooth farce, pound the meat (or fish) in a mortar with a pestle.

Push the mixture through a drum sieve a little at a time, using a scraper.

Basic Veal and Pork Farce

This makes a flavorful, all-purpose farce. You can bake it as is in pastry or fatback or garnish it with vegetables, diced meats, or mushrooms. Halve, double, or triple the recipe as needed.

YIELD: 1½ to 1¾ pounds uncooked farce

½ pound lean boneless veal shoulder
½ pound lean boneless pork butt
½ pound fresh rindless pork belly or fatback
¼ pound cotechino or garlic sausage meat
Seasonings to taste or according to recipe

Using any of the methods just described, combine and grind or chop the ingredients to the desired texture. Chill.

Basic Mousseline

A good mousseline is characterized by a fine, silky texture. The food processor ideally suits its preparation because it allows you to obtain the smoothest consistency without overworking the ingredients.

YIELD: about 6 cups

1½ pounds lean fillets of fish, shellfish, veal, or poultry, cut into 1-inch pieces
1 to 1½ teaspoons salt
½ teaspoon nutmeg
Pinch of cayenne or ¼ teaspoon Tabasco sauce
2 to 3 egg whites (less gelatinous fish and poultry require 3 egg whites)
2½ cups heavy cream

Combine the fish or meat and seasonings in the bowl of a food processor fitted with the metal blade. Process by frequently turning the machine on and off and scraping the mixture from the sides of the bowl until you achieve a smooth consistency.

With the food processor running, add the egg whites and slowly add the heavy cream through the feed tube. Process until the mixture is well blended and fluffy. Test the seasonings and correct if necessary.

Mousseline keeps, refrigerated, for about 1 day or for up to 3 months if frozen.

Cold Mousseline

A cold mousseline or mousse is prepared from cooked and chilled puree. This method allows you to quickly transform leftovers into delicious dishes.

YIELD: about 2 quarts

4½ cups cooked meat, fish, vegetable, or fruit puree, chilled
1⅛ to 1¼ cups melted aspic, cooled
1¾ cups Velouté Sauce
¼ teaspoon nutmeg
¼ to ½ teaspoon white pepper
Salt to taste
1¾ cups heavy cream, whipped to soft peaks

In a bowl set on ice, mix together the puree, aspic, velouté, and seasonings. When the mixture becomes cold and thickens, fold in the whipped heavy cream. Adjust the seasonings if necessary. Mold, chill, and serve.

Variations
Instead of using aspic and Velouté Sauce, you can substitute the combined amount (2⅞ to 3 cups) of one or the other.

Basic Seafood Mousseline

It is important to keep the fish, the mixing bowls, and the utensils chilled to prevent the fish from developing a gummy texture or the cream from curdling.

YIELD: about 2¼ pounds

1 pound fish fillets
⅓ pound crustless bread
1 medium onion, thinly sliced
1 tablespoon unsalted butter
2⅝ cups heavy cream
4 egg whites
1 teaspoon salt
½ teaspoon white pepper
¼ teaspoon nutmeg
1 to 2 tablespoons white wine

Slice the fish into thin strips and keep them well chilled. Slice the bread into thin strips and place them in a shallow platter or bowl. Sauté the sliced onion in the butter until limp and translucent but not browned.

Mix ⅝ cup (5 ounces) of the heavy cream with the egg whites. Pour over the bread and mix well.

Combine the fish, bread, onions, and spices, and pass them twice through a food grinder fitted with a fine grinding disk. Chill.

Next, push the mixture through a drum sieve a little at a time, using a scraper, or puree it until smooth in a food processor fitted with the metal blade. Chill.

Whip the remaining 2 cups of heavy cream until stiff but not dry. Beat enough white wine into the seafood puree to soften its texture.

While keeping the mousseline on a bed of ice, gradually fold in the whipped heavy cream until thoroughly blended. Test the seasonings and correct if necessary.

Alternate Method
To prepare a seafood mousseline with a food processor, cut the fish into 1-inch pieces and add the seasonings. Using the metal blade, grind the pieces of fish, frequently turning the machine on and off and scraping the mixture from the sides of the bowl, until you achieve the desired consistency. Chill.

Combine the fish, bread, onions, and spices, and puree the mixture until smooth. Chill again and continue as in the procedure above by adding the wine and the whipped heavy cream.

BASIC PROPORTIONS OF A FARCE OF MOUSSELINE

You can prepare endless varieties of charcuterie using these basic proportions as a guide:

- 1 cup meat farce weighs about ½ pound.
- To bind a meat farce with eggs, add 2 whole eggs for each 2 to 2¼ pounds of farce.
- Approximately ⅓ to ½ ounce of seasoning will flavor 2 pounds of meat farce.
- To preserve the pink or rosy color of the meat, add crystalline ascorbic acid to the farce in the proportion of ⅛ teaspoon for each 2½ pounds of meat.
- A 4-pound chicken prepared into a galantine or ballotine will hold about 2 pounds of farce.
- A 3½-pound eviscerated chicken yields approximately 1¼ to 1½ pounds of meat.
- Partially whip heavy cream when adding it to a mousseline made from cooked meat or fish. If it is fully whipped, the resulting texture will be drier and not as smooth. One cup heavy cream yields 1½ cups half whipped and 2 to 2½ cups fully whipped.
- Add 2 or 3 tablespoons of liquor to flavor about 1 pound of farce. Heat the alcohol to just below the boiling point and maintain that temperature long enough to evaporate the alcohol but keep the aroma.

TESTING SEASONINGS AND TEXTURE

It is always a good idea to test the seasonings and texture of a farce or mousseline before assembling and cooking the final dish. Test the farce or mousseline before mixing in the garniture. This allows you, if necessary, to grind or puree the mixture more finely or to blend in more seasonings.

COARSE MEAT FARCES

In a lightly greased skillet over medium heat, sauté about 1 tablespoon of farce for a few minutes, or until its juices run clear. Chill the sautéed farce before tasting it.

If the farce lacks flavor, correct the seasonings by adding more pâté spice, pepper, or salt.

To lighten a heavy, dense farce, add more chopped or ground fat or bread crumbs soaked in gelatinous stock.

MEAT OR FISH MOUSSELINES

Poach miniature quenelle-like dumplings (about a half teaspoon each) of mousseline in simmering stock or water. (Salting the poaching water is

PROPORTIONS OF INGREDIENTS

Use the following proportions of ingredients to develop new recipes:

ANY MEAT FARCE

2 parts lean meat
1 part fat
Or:
1 part lean meat
1 part fatty meat
Or:
3 parts lean meat
1 part fat

PORK OR SAUSAGE FARCE

1 part lean pork
1 part pork fat

PORK AND VEAL FARCE

1 part lean pork
1 part lean veal
2 parts pork fat

POULTRY FARCE

2 parts lean poultry
2 parts lean veal
2 parts lean pork
1 part liver (optional)
4 parts pork fat

GAME FARCE

2 parts lean game
1 part lean pork
2 parts pork fat
Or:
2 parts lean game and pork combination
1 part pork fat

GRATIN FARCE

Add sautéed and sieved liver to enrich a meat farce. Proportionally, the amount of gratin liver should not exceed a quarter of the weight of the farce.

FARCE WITH PANADA

2 parts meat or fish farce
1 part panada (or less)

MOUSSELINE

1 pound fish meat
½ pound panada (or less)
2 to 3 egg whites
2 cups heavy cream (for whipping)
1¾ to 2 teaspoons seasonings

MOUSSELINE

2¼ pounds meat or fish puree
4 egg whites
6½ cups heavy cream
4 to 5 teaspoons seasonings

COLD MOUSSELINE OR MOUSSE

4 parts cooked meat or fish puree
1 part melted aspic
1½ parts Velouté Sauce
1½ parts heavy cream (for whipping)

VEGETABLE MOUSSELINE

1½ to 2 pounds vegetable
3 to 4 eggs
2 tablespoons unflavored gelatin
1 cup heavy cream (for whipping)

optional.) Turn the dumplings so that they cook through. Remove, chill, then taste. If the mousseline needs more flavor, add more seasonings.

To lighten a heavy mousseline, mix in more whipped heavy cream. If the mousseline breaks apart and will not hold its shape, lightly whip an egg white and fold it into the mousseline.

VEGETABLE MOUSSELINES

In a small, lightly greased and covered ramekin set in a water bath, bake a tablespoon or two of the mixture in a 350°F oven. Or steam the covered ramekin in a saucepan of simmering water on top of the stove. Remove the ramekin and chill it before tasting. Correct the seasonings and texture as you would a meat or fish mousseline.

SEASONINGS

Combinations of herbs, spices, and seasonings develop the distinctive flavor of a farce. Savory blends may be robust and bold, or mild and delicate. Be adventurous in preparing your own spice mixtures.

Unless specified as fresh, the herbs in the recipes in this book are dried. When using fresh parsley, choose the Italian flat-leafed variety, which is more flavorful than the curly type.

Finely grind dried herbs and spices in a mill or blender and store them, tightly covered, in opaque containers kept in a dark, dry place. For each 2 pounds of farce, use approximately ½ ounce of seasoning. Allow your taste preference to be your guide.

Herb Bouquet (Bouquet Garni)

Tie together fresh parsley sprigs (8 parts), fresh thyme (1 part), and bay leaves (1 part) into a little faggot or bunch weighing 1 ounce. The quantities vary for each recipe. Herb bouquets for certain dishes may include basil, celery, chervil, fennel, garlic, leeks, tarragon, rosemary, or savory. Bouquets for light or white stocks and sauces are composed of only white vegetables. Remove the faggot before serving the dish.

Seasoning Sachet (Sachet d'Epices)

Seasoning sachets consist of any combination of herbs and spices tied in cheesecloth and cooked with meats, game stews, sauerkraut, beans, soups, and sauces.

Fine Herbs (Fines Herbes)

Fine herbs is a mixture of delicate herbs such as parsley, chervil, tarragon, and chives. The proportions are equal for all parts unless otherwise indicated.

Fine Spices (Epices Fines)

This blend of ground spices is a good all-purpose seasoning for meat marinades, pâtés, and terrines.

YIELD: about 14 ounces

6½ ounces white pepper
2¼ ounces allspice
1 ounce mace
½ ounce each—bay leaf, cinnamon, cloves, marjoram, nutmeg, rosemary, sage, summer savory

Four Spices (Quatre Epices)

This is a blend of four spices—pepper, nutmeg, clove, and either cinnamon or ginger—used primarily in charcuterie. Proportions vary, but pepper always predominates. A ratio of 8 parts pepper to 1 part each of ground nutmeg, clove, and cinnamon or ginger is often used. This recipe is a milder version.

YIELD: about 8 ounces

5 ounces white pepper
1½ ounces nutmeg
2 teaspoons cloves
¾ ounce ginger or cinnamon

Garlic Salt

YIELD: about 1 cup

1 cup Kosher or coarse salt
4 teaspoons fresh garlic, chopped

Chili Spice

YIELD: about 1½ cups

1 cup salt
1 onion, finely chopped
3 tablespoons chili powder
2 tablespoons finely chopped garlic
1 teaspoon (hot) red pepper flakes
½ teaspoon cayenne

Poultry Seasoning

As an all-around seasoning mixture, poultry seasoning goes especially well with chicken and duck.

YIELD: about 1¼ cups

1 cup garlic salt
2 tablespoons chopped fresh rosemary
¾ teaspoon commercial poultry seasoning
¾ teaspoon paprika
¾ teaspoon thyme
¾ teaspoon oregano
¾ teaspoon white pepper

Beef Seasoning

YIELD: about 2⅛ cups

1 cup Kosher or coarse salt
⅔ cup ground sage
⅓ cup thyme leaves
4 teaspoons oregano leaves
4 teaspoons cracked black pepper

SEASONING MIXTURES FOR FARCES

Many of the meat recipes list pâté seasoning among the ingredients. You can buy an all-purpose pâté spice* or blend one according to the following recipes by grinding all the ingredients together. Each recipe yields enough seasoning for several uses. Approximately ⅓ to ½ ounce of seasoning will flavor 2 pounds of meat farce. For variation and added zest, rub a sparing amount of pâté spice onto meats such as chicken or steak before roasting or broiling. Experiment and develop your own combinations.

Pâté Seasoning I

This is a good, all-purpose seasoning for pâtés and other charcuterie.

YIELD: about 5 ounces

⅔ ounce whole black peppercorns
⅔ ounce whole white peppercorns
⅔ ounce basil
½ ounce cloves
½ ounce ginger
½ ounce nutmeg
½ ounce sweet paprika
½ ounce thyme
⅓ ounce marjoram
¼ ounce mace
⅛ ounce bay leaves

* A flavorful blend of French mixed spices can be purchased for use as a base seasoning for meat pâtés from: Greene Baum, Inc., 165 Chambers Street, New York, NY 10007, which imports G.C. Bruck Mixed Spices, in 30-ounce tins, from Strasbourg, France.

Pâté Seasoning II

Another good, basic seasoning for any charcuterie.

YIELD: about 4½ ounces

⅔ ounce whole black peppercorns
⅔ ounce whole white peppercorns
½ ounce sweet paprika
⅓ ounce allspice
⅓ ounce basil
⅓ ounce cloves
⅓ ounce ginger
⅓ ounce mace
⅓ ounce thyme
¼ ounce hot paprika
¼ ounce oregano
⅛ ounce bay leaves

Pâté Seasoning III

For a light and fragrant blend, use this recipe to season white meats such as veal, chicken, and sweetbreads.

YIELD: about 6 ounces

1 to 1¼ ounces dried cepes or shiitake mushrooms
¾ ounce whole white peppercorns
¾ ounce basil
¾ ounce nutmeg
¾ ounce thyme
½ vanilla bean, scraped
⅓ ounce allspice
⅓ ounce coriander seeds
⅓ ounce mace
¼ ounce cinnamon
¼ ounce cloves
⅛ ounce bay leaves
⅛ ounce cardamom

Pâté Seasoning IV

Spicy and aromatic, this mixture accentuates the flavor of a coarse pork pâté, terrine, or sausage.

YIELD: about 5½ ounces

1½ ounces dried, whole green peppercorns
⅔ ounce sweet paprika
½ ounce summer savory
½ ounce thyme
⅓ ounce allspice
⅓ ounce basil
⅓ ounce coriander seeds
⅓ ounce mace
¼ ounce cloves
¼ ounce ginger
¼ ounce rosemary
⅛ ounce bay leaves

Pâté Seasoning V

The robust flavor of these spices enriches the taste and aroma of game.

YIELD: about 7 ounces

1¾ ounces dried shiitake mushrooms
⅔ ounce whole white peppercorns
⅔ ounce juniper berries
½ ounce whole black peppercorns
⅓ ounce basil
⅓ ounce cloves
⅓ ounce ginger
⅓ ounce mace
⅓ ounce nutmeg
⅓ ounce thyme
¼ ounce bay leaves
¼ ounce chervil
¼ ounce marjoram
¼ ounce summer savory
¼ ounce winter savory
⅛ ounce cayenne
⅛ ounce cinnamon
⅛ ounce sweet paprika

PANADAS

Most farces or forcemeats are bound with eggs. A panada can be substituted for, or used with, eggs to bind, extend, or lighten a farce or mousseline. Made of flour, bread, potato, or rice, they are used cold, except for the potato panada, which is used while still warm. Proportionally, the amount of panada added to a farce should not exceed half the weight of the primary ingredient (meat or fish). These recipes can be multiplied or divided to obtain the quantity needed.

Flour Panada

Flour panada adds body and a smooth, light texture to seafood and meat mousselines.

YIELD: about 1 pound

1¼ cups gelatinous stock, milk, or water
Pinch of salt
Pinch of white pepper
Pinch of nutmeg
¼ cup unsalted butter
1¼ cups all-purpose flour
3 egg yolks

In a saucepan, combine the stock, salt, pepper, nutmeg, and butter and bring to a boil. Remove from the heat, then mix in the flour. Return to medium heat and stir until the mixture becomes thick and dry, leaving the sides of the pan clean. While still warm but not hot, stir in the egg yolks.

If you want a silky smooth panada, push it through a drum sieve. Spread the panada onto a buttered flat tray and cover with a piece of buttered paper to prevent a skin from forming. Allow to cool before using.

Bread Panada

Bread panada is used in fish, veal, and poultry farces, and it will lighten the texture.

YIELD: about 1 pound

1¼ cups hot gelatinous stock, milk, or water
½ pound crustless bread or bread crumbs
Pinch of salt
Pinch of white pepper

In a saucepan, soak the bread in the hot stock. Season, then stir the mixture over medium heat until it becomes thick and dry, leaving the sides of the pan clean.

Spread the panada onto a buttered flat tray and cover with a piece of buttered paper to prevent a skin from forming. Allow to cool before using.

Potato Panada

Today potato panada is used infrequently because it must be used while still warm. It can be added to white meat or fish farces or sometimes to large stuffed quenelles.

YIELD: about 1 pound

1½ cups boiled, peeled, and thinly sliced potatoes
1½ cups gelatinous stock, milk, or water
4 teaspoons unsalted butter
Pinch of salt
Pinch of white pepper
Pinch of nutmeg

Combine all the ingredients and cook over low heat for 15 to 20 minutes. Mix well to obtain a puree or smooth paste.

Use this panada while still warm because it becomes elastic and gluey once cooled.

Rice Panada

Rice panada is used in various forcemeats and sausage mixtures.

YIELD: about 1 pound

1 cup rice, short grain or Italian
3 cups gelatinous White Stock
2 tablespoons unsalted butter

Combine all the ingredients and bring to a boil. Remove from the stove and bake in a moderate oven for 40 to 50 minutes. Blend well, until the rice forms a smooth mixture.

Spread the panada onto a buttered flat tray and cover with a piece of buttered paper to prevent a skin from forming. Allow to cool before using.

MIXING A PANADA INTO A FARCE

Combine the farce and egg whites in a mixing bowl set on ice. Add the panada and blend thoroughly. Chill.

Keeping the mixture in a bowl on ice, stir in the wine (optional), and mix in the heavy cream, a little at a time.

WORKING WITH FAT

Fat is an integral ingredient in traditionally prepared charcuterie; it helps bind the meat. Ground, diced, or cut into strips (lardons), pork fat gives the farce a tender, moist texture, a rich flavor, and an interesting pattern. The lardons can be artfully layered throughout the farce or threaded through fillets of lean meat used as garnitures. A lining of fatback, sliced into ⅛-inch sheets called leaves or bards, continually bastes the farce as it cooks.

Fatback retains a firm, even texture, making it convenient to use. It slices well and possesses a delicate taste. Fresh fatback is preferred, but you can substitute salted fatback if you blanch it for 5 minutes to remove the salt. You also can substitute fat sliced from the outside of a pork loin roast, but fat trimmed from the top of a fresh ham or a pork shoulder is too soft and lumpy. Caul fat, a web-like membrane from the stomach of a pig, also makes a delicate lining for charcuterie.

Rendered pork fat, or lard, is used to preserve terrines, confits, sausage, rillettes, and rillons in their molds or containers. Pour the melted lard over the cooled, cooked meat until the meat is covered with a half inch of fat. If necessary, once the fat cools and hardens, add more melted lard to fill any gaps. Store the charcuterie in a cold, dry place.

SLICING FATBACK

You can slice fatback on a commercial slicing machine, or you can slice it by hand using the following instructions.

Freeze the fatback for about an hour or until firm enough to handle before slicing it into bards. With the rind side down, steady the chilled slab of fatback by wedging it against the side of a cutting board. Cutting toward the board, slice the fat into ⅛-inch-thick sheets or bards (fig. 1-5). Do not use the rind.

Discard the rind. Cut the chilled fatback into ¼-inch-thick lardons or dice the lardons into ¼-inch-cubes.

HANDLING CAUL FAT

Caul fat requires gentle handling because it tears easily. Rinse fresh caul fat before using it. Soak frozen or dry-salted caul fat in warm water, with 1 tablespoon vinegar or lemon juice added per cup of water, for 15 to 30 minutes, until it becomes pliable.

RENDERING PORK FAT

Unrendered fat keeps for up to 6 months if frozen. Three pounds of pork leaf lard (fat surrounding the kidneys) yields about 6 cups.

Cut fatback (with rind on), belly fat, or kidney suet into 1-inch cubes. In a heavy pot, add the cubed fat with enough cold water to cover the pot bottom. Cook the fat, uncovered, over low heat for about 4 hours, until the liquid becomes clear. Stir occasionally to prevent the fat from sticking to the bottom of the pot.

1.5 Cutting toward the board, slice the fatback into ⅛-inch-thick bards.

1.6 Strain rendered lard through a strainer lined with cheesecloth.

Gently pour the rendered fat or lard through a strainer lined with a few layers of dampened cheesecloth or muslin into a heat-resistant bowl or container (fig. 1-6). Cover and chill. Use the remaining solid bits of fat, called cracklings, as a soup garnish, a snack, or in bread dough.

For your convenience, store the finished lard in smaller containers. It keeps for 2 months, refrigerated, 4 months if frozen. Render other fats into lard using this same procedure.

STOCKS, ASPICS, AND CHAUD-FROID

Stocks of meat, fish, or vegetables contribute to the full-bodied flavor of charcuterie. Once jelled into aspic, stocks add a tasty and decorative glaze to terrines, timbales, and galantines. Poured into a pâté after it is baked, aspic fills the gaps between the crust and the filling. It also serves to add moisture and bind ingredients in a mold.

The proper consistency for aspic is stiff enough to hold its shape when cut, but soft enough to melt in your mouth without chewing. Aspic is affected by weather. Make it a bit stiffer in warm weather or it will tend to melt. Avoid adding salt or wine to aspic after cooking or it may become cloudy.

Aspic and glazes made with aspic are vulnerable to bacteria and should not be touched with your hands, which could hasten their spoilage. Always handle them with clean utensils and refrigerate them immediately. It takes only a few hours for bacteria to spoil an aspic. Do not freeze aspic or it will develop a clouded, milky color, and the liquid may separate from the gelatin.

Chaud-froid (which means "hot-cold") is a savory glaze that is prepared hot and served cold; hence its name. Similar to aspic, but opaque instead of clear, it also is used to glaze terrines, timbales, and galantines.

Brown Stock

YIELD: about 1 gallon

6 pounds veal and/or beef bones, sawed into 2-inch pieces and rinsed
4 tablespoons fat
1 cup mushroom trimmings
4 carrots, sliced 1 inch thick
3 celery stalks, sliced 1 inch thick
1 large Spanish onion, cut into 8 wedges
1 whole leek, coarsely chopped
3/4 cup tomato puree
6 quarts cold water
2 ounces blanched pork rind (optional)
Seasoning sachet (10 fresh parsley sprigs, 2 small bay leaves, 4 garlic cloves, crushed but unpeeled)
Salt and pepper to taste

Preheat oven to 400°F. Brown the bones and fat in a roasting pan, turning and basting occasionally. When the bones are partially browned, add the cut vegetables and the tomato puree. The browning will take 40 minutes to 1 hour.

Transfer the bones and vegetables to a large stockpot. Pour off the fat from the roasting pan. Then deglaze the pan with a cup or two of water by heating it on the stove and scraping up all the concentrated juices. Cover the bones in the stockpot with the deglazing liquid, the remaining cold water, the pork rind, and the seasoning sachet. The water should cover the ingredients by about 2 inches. Bring the water to the boiling point, then simmer slowly, uncovered, for 8 to 12 hours. Occasionally skim off the fat or scum that accumulates on the surface. While the stock simmers, add more water as necessary.

Strain the stock through a colander lined with a double layer of cheesecloth. Simmer the strained stock to reduce it further, then lightly season with salt and pepper. Cool and refrigerate the stock. A congealed layer of fat will form on the surface and can easily be lifted off.

Freeze the stock in several small containers for up to 3 months. If refrigerated, bring it to a boil every 2 days in order to prevent bacteria growth and spoilage.

Variations

For a stronger stock, use approximately 2 pounds of bones for each quart of water.

White Stock

YIELD: about 1 gallon

6 pounds veal bones, sawed into 2-inch pieces and rinsed
Cold water to cover
1 large Spanish onion, cut into 8 wedges
2 celery stalks, sliced 1 inch thick
1 leek, white part only, coarsely chopped
6 quarts cold water
Seasoning sachet (10 fresh parsley sprigs; 1 small bay leaf; 1 fresh thyme sprig or 1/4 teaspoon dried leaves; 3 garlic cloves, crushed but unpeeled; 4 peppercorns, cracked; 3 whole cloves)
Salt to taste

Place the bones in a stockpot, cover with cold water, and heat to the boiling point to blanch. Drain the bones and return them to the pot. Add the vegetables, 6 quarts cold water, and seasoning sachet. The water should cover the ingredients by about 2 inches. Simmer the stock slowly, uncovered, for 4 to 6 hours. Occasionally skim off the fat or scum that accumulates on the surface.

Strain the stock through a colander lined with a double layer of cheesecloth. Simmer the strained stock to reduce it further, then lightly season with salt. Cool and refrigerate the stock. A congealed layer of fat will form on the surface and can easily be lifted off.

Freeze the stock in several small containers for up to 3 months. If refrigerated, bring it to a boil every 2 days in order to prevent bacteria growth and spoilage.

Variations

For a stronger stock, use approximately 2 pounds of bones for each quart of water.

Chicken Stock

YIELD: about 1 gallon

4 pounds chicken bones, rinsed
2 pounds veal bones, sawed into 2-inch pieces and rinsed
Cold water to cover
1 large Spanish onion, cut into 8 wedges
2 celery stalks, sliced 1 inch thick
1 leek, white part only, coarsely chopped
6 quarts cold water
Seasoning sachet (10 fresh parsley sprigs; 1 small bay leaf; 1 fresh thyme sprig or 1/4 teaspoon dried thyme leaves; 2 garlic cloves, crushed but unpeeled; 3 whole cloves; 5 peppercorns, cracked)
Salt to taste

Place the bones in a stockpot, cover with cold water, and heat to the boiling point to blanch. Drain the bones and return them to the pot. Add the vegetables, 6 quarts cold water, and seasoning sachet. The water should cover the ingredients by about 2 inches. Simmer the stock slowly, uncovered, for about 4 hours. Occasionally skim off the fat or scum that accumulates on the surface.

Strain the stock through a colander lined with a double layer of cheesecloth. Simmer the strained stock to reduce it further, then lightly season with salt. Cool and refrigerate the stock. A congealed layer of fat will form on the surface and can easily be lifted off.

Freeze the stock in several small containers for up to 3 months. If refrigerated, bring it to a boil every 2 days in order to prevent bacteria growth and spoilage.

Variations

For a stronger stock, use approximately 2 pounds of bones for each quart of water.

Game Stock

YIELD: about 1 gallon

6 to 8 pounds game bones, preferably from older animals (neck, breasts, and trimmings of venison; hare bones and trimmings; bones and trimmings from old pheasants, partridges, or wild rabbits)
2½ ounces pork rind
4 tablespoons fat
3 carrots, sliced 1 inch thick
2 celery stalks, sliced 1 inch thick
1 large Spanish onion, cut into 8 wedges
1 cup red wine
6 quarts cold water
Seasoning sachet (5 juniper berries; 1 fresh sage sprig or 3 to 5 dried leaves; 2 cloves garlic, crushed but unpeeled; 4 peppercorns, cracked)
Salt to taste

Place the bones, rind, and fat in a large pan and brown on top of the stove. Add the vegetables and continue browning. Transfer the bones and vegetables to a stockpot. Pour off the fat from the pan. Deglaze the pan with wine and 1 cup water by heating it on the stove and scraping up all the concentrated juices. Cover the bones in the stockpot with the deglazing liquid, the remaining cold water, and the seasoning sachet. The water should cover the ingredients by about 2 inches. Simmer the stock slowly, uncovered, for about 4 hours. Occasionally skim off the fat or scum that accumulates on the surface.

Strain the stock through a colander lined with a double layer of cheesecloth. Simmer the strained stock to reduce it further, then lightly season with salt. Cool and refrigerate the stock. A congealed layer of fat will form on the surface and can easily be lifted off.

Freeze the stock in several small containers for up to 3 months. If refrigerated, bring it to a boil every 2 days in order to prevent bacteria growth and spoilage.

Variations
For a stronger stock, use approximately 2 pounds of bones for each quart of water.

Fish Stock

YIELD: about 1¼ gallons

6 to 8 pounds fish bones, rinsed (such as sole, flounder, whiting, halibut, or carp)
1 large Spanish onion, cut into 8 wedges
2 celery stalks, sliced 1 inch thick
⅔ cup mushroom trimmings (optional)
1 leek, white part only, coarsely chopped
Juice of ½ lemon
1 cup white wine
5 quarts cold water
Seasoning sachet (1 bay leaf; 2 whole cloves; 3 white peppercorns, cracked)
Salt to taste

Place the bones, vegetables, lemon juice, wine, and water in a large stockpot. Quickly bring to a boil and simmer gently for 20 minutes, skimming off the fat or scum that accumulates on the surface. Add the seasoning sachet and continue to simmer for another 10 minutes.

Strain the stock through a colander lined with a double layer of cheesecloth, then lightly season with salt. Cool and refrigerate the stock. If a congealed layer of fat forms on the surface, carefully lift it off.

Freeze the stock in several small containers for up to 3 months. It keeps, refrigerated, for 2 or 3 days.

Variations
For a stronger stock, use approximately 2 pounds of bones for each quart of water.

Vegetable Stock

YIELD: about 1 gallon

1 Spanish onion, sliced
1 whole leek, sliced
4 tablespoons unsalted butter or vegetable oil
3 celery stalks, sliced ½ inch thick
1 cup shredded cabbage
1 cup quartered mushrooms or mushroom trimmings
1 small turnip, ½-inch diced
1 small parsnip, sliced
2 carrots, sliced
2 plum tomatoes, each cut into 6 wedges
1 unpeeled potato, ½-inch diced
1 fennel stalk, sliced
Juice of 1 lemon
5 quarts cold water
Seasoning sachet (1 bay leaf; 10 fresh parsley sprigs; 2 whole cloves; 5 garlic cloves, crushed but unpeeled; 4 peppercorns, cracked)
Salt to taste

Sauté the onion and leek in the butter. Add the remaining vegetables and continue to sauté. Transfer the crisply sautéed vegetables to a stockpot and add the lemon juice, water, and seasoning sachet. Bring to the boiling point, then slowly simmer for about 1 hour. Occasionally skim off any fat or scum that accumulates on the surface.

Strain the stock through a colander lined with a double layer of cheesecloth, then lightly season with salt. Cool and refrigerate the stock. If a congealed layer of fat forms on the surface, carefully lift it off.

Freeze the stock in several small containers for up to 3 months. It keeps, refrigerated, for 2 or 3 days.

Court Bouillon

You can poach fish, poultry, or vegetables in a court bouillon. Obtain different flavorings by substituting or adding fresh herbs and their seeds, such as dill, coriander, or fennel, to the liquid.

YIELD: about 1 quart

3 cups water
1 cup white wine
3 lemon slices (optional)
1 to 2 carrots, finely sliced
1 celery stalk, finely sliced
1 small onion or 2 small leeks, finely sliced
4 parsley sprigs
1 fresh tarragon sprig or ½ tarragon sprig in vinegar or ⅛ teaspoon dried tarragon
1 bay leaf
12 peppercorns, cracked
Salt to taste

In a stainless steel or enamel saucepan, combine the ingredients and simmer for 30 minutes. Strain.

Meat or Fish Glazes

YIELD: about 1 cup

Vigorously reduce 1 gallon of strained meat or fish stock until it reaches the consistency of oil. Strain it through a sieve lined with cheesecloth and place it in a heavy, small pot. Slowly reduce the thickened stock to the consistency of syrup or marmalade.

Pour the glaze into a lightly greased metal ice-cube tray and refrigerate. Once hardened, unmold, cut into cubes, and freeze.

Basic Aspic

YIELD: about 2 quarts

2 pounds veal knuckles
1/2 pound beef knuckles
1 1/2 pounds veal bones, sawed into 2-inch pieces
2 calf's or pig's feet, split in half lengthwise
1/4 pound pork rind
Cold water to cover
4 quarts cold White Stock
1 whole clove
Pinch of salt
3/4 pound lean beef, ground
2 to 3 egg whites, beaten until just frothy
1 onion, chopped
2 carrots, chopped
2 celery stalks, chopped
Seasoning sachet (5 fresh parsley sprigs; 1 fresh thyme sprig or 1/8 teaspoon dried leaves; 1 bay leaf; 3 garlic cloves, crushed but unpeeled; 4 peppercorns, cracked)
Salt to taste
3/4 cup Madeira, sherry, or wine (optional)

Blanch the veal and beef knuckles, veal bones, calf's feet, and pork rind in cold water. Drain and rinse well. Return to the stockpot and add the cold stock, clove, and salt. Bring to a boil and simmer, uncovered, for 4 to 6 hours. Skim off the fat or scum as it accumulates on the surface.

Strain the stock through a colander and cool. If a congealed layer of fat forms on the surface, carefully lift it off. Reduce the stock to 3 quarts by cooking it over medium heat.

To clarify the stock, return it to the pot, mix in the remaining ingredients except the Madeira, and simmer for 1 to 1 1/2 hours. Adjust the seasonings and add the Madeira. Occasionally stir the stock slowly. Remove it from the heat and let stand, undisturbed, for about 10 minutes, until the raft (crust of ingredients floating on the surface) settles to the bottom of the pot. Carefully ladle the stock through a colander or sieve lined with a double layer of cheesecloth. The stock should be clear and free of particles. Refrigerate a couple of tablespoons to test the consistency of the aspic. Reduce further if necessary. Chill.

Refrigerated, aspic keeps for 2 to 3 days and up to 1 week if not touched with your hands. Do not freeze. To keep aspic longer, bring it to a boil every 2 days and simmer gently for 30 minutes to 1 hour.

Variations
If you reduce the stock further, it will form a thicker natural jelly. Veal bones are particularly gelatinous.

If the jelly does not set sufficiently, add gelatin—approximately 1 1/2 teaspoons unflavored gelatin powder per pint of stock.

For a darker aspic, instead of blanching, brown the knuckles, bones, calf's feet, and pork rind and substitute brown stock for the white stock. Proceed as in the original recipe.

Chicken Aspic

YIELD: about 2 quarts

Follow the recipe for Basic Aspic, but make the following changes:

- Substitute 1½ pounds chicken or other fowl bones for the 1½ pounds veal bones.
- Substitute Chicken Stock for the White Stock.
- Add 2 whole browned chickens with hearts but not livers to the stock.
- To clarify, substitute chopped poultry skeletons for the ground beef.

Game Aspic

YIELD: about 2 quarts

Follow the recipe for Basic Aspic, but make the following changes:

- Substitute Game Stock for the White Stock.
- To clarify, substitute game, such as venison, hare, or wild rabbit, for the ground beef.

Fish Aspic

YIELD: 2 quarts

2 quarts warm Fish Stock
2 to 3 egg whites, beaten until just frothy
1 cup finely diced carrots for color (optional)
Pinch of saffron for color (optional)
Seasoning sachet (5 fresh parsley sprigs; 1 bay leaf; 1 fresh tarragon and/or thyme sprig or ⅛ teaspoon dried leaves; 4 white peppercorns, cracked)
Juice of ½ lemon
¾ cup white wine
2 to 4 tablespoons (envelopes) unflavored gelatin
Pinch of salt

In a stockpot over low heat, whisk all the ingredients into the warm fish stock. Keep mixing until it comes to a boil. Gently simmer, undisturbed, for 2 minutes, or until the egg whites form a crust on the surface. Carefully ladle the stock through a colander or sieve lined with a double layer of cheesecloth. The stock should be clear and free of particles. Refrigerate a couple tablespoons to test the consistency of the aspic. Add more gelatin if necessary. Cool.

Refrigerated, aspic keeps for 2 or 3 days. Do not freeze.

Vegetable or Fruit Aspic

YIELD: about 1 quart

2½ tablespoons (envelopes) unflavored gelatin
½ cup cold water
4 cups clear vegetable stock or fruit juice

Sprinkle the gelatin into the cold water, and allow it to stand about 15 minutes to soften. Over simmering water, heat the mixture to dissolve the gelatin. Add it to the stock or juice and blend well.

Note: Fresh pineapple contains an enzyme that prevents jelling. Either heat the fresh juice to destroy the enzyme or use canned juice.

Quick Aspic

If you do not have time to make aspic from scratch, rely on this recipe to prepare a quick aspic. The texture and taste are different but quite acceptable.

YIELD: about 2 cups

2 tablespoons (envelopes) unflavored gelatin
2 cups hot Brown, Fish, or Vegetable Stock
1½ tablespoons Madeira, wine, or sherry (optional)
½ teaspoon white vinegar or lemon juice

Dissolve the gelatin in the hot stock and add the Madeira and vinegar. Refrigerate a couple of tablespoons to test the consistency of the aspic. Adjust as necessary. Chill.

Variations
Canned (jellied) consommé Madrilène, flavored with wine or sherry, makes a quick and tasty base for aspic. Add more gelatin if needed.

Classic Chaud-Froid

YIELD: about 1 quart

1½ to 2 tablespoons (envelopes) unflavored gelatin
2 cups heavy cream
2 cups White Stock, warmed
Pinch of salt
1 drop Tabasco sauce or pinch of cayenne
1 egg yolk

Sprinkle the gelatin into 1 cup of the heavy cream and allow it to stand about 15 minutes to soften. Add to the warmed stock and heat to dissolve the gelatin. Season with salt and Tabasco. Gently simmer for 5 to 10 minutes. Combine the remaining cream with the egg yolk and add to the sauce. Pour the sauce through a strainer lined with a double layer of cheesecloth. Chill.

Refrigerated, chaud-froid keeps for 2 or 3 days. Handle like aspic.

White Chaud-Froid

YIELD: about 1 quart

8 cups clear White, Chicken, Fish, or Vegetable Stock
¼ cup cornstarch
1 tablespoon white wine or stock
2 to 2½ tablespoons (envelopes) unflavored gelatin
3 tablespoons hot water
1¼ cups heavy cream
White pepper to taste
Salt to taste

Bring the stock to a boil and simmer over medium heat until reduced to 3 cups. Blend the cornstarch with the white wine and whisk into hot stock. Return to the boil. Simmer over medium heat for 1 minute, stirring constantly. Sprinkle the gelatin into the hot water and stir until dissolved. Pour the gelatin mixture into the stock and blend well. Stir in the cream. Strain the chaud-froid through a fine sieve. Season to taste. Chill.

Refrigerated, chaud-froid keeps for 2 or 3 days. Handle like aspic.

Red or Pink Chaud-Froid

YIELD: about 1 quart

½ teaspoon sweet paprika
¼ to ½ cup tomato paste
1 quart Classic, White, or Mayonnaise Chaud-Froid

Mix the paprika and a sufficient amount of the tomato paste into the chaud-froid until you obtain the color desired. Do not use food coloring.

Refrigerated, chaud-froid keeps for 2 or 3 days. Handle like aspic.

Green Chaud-Froid

YIELD: about 1 quart

1 quart Classic, White, or Mayonnaise Chaud-Froid
4 ounces spinach leaves
4 ounces watercress leaves
4 ounces fresh parsley or dill sprigs

In a food processor or blender, puree ½ cup chaud-froid with the spinach, watercress, and parsley. Quickly bring the mixture to a boil, then strain it through cheesecloth. Blend the resulting sauce into the remaining chaud-froid. Cool it quickly so that it does not lose its color.

Refrigerated, chaud-froid keeps for 2 or 3 days. Handle like aspic.

Brown Chaud-Froid

YIELD: about 1 quart

1½ cups Meat Glaze
2 cups Basic, Chicken, or Game Aspic
¼ to ½ cup tomato sauce
Madeira or sherry to taste

Melt the meat glaze and aspic. Add the tomato sauce a little at a time until you reach the color desired. Flavor with Madeira or sherry. Chill.

Refrigerated, chaud-froid keeps for 2 or 3 days. Handle like aspic.

Mayonnaise Chaud-Froid

YIELD: about 1 quart

2 cups mayonnaise
2 cups cold liquid aspic

Slowly mix the cold, liquid aspic into the mayonnaise. Avoid whipping, as bubbles may form.

If you make your own mayonnaise, do not heat the chaud-froid to remelt it once it solidifies, or it may break. A chaud-froid made with commercially prepared mayonnaise can be reheated without breaking.

Note: Choose an aspic that best complements the food to be glazed. The Basic Aspic can be used with most items, except fruit and sometimes vegetable preparations.

DECORATIVE GLAZING

Decorated terrines, timbales, and galantines enhance the beauty of a dining table or buffet. The presentation may be elegant or rustic, but the garnish should always be simple and complementary so as not to distract from the dish itself. For a buffet, glaze precut servings with a thin coat of clear aspic. The aspic will prevent the slices from drying out. Arrange the cut portions on a platter around the unsliced terrine or galantine. This presentation looks exciting, and guests may easily help themselves without disrupting the arrangement.

To glaze a terrine, timbale, or galantine, first unmold or unwrap it. Wipe away any excess fat or jelly, then thoroughly chill. The surface must be cold for the aspic to adhere.

Blanch, or steam for a few seconds, any herbs or vegetables to be used as a garnish. Pat them dry, then chill. Ladle some of the melted aspic into a bowl and stir it over ice until it turns syrupy. Quickly spoon a few layers over the terrine, timbale, or galantine, chilling for a couple of minutes between layers.

1.7 Arrange aspic-dipped garnish on galantine and spoon on more aspic to set.

Dip each piece of chilled garnish into aspic and arrange it on the charcuterie. Cover everything with a final layer of aspic (fig. 1-7). Chill and serve.

If you use chaud-froid, you may coat the terrine, timbale, or galantine with a layer of clear aspic first, then add several layers of chaud-froid. If desired, ladle a final layer of clear aspic over all. Chill and serve.

CHAPTER TWO

Pâtés, Terrines, and Savory Pies

PATES AND TERRINES

Perfumed with freshly chopped herbs and aromatic spices, a mélange of succulent ingredients distinguish pâtés and terrines as some of the most delectable of food preparations. Dot pâtés and terrines with truffles, peppercorns, or nuts, and lace them with a rich aspic hinting of eau de vie. In essence, a pâté is a savory or sweet golden-crusted pie, and a terrine, though similar to a pâté, differs in that it is commonly baked without a crust in a bacon- or fat-lined dish or mold. Traditionally, pâtés are served hot or cold, while terrines are served cold. The two terms sometimes are used interchangeably.

Pâtés and terrines can be basic or fancy, inexpensive or costly. Cooked either free-standing or formed into a container, they take on a multitude of shapes and sizes—large, small, rectangular, oval, round, cylindrical, or carved. Terrines are cooked, stored, and sometimes even served in their decorative molds crafted of enameled iron, glass, porcelain, ceramic, and pottery. Pâtés, prepared in removable tin molds, feature a delicate pastry as their ornamental container.

CRAFTING AND COOKING

Before being combined with other ingredients, the meat or fish in a pâté or terrine is often marinated in a minimum amount of liquid and sometimes partially precooked. Adding 1½ to 2 ounces of bread crumbs to each pound of farce lightens the mixture. Presoak the bread crumbs in a little stock or melted aspic to soften them. This contributes additional flavoring and helps bind the preparation. Nonfat dry milk or a meat or fish glaze serves as a good binder. Nonfat dry milk, for example, imparts a creamy taste and texture to liver terrine, while a meat or fish glaze intensifies the rich gelatinous quality of a farce. Add some unflavored gelatin powder or egg white to a turkey farce to compensate for the meat's lack of moisture and natural jelly. For extra fragrance, at the last minute fortify an aspic or farce with eau de vie, wine, or another liquor.

Avoid the use of saltpeter or other nitrate additives. If you want to preserve the pink or rosy color of the meat, you can add crystalline ascorbic acid to the farce in the proportion of ⅛ teaspoon for each 2½ pounds of meat.

Baking pâtés and terrines in a slow to moderate oven causes the fat and juice to constantly baste them, developing a harmonious medley of flavors. Cook terrines on an inverted cake rack in a pan filled with enough hot, but not boiling, water to rise two-thirds of the way up the sides of the mold. (Though not the preferred method, terrines can be cooked on the stove, like a steamed pudding.) The water bath ensures a moist, gentle, even heat. *Pâté de campagne,* actually a terrine, is an exception to the rule. Encased in caul fat and mounded high, this country terrine is cooked on a baking sheet like a pâté (to catch any juices that might spill), in the lower third of a preheated oven.

Cooking times vary with different meats and fish and with different size molds. A larger pâté or terrine will cook in proportionally less time per pound than smaller ones. If a trussing needle or metal skewer inserted into the center of a pâté feels hot when it is removed, the pâté is done. Test seafood and vegetable pâtés and terrines for doneness as you would a custard. If the trussing needle or metal skewer comes out nearly clean, it is cooked through. Cooked terrines feel firm to the touch and their juices run clear. In either case, if you are uncertain, use an instant-reading food thermometer to check. The filling should reach 150°F to 160°F. Those preparations made with whole meat fillets or chunks of meat can be served slightly rare at about 145°F. Keep in mind the pâté or terrine continues to cook for a short time after it is removed from the oven.

Once the terrine is removed from the oven, place it on a shallow, dry pan. With the foil still intact, chill the terrine or allow it to rest for 30 minutes, then weight it. When a recipe requires, weight meat terrines with a 1- to 2-pound weight. Remove the weight only after the terrine has chilled or set overnight. This process compacts and binds the forcemeat, preventing it from crumbling when sliced and served. Seafood and vegetable terrines need little or no weighting. In especially light preparations, no weight is required. Since pâtés cannot be weighted, aspic is poured into them (through the steam hole) while they are still hot. The aspic binds the forcemeat, fills in any gaps, and adds flavor and texture to the pâté. After chilling, pour in more aspic until it reaches the top of the steam hole. Chill the pâté overnight before unmolding it.

STORING PATES AND TERRINES

Refrigerate meat pâtés and terrines for 2 or 3 days to ripen their flavor. Covered and refrigerated, they keep for about a week. Terrines will keep for several weeks if sealed with a ½-inch layer of melted lard or rendered goose fat and refrigerated. If you need to store them longer, remove the terrines from their molds and wipe off any excess fat and jelly. Return them to clean, dry molds and seal them with fat. You may decorate the fat with sprigs of herbs or dried spices before securely covering the terrine in foil.

Avoid freezing meat pâtés and terrines; it alters the texture of both the farce and the pastry. If you must, charcuterie is better frozen uncooked rather than cooked. However, if the fat content is 50 percent or more, as in a rillette, freezing works well. In France, bottling terrines in jars (like fruits) is a popular method of preservation. Prepared on the stove like a steamed pudding, they take about 2 hours to cook.

Seafood and vegetable pâtés and terrines should be refrigerated at least overnight before serving, and taste best after one day. Some keep for as long as 5 to 7 days, but their taste changes as they age. Shrimp and scallop terrines freeze quite well, with little change in flavor, but their texture softens.

SETTING THEM OUT

Well-chilled pâtés and terrines slice best. Like cheese, however, they taste best closer to room temperature. After slicing a loaf, allow it to stand for an hour before serving. In this way, all the subtleties of flavor have a chance to emerge. On the other hand, those made of seafood are quite perishable and should not remain at room temperature for an extended time. For buffets, arrange and refrigerate several smaller platters and serve them as needed.

You may prefer to remove the border of fat from the slices of a meat terrine prior to serving them. If you are not offended by this thin outline of fat, leave it to add a nice frame to the slice.

BASICS OF ASSEMBLING AND BAKING A PATE

Although most containers make suitable molds for pâtés, collapsible or hinged metal forms are preferable. You can remove the clip or pin to pull the sides of the form away from the pâté without damaging the crust. Crusts also bake more evenly in metal molds.

Roll out the dough to 3⁄16 inch thick for the bottom and sides of the pâté and to 1⁄8 inch for the top cover or lid. The thicker crust absorbs more of the melting fat as the pâté bakes. Line the dough with fresh fatback bards or spread it with a layer of fine mousseline to help prevent the pastry from becoming soggy. Seal any seams in the dough with egg wash.

One and a half pounds of dough will line a 6-cup mold (8½ by 4½ by 2½ inches), a 6½-cup kugelhopf mold (8 by 4½ inches), or a hinged metal mold (14 by 3 by 3½ inches). Two pounds of dough will line a 5½-cup fluted brioche mold (8 by 4 inches) or a 13-cup mold (10½ by 5½ by 4 inches). A 4-cup saddle mold (10 by 4½ by 2 inches) requires 1½ pounds of dough.

Roll out the dough into a rectangle 3⁄16 inch thick for the bottom and sides of the pâté and 1⁄8 inch thick for the lid. To line the mold with one piece of dough (excluding the lid), make the rectangle about 2 inches longer and wider than the total dimension of the bottom plus both sides. This provides a ½- to ¾-inch overhang on each side. Lightly press the bottom and sides of the mold onto the dough to outline the size, then cut (fig. 2-1).

Grease the sides of the mold with butter or oil. Flour the dough and fold it in thirds lengthwise to transfer into the mold. Gently fit it to the shape of the mold, taking care not to puncture or tear the dough (fig. 2-2).

Use a small, floured ball of dough to press the pâté dough firmly onto the sides of the mold. Working from the bottom up, use your fingers to press the dough evenly into the corners without pulling or tearing it (fig. 2-3). Trim the edges with scissors or a sharp paring knife, leaving a ½- to ¾-inch overhang. You may wrap the dough-lined mold and lid in plastic and refrigerate until ready to use.

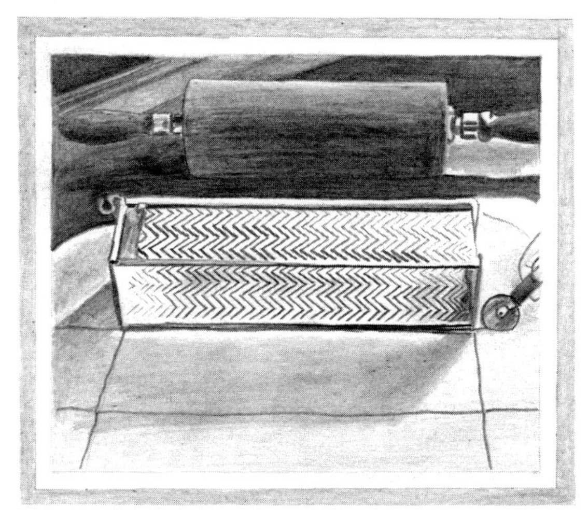

2-1. Lightly press the mold into the dough and then cut the outlined dough, allowing ½- to ¾-inch overhang on each side.

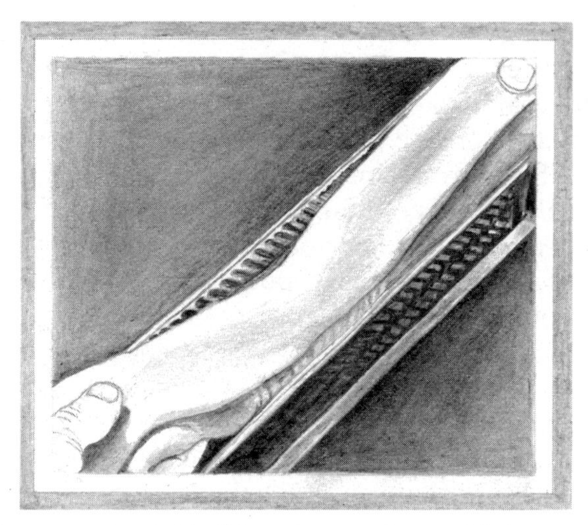

2-2. Gently place the folded dough into the mold, being careful not to puncture or break it.

Line the bottom and sides of the dough with overlapping fresh fatback bards, leaving a ¾- to 1-inch overhang (fig. 2-4). Or, instead of fatback, spread the dough with a ½- to 1-inch layer of fine mousseline. Press the fatback or mousseline snugly into the corners to avoid air bubbles.

Fill the mold with alternating layers of farce and garniture or with any arrangement of ingredients a recipe calls for. End with a layer of farce or

2-3. Working from the bottom up, press the dough evenly into the corners of the mold.

2-4. Line the dough with overlapping bards of fatback or with a ½- to 1-inch layer of mousseline.

mousseline. Fold the fatback over the top to seal in the filling completely. Firmly tap the pâté several times on a towel-lined counter to settle the filling.

Fold the overhanging edges of dough over the top of the pâté. If necessary, add an extra strip of dough to cover the filling completely. Brush the top with egg wash and fit the lid in place. Gently press the lid onto the pâté (fig. 2-5).

Crimp the edges of the lid to seal. Use a small pastry cutter or sharp paring knife to cut steam holes in the top. Cut the holes through both the dough and the fatback if used. Usually one hole adequately vents a pie-shaped pâté, while two or three may be required for a long rectangular pâté. Brush the lid with egg wash.

Decorate the lid with egg-washed dough cutouts or lightly score it in a patterned design. Roll a doubled piece of foil into a 2-inch collar. Place this chimney into the steam hole to prevent the pâté juices from spilling onto the crust while baking. Cook the pâté on a baking sheet (to catch any juices that might spill) in the lower third of a preheated oven.

To test for doneness, insert a trussing needle or metal skewer into the center of the pâté until it almost reaches the bottom. Remove the skewer after 15 seconds and place it against your lip. If the pâté is cooked, the skewer should feel warm where it passed through the center of the pâté and hot where it passed through the top and bottom. Or test the absolute center of the pâté (not through a steam hole) with an instant-reading ther-

2-5. Brush egg wash onto the top of the pâté; then cover with the lid.

mometer. Most pâtés are cooked when they reach an internal temperature of 150°F to 160°F or about 145°F for a slightly rare garniture.

After chilling the pâté, pour cooled, melted aspic into the steam holes until the aspic reaches the top. Chill again. Unmold when ready to serve.

BASICS OF ASSEMBLING AND BAKING A TERRINE

Assemble a terrine like a pâté without a crust. Line the mold with thin fatback bards slightly overlapped to seal in the filling or with a large rectangular piece of caul fat. If you prefer not to use fat, you can grease the mold with shortening or oil and line it with roasting film, parchment, or aluminum foil. Make certain to remove the film, paper, or foil before slicing and serving the terrine.

Follow "Basics of Assembling and Baking a Pâté" to line the terrine with fatback and fill. Arrange the overlapping fatback bards so that one piece of fat turns each corner without a seam (fig. 2-6). Leave a 2- to 3-inch overhang of fat on all sides.

Fold the overlapping edges of fat over the top of the filled terrine. Add an extra piece of fatback to cover the top completely. Firmly tap the terrine several times on a towel-lined counter to settle the filling. Decorate the top with herbs and spices used in the seasoning.

Cover the terrine with a double layer of well-greased aluminum foil, crimped tightly around the edges of the mold. Cook the terrine in a water bath. Place it on an inverted cake rack in a pan filled with enough hot (176°F), but not boiling, water to rise two-thirds of the way up the sides of the mold.

2-6. Line the terrine with overlapping fatback bards, making sure there are no seams at the corners.

A cooked terrine feels firm to the touch, and its juices run clear. Test a meat terrine as you would a pâté, using a trussing needle, metal skewer, or instant-reading thermometer. Most meat terrines are cooked until they reach an internal temperature of 150°F to 160°F, or about 145°F for a slightly rare garniture. Test seafood and vegetable terrines like a custard. They are cooked through when a metal skewer comes out nearly clean. Cool the terrine on a wire rack and allow it to rest for 30 minutes. Then, if the recipe requires, weight and chill the terrine (fig. 2-7). Pour cooled, melted aspic into the cold terrine and chill again.

2-7. After it cools, weight the terrine.

SHAPING EROTIC PATES AND OTHER FREE-FORM DELIGHTS

Pâtés can take the form of erotic Adam and Eve cupids, Valentine hearts, Christmas trees, or anything else you can dream up to suit an occasion. Since they are not contained by molds, free-standing pâtés require a firm yeast or egg-dough crust to seal in and support the filling. Choose almost any meat, fish, vegetable, or fruit filling. For best results, mound the filling no higher than 1 to 3 inches, depending on the size of the pâté. If the crust browns too quickly, cover it with an aluminum foil tent for the remainder of the baking time.

Roll out the dough to ⅓ inch thick. Cut out two of the desired shapes, making them about 3 inches larger than the final size. Set the pastry base on a greased baking sheet and lay out long overlapping strips of fresh fatback with which to enclose the filling.

Following the outline of the cutout, mound the filling no higher than 1 to 3 inches on top of the pastry and fatback base, leaving a 3-inch border of dough under the fatback (fig. 2-8). Fold the overhanging edges of fatback

2-8. You can make pâtés in any form. Line the dough cutout with fatback, leaving a 3-inch overhang of dough, and then fill with pâté. Cover with a second dough cutout.

over the top to seal in the filling completely. Brush the dough border with egg wash and press it up over the sides of the filling. Egg wash the top.

Gently cover the top with the remaining dough cutout. Trim and press the cutout into place. Using a small pastry cutter or a sharp paring knife, cut one or two steam holes in the top. Cut the holes through both the dough and the fatback. Brush the pâté with egg wash.

Decorate the pâté with dough cutouts or lightly score it in a patterned design. Brush the decorated pâté with egg wash. To complete, follow the baking procedure in "Basics of Assembling and Baking a Pâté."

SAVORY MEATS

Rabbit and Pheasant Terrine

The meat of a hen pheasant is more tender than that of the cock, but the cock is meatier. Unlike hare, rabbit meat is tender and delicate in flavor, somewhat like poultry.

YIELD: 1 terrine, about 3 pounds

Marinade
1/2 cup port wine
1/4 cup brandy
1 onion, minced
4 to 5 garlic cloves, minced
1/4 teaspoon thyme
2 bay leaves

Meat (about 1 1/3 pounds) plus liver from 1 rabbit
Meat (about 1 pound) from 1 hen pheasant
1 pound fresh rindless pork belly or fatback
1 1/2 tablespoons all-purpose flour
1 egg
1 tablespoon Pâté Seasoning III
1 teaspoon chopped fresh lovage
1/2 teaspoon allspice
1/4 teaspoon thyme
1/8 teaspoon cardamom
Black pepper to taste
Salt to taste
1/2 cup pimiento, 1/2-inch diced
1 pound fresh fatback, thinly sliced to line mold
1 fresh thyme sprig
2 cups Basic Aspic flavored with port wine

Combine the ingredients for the marinade. Pour them over the rabbit and pheasant, cover, and marinate, refrigerated, for 1 hour, occasionally turning the meat.

Remove the meat and bay leaves from the marinade and reserve. Dice half the meat from the rabbit (including the liver), pheasant, and pork belly into 5/8-inch cubes. Finely grind the remaining undiced meats and fat. Chill.

Reduce the unstrained marinade to about 3 tablespoons of liquid plus the onion and garlic. In a bowl, combine the reduced marinade with the flour. Beat in the egg, pâté seasoning, lovage, allspice, thyme, cardamom, pepper, and salt. Add this mixture and the pimiento to the diced and ground meats.

Line a 6-cup mold (8½ by 4½ by 2½ inches) with fatback and fill it with farce. Cover the farce with fatback and place the reserved bay leaves and thyme sprig on top. Seal the mold with greased aluminum foil.

Bake in a water bath in a preheated 350°F oven for approximately 1 hour, or until done. Chill and weight the terrine for 3 to 5 hours with a 1-pound weight. Remove the weight, pour in cooled, melted aspic, and rechill.

Serving Suggestions
Garnish the terrine with marinated roasted red peppers sprinkled with a julienne of chopped lovage.

Wild Boar Pâté With Truffles

Wild boar is an undomesticated mammal somewhat similar to pig. Though they often live for 30 years, only the flesh of young boars (a year or younger) is worth cooking. The older animals develop an overpowering gamy taste and leathery texture. Usually only the head of an older boar is used for cooking.

YIELD: 1 pâté, about 5 pounds

Marinade
½ cup red wine
2 tablespoons brandy
3 shallots, chopped
1 garlic clove, minced
Grated zest of ½ orange
5 white peppercorns, crushed
4 juniper berries, crushed
1 teaspoon marjoram
½ teaspoon thyme
1 bay leaf
Pinch of cloves

1¾ pounds boneless wild boar meat, cut into strips
½ pound calves liver, cut into strips
½ pound bacon strips
2 teaspoons Pâté Seasoning V
1 egg
1½ to 2 tablespoons game or brown glaze
¼ pound diced fresh fatback, ⅜-inch cubed
1 ounce truffles, finely diced
¼ cup chopped pistachio nuts
2 pounds Pâté or Short-Crust Pastry, rolled out to 3/16 inch thick
¾ pound fresh fatback, thinly sliced to line mold
Egg wash
3 cups melted Game or Basic Aspic

Combine the ingredients for the marinade. In a ceramic or stainless steel bowl, pour the marinade over the strips of wild boar, calves liver, and bacon. Refrigerate for at least 24 hours.

Remove the bay leaf, drain off the liquid marinade, and discard. Sprinkle the marinated meats with the pâté seasoning and pass them twice through the fine disk of a food grinder. Beat in the egg and the glaze. Stir in the diced fatback, truffles, and chopped pistachios.

Grease a 2-quart mold. Line it with pastry dough and line the dough with fatback. Fill the lined mold with farce. Cover the farce with the remaining fatback, then fold over the dough edges and brush them with egg wash. Seal the pâté with a pastry lid. Cut out a steam hole; decorate and egg wash the top.

Insert a foil chimney and bake in a preheated 425°F oven for 10 minutes. Lower the temperature to 325°F and bake for 45 minutes to 1 hour longer.

Chill the pâté and pour cooled, melted aspic into the steam hole until the aspic reaches the top. Chill and unmold when ready to serve.

Serving Suggestions

Garnish the pâté with sliced fresh persimmon and Persimmon Sauce on the side.

Variations

Substitute chicken or beef liver for the calves liver.

Substitute fresh pork belly for the bacon.

Venison Pâté

YIELD: 1 pâté, about 3½ pounds

Marinade
¼ cup red wine
1½ tablespoons red wine vinegar
1 tablespoon brandy
1 teaspoon vegetable oil
1 teaspoon brown sugar, honey, or molasses
5 juniper berries, crushed
3 black peppercorns, crushed
1 garlic clove, minced
½ bay leaf
Pinch of rosemary
Pinch of thyme

¾ pound lean boneless venison, cut into finger-size strips
2 venison fillets, about ¼ pound each
1 teaspoon vegetable oil
3 shallots, minced
1 garlic clove, minced
½ pound boneless pork butt, cut into finger-size strips
2½ teaspoons Pâté Seasoning V
½ pound fresh rindless pork belly, cut into finger-size strips
½ pound cooked skinned tongue, ½-inch cubed
¼ pound fresh fatback, ½-inch cubed
2 tablespoons chopped black walnuts
2 tablespoons julienned black olives
1½ pounds Pâté or Short-Crust Pastry seasoned with ground juniper, rolled out 3/16 inch thick
3 to 4 slices fresh fatback, ⅛ inch thick
Egg wash
2½ cups Basic Aspic flavored with Madeira

Combine all the ingredients for the marinade and bring them to a boil. Let cool for 5 to 10 minutes. In a ceramic or stainless steel bowl, pour the marinade over the venison strips and the two fillets. Cover and refrigerate for at least 4 hours or overnight.

Remove the venison and set it aside. Strain the marinade, discarding the solid ingredients. Over high heat, reduce the marinade to 3 tablespoons and add the shallots and garlic to soften. Toss the strips of venison (but not the two venison fillets) and pork butt with the pâté seasoning and pass them through the fine disk of a food grinder. Add the strips of pork belly to the ground meat and again pass the mixture through a food grinder. Mix together the ground meats, reduced marinade, diced tongue and fatback, walnuts, and black olives. Refrigerate the farce.

Grease a 1½-quart hinged metal mold and line it with dough. Press half the farce into the bottom of the mold, forming a slight groove down the center of the farce. Roll each venison fillet in sliced fatback and place it in the groove. Add the remaining farce. Fold over the dough edges and brush them with egg wash. Seal the pâté with a pastry lid. Cut a steam hole in the center; decorate and egg wash the top.

Insert a foil chimney and bake in a preheated 425°F oven for 15 minutes. Lower the temperature to 350°F and bake for another 25 to 30 minutes, or until done.

Chill the pâté and pour cooled, melted aspic into the steam holes until the aspic reaches the top. Chill and unmold when ready to serve.

Serving Suggestions
Puree either a little Orange Cranberry Relish or chutney and mix it with some whipped cream to garnish the pâté. Or serve the pâté with Chestnut Sauce.

Variations
Substitute ham or boneless pork butt for the tongue.

Meat-Market Pâté

This is chef Arnold Fanger's recipe for a pâté that was quite popular at the Market Bar and Dining Room in the World Trade Center. See the color insert for a photograph of this pâté.

YIELD: 1 pâté, about 8 pounds

3/4 pound boneless pork butt, 5/8-inch cubed
1/3 pound boneless veal shoulder, 5/8-inch cubed
1/3 pound chicken livers, 5/8-inch cubed
1 1/2 tablespoons bacon fat
1/3 cup finely diced shallots
1/2 unpeeled apple, cored and chopped
1 1/2 tablespoons minced garlic
1 3/4 tablespoons Pâté Seasoning IV
1/2 teaspoon thyme
1/4 cup brandy
1/4 cup port wine
1 3/4 pounds boneless pork butt, coarsely ground
1 1/2 pounds fresh rindless pork belly or fatback, coarsely ground
2/3 pound boneless veal shoulder, coarsely ground
2/3 pound chicken livers, coarsely ground
3/4 cup softened and julienned shiitake mushrooms
1/3 cup shelled pistachio nuts
4 pounds Pâté Pastry, rolled out 3/16 inch thick
2 1/2 pounds fresh fatback, thinly sliced to line mold
Egg wash
1 quart Basic Aspic flavored with port wine

Sear the diced pork, veal, and chicken livers in the bacon fat. Add the shallots, apple, garlic, pâté seasoning, and thyme. After a couple of minutes, pour in the brandy and port wine and heat long enough to evaporate the alcohol. Chill.

Mix together the ground pork, pork belly, veal, and chicken livers. Add the shiitake mushrooms, pistachios, and the chilled sautéed meats. Test the seasonings and correct if necessary.

Grease an 18- by 5½- by 4-inch mold. Line it with pastry dough and line the dough with fatback. Fill the lined mold with farce. Cover the farce with the remaining fatback, then fold over the dough edges and brush them with egg wash. Seal the pâté with a pastry lid. Cut out a steam hole; decorate and egg wash the top.

Insert a foil chimney and bake in a preheated 425°F oven for 10 minutes. Lower the temperature to 350°F and bake for 1 to 1½ hours longer.

Chill the pâté and pour cooled, melted aspic into the steam hole until the aspic reaches the top. Chill and unmold when ready to serve.

Serving Suggestions
Garnish the pâté slices with Orange Cranberry Relish.

Spinach and Cheese Terrine

Distinctively flavorful and moist, this unorthodox terrine is inexpensive and quick to prepare. (This terrine is an adaptation of Nancy Giambona's recipe.)

YIELD: 1 terrine, about 2½ pounds (about 26 ½-inch slices)

Farce
4 slices bread
2 tablespoons Brown Stock
1½ pounds ground pork, veal, and beef (½ pound each)
¼ cup grated Parmesan cheese
½ bunch Italian parsley, chopped
2 garlic cloves, minced
1 egg
¼ teaspoon black pepper
Pinch of salt

1 pound spinach leaves, washed, stems removed
1 garlic clove, minced
1 tablespoon olive oil
1 cup ricotta or low-fat cottage cheese
1 egg
¼ cup grated Parmesan cheese
⅛ teaspoon black pepper
14- by 17-inch piece caul fat
2 ounces thinly sliced prosciutto or ham (about 4 to 5 slices)
2 ounces mozzarella cheese, shredded
1 cup Chicken, White, or Brown Stock

Moisten the bread with the 2 tablespoons meat stock and break it into small bits. Combine all the ingredients for the farce and thoroughly blend them with the moistened bread. If the meat farce is too moist, add some bread crumbs.

Steam or blanch the spinach leaves until they are limp but still bright green in color. Squeeze out the excess water and chop. Lightly sauté the garlic and spinach in olive oil. Cool the spinach. In a bowl, combine the cooled spinach with the ricotta, egg, grated Parmesan, and black pepper.

Spread out the caul fat and form the meat farce into a 10- by 14-inch rectangle on top of the fat. Leaving a 1-inch border of meat, spread the spinach-and-cheese mixture over the farce. Add a layer of sliced prosciutto, then shredded mozzarella.

Carefully roll the terrine (starting with the 10-inch side) in a spiral fashion as you would a jelly roll. Smooth the seam together and pinch the edges to make sure the filling does not leak out. Wrap the caul fat around the loaf, placing the seam side on the bottom. Tightly wrap the pâté in foil and refrigerate for 2 hours or overnight before cooking.

Preheat the oven to 375°F. Remove the pâté from the foil and bake it in a roasting pan with the meat stock for approximately 1 hour, basting it occasionally.

Serving Suggestions
Serve the terrine hot with a marinara sauce, an onion sauce, or with the degreased and thickened pan juices. Garnish with sliced mushrooms and fresh herbs. Let the loaf sit for about 15 minutes before slicing. Serve the terrine cold with a tomato salad or with pickles and relish. It also makes a tasty sandwich.

Variations
If you use frozen spinach (one 10-ounce package), simply defrost the spinach and eliminate the blanching. Escarole, kale, or other leafy greens may be substituted for the spinach.

This terrine also can be assembled in layers. Divide the meat farce into three equal portions and divide the fillings into two. Form the farce into three separate 7- by 12-inch rectangles. Place one layer of meat farce on the caul fat. Leaving a 1-inch border of farce, spread half the filling over it. Gently place the second layer of farce over the filling. Crimp the edges of the meat together, sealing in the mixture. Follow this procedure to add the remaining filling, and finish it with the third layer of farce. Wrap the loaf in caul fat and follow the above recipe.

Farmhouse Terrine

This recipe makes a rough, chunky-textured terrine.

YIELD: 1 terrine, about 8½ pounds

1½ pounds Basic Veal and Pork Farce or sausage meat
1½ pounds fresh rindless pork belly, ¾-inch cubed
1¼ pounds lean boneless pork butt, 1-inch cubed
1⅛ pounds lean boneless veal shoulder, 1-inch cubed
1⅛ pounds cooked tongue, ham, or smoked ham, 1-inch cubed
¾ pound soaked and trimmed beef sweetbreads, ¾-inch cubed
¼ cup chopped fresh dill
1¾ tablespoons Pâté Seasoning I or II
1 teaspoon black pepper
1 teaspoon salt
2½ pounds fresh fatback, thinly sliced to line mold
3 bay leaves
3 cups Melted Basic Aspic

Mix together all the ingredients except the fatback, bay leaves, and melted aspic. Test the seasonings and correct if necessary.

Line an 18- by 5½- by 4-inch mold with fatback and fill it with farce. Cover the farce with the remaining fatback and place the bay leaves on top. Seal the mold with greased aluminum foil.

Bake in a water bath in a preheated 350°F oven for approximately 1½ hours, or until cooked. Chill, then weight the terrine for 2 hours with two 1-pound weights. Remove the weight, pour in cooled, melted aspic and rechill. Unmold when ready to serve.

Serving Suggestions
Garnish the sliced terrine with julienned Jerusalem artichoke tossed in spicy Mustard Sauce.

Variations
Substitute another meat for the sweetbreads or eliminate them completely and use ¾ pound of pork, veal, or tongue instead.

Haymarket Pâté

Since this makes a large pâté, you may want to halve the ingredients or form the farce into two or three smaller molds. If this is the case, you will need extra fatback and dough to line the additional molds. You might also consider making the mixture into one pâté and one terrine.

YIELD: 1 pâté, about 9 pounds

2 pounds boneless veal shoulder, medium ground twice
2 pounds boneless pork butt, medium ground twice
2 pounds fresh rindless pork belly or fatback, coarsely ground
1 pound garlic sausage, skinned and coarsely ground
1/4 cup applejack brandy, heated to evaporate alcohol and cooled
1 3/4 tablespoons Pâté Seasoning IV
1 teaspoon black pepper
1 teaspoon salt
4 pounds Pâté Pastry, rolled out 3/16 inch thick
2 1/2 pounds fresh fatback, thinly sliced to line mold
Egg wash
1 quart melted Basic Aspic

Mix together the veal, pork, pork belly, sausage, applejack, and seasonings. Test the seasonings and correct if necessary.

Grease an 18- by 5 1/2- by 4-inch mold. Line it with pastry dough and line the dough with fatback. Fill the lined mold with farce. Cover the farce with the remaining fatback, then fold over the dough edges and brush them with egg wash. Seal the pâté with a pastry lid. Cut out a steam hole; decorate and egg wash the top.

Insert a foil chimney and bake in a preheated 400°F oven for 10 to 15 minutes. Lower the temperature to 350°F and bake for 1 to 1 1/2 hours longer. If you use smaller molds, bake the pâtés for less time.

Chill the pâté and pour cooled, melted aspic into the steam hole until the aspic reaches the top. Rechill and unmold when ready to serve.

Serving Suggestions
Garnish the pâté slices with Apple Chutney.

Variations
Use any combination of pork and veal.

Country-Style Pâté

This country-style pâté, known as *pâté de campagne,* actually is a terrine and is baked as such. Its coarse texture is reminiscent of the flavorful, no-fuss loaves made by French farmers.

YIELD: 1 pâté, about 2¾ pounds

½ pound pork liver, ⅝-inch cubed
¾ cup milk
½ pound ground pork
½ pound ground veal
2 eggs
½ pound boneless lean pork, ⅝-inch cubed
½ pound fresh fatback, ⅝-inch cubed
2 tablespoons brandy, heated to evaporate alcohol and cooled
3 garlic cloves, minced
Grated zest of 1 orange
1½ tablespoons Pâté Seasoning II
¾ pound fatty bacon strips to line mold
3 juniper berries
2 bay leaves
1 fresh thyme sprig
1 fresh sage sprig

Soak the diced pork liver in the milk for 4 hours or overnight. Combine the ground pork and veal with the eggs. Mix in the diced pork and fatback, brandy, garlic, orange zest, and pâté seasoning. Drain and discard the milk from the liver, then add the liver to the farce.

Line the bottom and sides of a 6-cup rectangular mold with bacon strips and fill the mold with farce. Crisscross any remaining bacon strips over the farce. Place the juniper berries, bay leaves, and herb sprigs on top. Cover the mold with a well-greased piece of parchment paper cut to fit the top.

Bake the pâté in a preheated 425°F oven for about 1 hour or bake it at 350°F to 375°F in a water bath for 1 to 1½ hours.

Serving Suggestions
Garnish the pâté with a dab of coarse, spicy mustard, cornichons, and pickled pearl onions.

Variations
Eliminate the ground veal and use ¼ pound diced pork liver and ¼ pound ground pork instead.

Line the terrine with caul fat or fatback instead of bacon strips.

Pork and Veal Terrine with Shiitake and Pears

See the color insert for a photograph of this terrine.

YIELD: 1 terrine, about 5 pounds

2¼ pounds boneless pork butt, finely ground
1¾ pounds boneless veal shoulder, finely ground
1 pound fresh rindless pork belly or fatback, medium ground
⅓ pound garlic sausage, casings removed
¾ cup softened and julienned shiitake mushrooms
2 firm unpeeled pears, cored and cut into ⅜-inch cubes
¼ cup minced onion
1⅔ to 2⅓ tablespoons Pâté Seasoning IV
⅔ teaspoon thyme
5 tablespoons pear william, heated to evaporate alcohol and cooled
3 tablespoons medium sherry, heated to evaporate alcohol and cooled
Black pepper to taste
Salt to taste
2 pounds fresh fatback, thinly sliced to line mold
2 bay leaves
1 fresh thyme sprig

Combine all the ingredients. Test the seasonings and correct if necessary.

Line a 13-cup mold (10½ by 5½ by 4 inches) with fatback and fill it with farce. Cover the farce with fatback and place the bay leaves and thyme sprig on top. Seal the mold with greased aluminum foil.

Bake in a water bath in a preheated 350°F oven for 1½ to 1¾ hours, or until cooked. Chill and weight the terrine for 2 hours with a 2-pound weight.

Serving Suggestions
Serve with Cabbage Pear Relish.

Rustic Pie

Rustic Pie, or *pizza rustica* as the Italians call it, is a traditional Eastertime dish.

YIELD: 1 pâté, about 9 pounds

12 eggs
3 pounds ricotta cheese
1 pound lean prosciutto, 1/2-inch cubed
1 pound Genoa salami, 1/2-inch cubed
1 pound sopressata or salemetti dried sausage, 1/2-inch cubed
1 pound mozzarella cheese, 1/2-inch cubed
2 pounds Rustic Piecrust dough, rolled out 3/16 inch thick
Egg wash

In a large bowl beat the eggs into the ricotta. Mix in the diced prosciutto, salami, sopressata, and mozzarella.

Grease an 11- by 16- by 2½-inch baking pan and line it with dough. Fill the lined pan with the cheese-meat mixture. Brush the edges of the dough with egg wash and seal the pâté with a dough lid. Crimp the edges and trim away any excess dough. Decorate and egg wash the top, then pierce the lid with a fork in several places to allow steam to escape.

Bake the pâté in a preheated 375°F oven for 1½ to 2 hours.

Serving Suggestions

Serve the Rustic Pie, just warmed or chilled, as the first course of a holiday dinner. The pie also makes a hearty main course, accompanied by various garlicky pickled vegetables, such as hot peppers, green tomatoes, and julienned eggplant.

Variations

Substitute Monterey Jack cheese for mozzarella.

Substitute cooked ham, smoked ham, or tongue for prosciutto.

Substitute an assortment of other dried sausage such as pepperoni, chorizo, and felinetti for the salami and/or sopressata.

Headcheese

Though not the traditional German fare, this recipe produces a respectable, good-tasting variation. Flavorful aspic is crucial for best results.

YIELD: 1 terrine, about 8 pounds

6 cooked pig's feet, boned (about 4½ pounds with bones)
½ cooked beef tongue, skinned and trimmed (about 1½ pounds)
¾ pound ham
⅜ cup coarsely chopped fresh parsley
2 tablespoons coarsely chopped fresh dill
10 to 12 cups strong Basic Aspic

Cut all the meat into 1- by 4-inch strips. Mix the dill and parsley together. In the mold, randomly layer the meats and sprinkle them with herbs. Once all the meats and herbs are layered in the mold, gently ladle in the aspic until it comes to the top. Cover the mold and chill until firmly set.

Serving Suggestions
Serve Headcheese with Mustard or Horseradish Sauce.

Rosemary Lamb Pâté

The Greeks make a stuffed lamb wrapped in pastry as part of their traditional Easter repast. The pastry is decorated with dough cutouts of religious symbols of their holiday, such as leaves, flowers, small birds, and braids.

YIELD: 1 pâté, about 5½ pounds

¼ pound lean ground pork
½ to ¾ cup mango chutney
¼ cup chopped fresh parsley
1 to 2 tablespoons Dijon-style mustard
¼ teaspoon cumin
Black pepper to taste
Salt to taste
1 egg
3½ to 4 pounds dough (Classic Brioche, White Yeast, or Classic Puff Pastry)
1 3-pound rack of lamb, boned and trimmed of excess fat
3 tablespoons vegetable oil
2 to 3 garlic cloves, pressed
1 teaspoon crushed rosemary
Egg wash

In a bowl combine the ground pork, chutney, parsley, mustard, cumin, pepper, salt, and egg. Test the seasonings and correct if necessary.

Roll the dough out into a rectangle ¼ inch thick and chill.

Spread the stuffing onto the flap of the boned rack of lamb, leaving a ½-inch border. Fold the flap over the rib-eye meat and tie the stuffed roast closed with butcher's twine. In a large skillet over medium-high heat, sear the lamb in the oil for 8 to 12 minutes, turning it on all sides. Remove the roast from the skillet and set it aside to cool. Once the lamb is cool enough to handle, remove the twine and rub the meat with garlic and rosemary.

Set the stuffed lamb on the rectangle of dough. Brush the edges of the dough with egg wash and fold them over the lamb, lightly pressing the seams together. Place the lamb, seam side down, on an oiled baking sheet. Decorate with dough scraps and cut three 1½-inch-long slashes in the top. Refrigerate for 15 to 20 minutes.

Brush the pastry with egg wash and bake in a preheated 400°F oven for 15 minutes. Reduce the heat to 375°F and bake the lamb for another 10 minutes, until golden. If you want the lamb pinker, check the internal temperature of the rib eye after it has baked for 5 to 7 minutes at 375°F. Let the lamb sit for 10 minutes before transferring it to a platter.

Serving Suggestions
Serve Rosemary Lamb Pâté hot with lemon-flavored rice pilaf speckled with freshly chopped mint and chutney on the side.

Veal Terrine with Truffles

YIELD: 1 terrine, about 6 pounds (12 to 15 servings)

1 egg
1⅔ pounds boneless pork butt, finely ground
1¼ pounds boneless veal shoulder, finely ground
¾ pound fresh rindless pork belly or fatback, finely ground
¼ pound cotechino or garlic sausage, removed from casings and crumbled
2 tablespoons minced onion
½ unpeeled apple, cored and minced
2 garlic cloves, pressed
1 to 1¾ tablespoons Pâté Seasoning III
½ teaspoon thyme
Black pepper to taste
Salt to taste
4½ tablespoons Cognac, heated to evaporate alcohol and cooled
2⅓ tablespoons Madeira, heated to evaporate alcohol and cooled
2 tablespoons shelled pistachio nuts
1 tablespoon chopped fresh tarragon
¾ to 1 ounce black truffle, finely diced
6 veal scallops (about 1½ pounds), pounded thin
2 pounds fresh fatback, thinly sliced to line mold
2 bay leaves
2 fresh tarragon sprigs
2½ cups Basic Aspic flavored with Madeira

Beat the egg into the ground pork butt, veal shoulder, pork belly, and cotechino for 5 to 10 minutes. Mix in the onion, apple, garlic, pâté seasoning, thyme, pepper, salt, Cognac, and Madeira. Test the seasonings and correct if necessary. Chill the farce.

In a food processor, puree the pistachios with 1 cup of the farce. Add the tarragon and reserve. Meanwhile, mix the truffle into the remaining farce.

Place three veal scallops on a layer of thinly sliced fatback the length of the mold. Spread with half of the pistachio mixture and roll up, jelly-roll style. Make a second veal roll.

Line a 10-cup mold (12 by 4¼ by 4 inches) with fatback. Press one-third of the farce into the bottom of the mold, forming a slight groove down the center of the farce. Place the first veal roll in the groove. Cover with another third of the farce, and set the second veal roll in place. Add the remaining farce. Cover the farce with fatback and place the bay leaves and tarragon sprigs on top. Seal the mold with greased aluminum foil.

Bake in a water bath in a preheated 350°F oven for 1 to 1¼ hours, or until cooked. After baking, weight the terrine for an hour with a 1-pound weight. Remove the weight, pour in cooled, melted aspic, and rechill. Unmold when ready to serve.

Serving Suggestions
Serve the terrine warm with Lemon Herb Butter Sauce, or chilled with a tarragon-flavored mayonnaise or crème fraîche.

Variations
Substitute turkey for the veal.

Substitute black olives for the truffle.

Veal, Ham, and Quail Egg Pâté

Veal, ham, and egg pie, the British version of pâté and a popular fast food in England, is often served at local pubs with frothy mugs of stout. Unlike the "aristocratic" pâtés of old France, savory pies were fancied by commoners and nobility alike in England. The ingredients, however, differed greatly. In fact, during the reign of Elizabeth I (1558 to 1603), vendors made and sold their pies at a special corner near the Smithfield meat market known as Pie Corner.

Made with quail eggs, this pâté is a smaller, more delicate variation of the English veal, ham, and egg pie.

YIELD: 1 14-inch pâté, about 3½ pounds

Farce
¾ pound ground veal
¾ pound boneless veal shoulder, ⅝-inch cubed
½ pound smoked ham, ⅝-inch cubed
½ pound boneless pork butt, ⅝-inch cubed
¼ pound fresh rindless pork belly, ⅝-inch cubed
¼ cup finely chopped onion
5 tablespoons brandy
3 tablespoons sweet vermouth
3 tablespoons chopped fresh parsley
2 tablespoons chopped fresh sage (or ½ teaspoon dried)
Cracked black pepper
Salt to taste

1½ pounds Pâté Pastry, rolled out 3/16 inch thick
1 pound fresh fatback, thinly sliced to line mold
12 quail eggs, hard cooked and peeled
Egg wash
2½ cups Basic Aspic flavored with Vermouth

Mix together all the ingredients for the farce. Test the seasonings and correct if necessary.

Grease a hinged metal mold, 14 by 3 by 3½ inches. Line it with pastry dough and line the dough with fatback. Fill the lined mold with a little less than half the farce. Press a groove down the center of the farce. Trim a bit from the ends of each egg and line them tightly up in the groove (fig. 2-9). Add the remaining farce, firmly packing it into the mold. Cover the farce with fatback and brush the edges of the dough with egg wash. Seal the pâté with a pastry lid. Crimp the edges by pinching the dough between two fingers and trim away any excess. Cut out two steam holes; decorate and egg wash the top.

Insert foil chimneys and bake in a preheated 425°F oven for 15 minutes. Lower the temperature to 350°F and bake for another 30 to 35 minutes, or

2-9. Line the quail eggs tightly along the groove in the farce.

until cooked. While still warm, fill the pâté with cooled, melted aspic. Chill. Pour more aspic into the steam holes until the aspic reaches the top. Chill again and unmold when ready to serve.

Serving Suggestions
Serve the Veal, Ham, and Quail Egg Pâté with Mustard Horseradish Sauce or Mustard Herb Sauce.

Variations
Substitute cooked tongue or smoked ham for all or part of the ham.

Substitute veal for the pork butt and belly.

Sweetbread Terrine with Straw Mushrooms and Morels

To prepare sweetbreads, soak them in cold water for 2 to 4 hours. Blanch them in boiling water or stock, then trim any sinew and veins.

YIELD: 1 terrine, about 3½ pounds

1½ pounds veal sweetbreads, soaked, blanched, and trimmed
1½ tablespoons butter
¼ cup Drambuie
½ cup rich, gelatinous White or Chicken Stock
⅛ teaspoon allspice
⅛ teaspoon mace
Pinch of cayenne
1 pound boneless veal shoulder, finely ground
½ pound fresh rindless pork belly, finely ground
4 shallots, minced
1 tablespoon Pâté Seasoning III
Pinch of cinnamon
2 egg whites
⅝ cup heavy cream
1 tablespoon chopped fresh chervil
¾ cup straw mushrooms, halved
½ cup morels, cleaned and halved
¾ pound fresh fatback, thinly sliced to line mold
2 bay leaves

Separate the sweetbreads into pieces and quickly sauté them in butter, not cooking them through. Set the sweetbreads aside. Add the Drambuie, stock, allspice, mace, and cayenne to the skillet and reduce to a syrupy glaze. Pour over the sweetbreads and toss. Chill.

Combine the ground veal, pork belly, shallots, pâté seasoning, and cinnamon. Puree the ground mixture in a food processor until smooth. Chill. In a separate bowl blend the egg whites with the cream, then slowly beat into the pureed farce. Stir in the chervil. Fold in the glazed sweetbreads, straw mushrooms, and morels. Test the seasonings and correct if necessary.

Line an 8-cup mold with fatback and fill it with farce. Cover the farce with fatback and place the bay leaves on top. Seal the mold with greased aluminum foil.

Bake in a water bath in a preheated 375°F oven for 1 to 1½ hours, or until cooked. Chill and weight the terrine for 2 hours with a 2-pound weight.

Serving Suggestions
Serve cold with Spiced Raisins in Wine.

Variations
Substitute turkey for the veal.

Substitute lightly sautéed common mushrooms for the morels and/or straw mushrooms.

Duck Terrine with Veal and Green Peppercorns

Since duck contains a lot of fat, there is no need to line the mold with fatback in this recipe.

YIELD: 1 terrine, about 3¼ pounds

Marinade
2 tablespoons vegetable oil
¼ cup strong red wine
1 teaspoon rosemary
6 juniper berries, crushed
1 bay leaf
Grated black pepper

1 5-pound duck, boned as for a galantine—see chapter 4 (dice the liver and add to the farce)
¾ pound veal eye of round
1 small onion, minced
2 garlic cloves, pressed
1 tablespoon grated orange zest
2 tablespoons Cognac
1¼ pounds sausage meat or Basic Veal and Pork Farce
1 to 2 tablespoons Pâté Seasoning I
1 teaspoon Dijon-style mustard
1 tablespoon coarsely chopped green peppercorns, drained
½ teaspoon cracked black pepper
¼ teaspoon thyme
⅛ teaspoon cinnamon
Pinch of nutmeg
Pinch of cloves
Bay leaf
Fresh rosemary sprig
Fresh thyme sprig
3 juniper berries

Combine the ingredients for the marinade and pour over the boned duck and the veal fillets. Cover and marinate, refrigerated, for 6 hours to 3 days, occasionally turning the meat.

Heat the onion, garlic, and orange zest in Cognac to soften the ingredients and evaporate the alcohol. Mix into the sausage meat, along with the pâté seasoning, mustard, green peppercorns, cracked black pepper, thyme, cinnamon, nutmeg, and cloves. Test the seasonings and correct if necessary. Chill.

Drain off and discard the marinade. Line a 6-cup triangular mold (7½ by 3¾ by 3½ inches) with the boned duck, skin side out. Press half the farce into the bottom of the mold, forming a slight groove down the center of the farce. Place the marinated veal fillets in the groove. Add the remaining farce. Fold over the edges of the duck and sew them closed or secure them together with toothpicks. Place the bay leaf, rosemary and thyme sprigs, and juniper berries on top. Seal the mold with aluminum foil.

Bake in a water bath in a preheated 350°F oven for approximately 1¼ hours. After baking, chill and weight the terrine for 3 hours with a 2-pound weight. Unmold when ready to serve.

Serving Suggestions
Garnish the sliced terrine with fresh orange wedges and a bit of Spicy Orange Relish.

Variations
Eliminate the marinade altogether.

Substitute turkey for the veal or eliminate the ingredient altogether.

Turkey and Spinach Terrine

This recipe works well with any poultry or game bird.

YIELD: 1 terrine about 5 pounds (12 to 15 servings)

Turkey Mousseline
3 pounds boneless turkey, finely ground
4 egg whites
1½ teaspoons white pepper
1½ teaspoons salt
3 cups heavy cream
⅓ cup chopped fresh dill

Spinach Filling
1 pound spinach, cooked, drained, and chopped
1 pound smoked ham, ¼-inch cubed
⅔ cup chopped walnuts
1 small onion, finely diced
2 to 3 eggs
¼ teaspoon nutmeg
Black pepper to taste
Salt to taste
1¼ cups heavy cream

Combine the ground turkey with the egg whites, pepper, and salt. Puree one-third of the turkey in a food processor until smooth. With the machine running, slowly pour in 1 cup of the heavy cream. Prepare two more batches in the same way. Combine the three batches and fold in the dill. Test the seasonings and correct if necessary.

Combine all the ingredients for the spinach filling except the heavy cream. Beat in the heavy cream a little at a time.

Grease a 10-cup mold (12 by 4 by 4 inches). Starting and ending with the turkey mousseline, assemble alternating layers of the turkey and spinach mixtures. Seal the mold with greased aluminum foil.

Bake in a water bath in a preheated 350°F oven for 30 to 40 minutes. After baking, chill the terrine.

Serving Suggestions
Serve the terrine with Caper Dill Sauce.

Chicken, Shiitake, and Spinach Torte

YIELD: 1 10-inch pie

Marinade
1/4 cup Madeira
1/4 cup Chicken Stock
1 tablespoon Pâté Seasoning III
1 tablespoon chopped fresh parsley
1 garlic clove, minced
Pinch chopped fresh thyme

1 1/2 pounds chicken cutlets, lightly pounded
2 tablespoons olive oil
1 1/2 ounces dried shiitake mushrooms, softened
3/4 pound untrimmed boneless pork butt, finely ground
1/2 pound boneless chicken, finely ground
1/4 pound fresh fatback, finely ground
1 to 1 1/2 tablespoons Pâté Seasoning III
1 egg white, lightly beaten
1/2 cup heavy cream, whipped to soft peaks
1 1/2 cups sautéed chopped spinach, drained
1/4 teaspoon nutmeg
Pepper to taste
Salt to taste
2 pounds Short-Crust Pastry or White Yeast Dough
Egg wash

Combine the ingredients for the marinade. Brown, but do not cook, the chicken cutlets in the oil. Toss the browned cutlets and softened shiitake mushrooms in the marinade. Cover and refrigerate for 4 hours to 1 day.

Beat together the ground pork, chicken, and fatback for 5 to 10 minutes and mix in the pâté seasoning and egg white. Test the seasonings and correct if necessary. Fold in the whipped heavy cream. In a separate bowl, season the spinach with nutmeg, pepper, and salt.

Remove the cutlets and mushrooms from the marinade and reduce the marinade to a glaze. Coat the cutlets with the glaze.

Roll out the dough to line a greased 10-inch cake pan. Press two-thirds of the pork farce onto the bottom and up the sides of the dough-lined pan. Add a layer of spinach to the bottom, followed by the shiitake mushrooms and the glazed chicken cutlets. Spread the remaining farce over the top.

Fold over the dough edges and brush them with egg wash. Seal the torte with a pastry lid. Cut a steam hole in the center; decorate and egg wash the top.

Insert a foil chimney and bake in a preheated 425°F oven for 50 to 55 minutes. Let the torte rest awhile before cutting into it so that the ingredients can settle.

Serving Suggestions
Serve the Chicken, Shiitake, and Spinach Torte hot with either Bordelaise or Cumberland Sauce.

Variations
Substitute turkey for the chicken.

Substitute another mushroom for the shiitakes.

Chicken Terrine

This simple, inexpensive recipe can be assembled and frozen uncooked, then baked another time. (This terrine is based on Barbara Ewton's recipe.)

YIELD: 1 terrine, about 2¼ pounds

1 pound sausage meat
¾ cup chopped onion
1 garlic clove, minced
1 teaspoon Pâté Seasoning III
3 tablespoons brandy
¼ cup chopped fresh parsley
Black pepper to taste
Salt to taste
1 pound sliced bacon
1 pound chicken breast cutlets, sliced and flattened to ¼ inch thick
1 bay leaf

Sauté together the sausage, onion, garlic, and pâté seasoning. Add the brandy and heat to evaporate the alcohol. Remove from the heat and mix in the parsley, pepper, and salt. Test the seasonings and correct if necessary. Allow to cool.

Line a 9- by 5- by 3-inch mold with bacon strips. Starting and ending with chicken cutlets, assemble alternating layers of cutlets and the sausage mixture. Cover the farce with the remaining bacon and place the bay leaf on top. Seal the mold with greased aluminum foil.

Bake the terrine in a preheated 400°F oven for 40 to 45 minutes. During the last 15 minutes, unmold the terrine onto a baking sheet in order to brown the bacon. After browning, return the terrine to its mold. Drain and chill the terrine under a 1-pound weight.

Serving Suggestions
Serve the chilled terrine with Rustic Sauce.

Liver Terrine

This was another popular dish served at the Market Bar and Dining Room in the World Trade Center. The following is an adaptation of chef Arnold Fanger's recipe. See the color insert for photographs of this terrine.

YIELD: 1 terrine, about 7½ pounds

2¼ pounds chicken livers
⅓ pound fatty boneless pork butt, diced
½ cup chopped shallots
½ cup unpeeled chopped apple
1½ teaspoons Pâté Seasoning IV
1 teaspoon white pepper
1 teaspoon salt
½ teaspoon thyme
¼ teaspoon nutmeg
⅓ teaspoon crystalline ascorbic acid (optional)
⅓ cup Armagnac brandy
2¾ pounds chicken livers
1 pound boneless pork butt, cut into strips
⅔ pound fresh rindless pork belly or fatback, cut into strips
2½ pounds fresh fatback, thinly sliced to line mold
½ to ¾ pound chicken livers (for center garniture)
2 bay leaves
1 fresh thyme sprig
2½ cups Basic Aspic flavored with sherry

Sauté the 2¼ pounds of chicken livers with the ⅓ pound diced pork butt. Add the shallots, apple, pâté seasoning, pepper, salt, thyme, and nutmeg. Stir the ascorbic acid into the Armagnac and add it to the sautéed mixture. Heat until the alcohol evaporates. Cool the mixture.

Combine the sautéed mixture with the 2¾ pounds chicken livers and the pork butt and pork belly strips. Pass the mixture twice through a food grinder fitted with a fine disk (about ⅛-inch holes). Test the seasonings and correct if necessary. Chill.

Line a 13-cup mold (10½ by 5½ by 4 inches) with fatback. Also wrap fatback around the remaining livers to form a cylinder long enough to fit down the center of the terrine. Pat half the farce into the bottom of the mold. Set the fat-rolled livers down the center of the farce. Add the remaining farce. Cover the farce with fatback, and place the bay leaves and thyme sprig on top. Seal the mold with greased aluminum foil.

Bake in a water bath in a preheated 350°F oven for approximately 1 hour. After baking, weight the terrine for 2 hours with a 1½-pound weight. Remove the weight, pour in cooled, melted aspic, and chill. Unmold when ready to serve.

Serving Suggestions
Serve the terrine with thinly sliced raw onion rings, cornichons, and halved hard-cooked eggs.

Variations
Eliminate the ⅔ pound fresh rindless pork belly or fatback, and use ⅔ pound fatty pork butt instead.

Apple Liver Strudel

This makes an unusual sweet-and-savory appetizer.

YIELD: 1 10-inch strudel (about 6 servings)

¾ pound chicken livers, diced
2 teaspoons bacon fat
1 small onion, finely diced
½ pound unpeeled, cored apples, thinly sliced
5 tablespoons rich, gelatinous Brown Stock
1 teaspoon Madeira
Pinch of sage
Black pepper to taste
Salt to taste
½ pound commercial Filo or strudel dough, 12- by 18-inch leaves
¼ cup melted butter
½ cup bread crumbs browned in 1½ tablespoons butter

Quickly sear the chicken livers in the bacon fat, then remove. Sauté the onions in the remaining fat until they turn translucent. Add the apples and sauté until almost soft. Return the livers to the pan and add the brown stock and Madeira. Continue to cook for 2 to 3 minutes. Season with sage, pepper, and salt. Allow the mixture to cool until it is easy to handle.

Brush each strudel leaf with melted butter and sprinkle it with browned bread crumbs. Layer the leaves one on top of the other on a pastry cloth or sheet of wax paper. Shape the apple-liver filling into a 10-inch cylinder along the 12-inch side of the dough, leaving a 1-inch border at each end. Fold the dough borders over the filling. Using the cloth or wax paper as support, loosely roll up the strudel. Place the strudel, seam side down, on a buttered baking sheet and brush the top with melted butter.

Bake the strudel in a preheated 350°F oven until golden brown.

Serving Suggestions
Serve warm Apple Liver Strudel with honey-glazed apple slices and a sprig of sage for decoration.

Variations
Substitute turkey, duck, or goose livers for the chicken livers.

Bake the filling in a thin layer of Puff Pastry (about 1 pound) rather than strudel dough.

Quick Chicken-Liver Terrine

A real no-muss, no-fuss dish.

YIELD: 1 terrine, about 1¾ pounds

1 pound chicken livers, finely diced
½ pound streaky bacon, finely diced
1 onion, chopped
1 garlic clove, minced
⅓ cup rich, gelatinous Chicken Stock
2 tablespoons brandy
½ teaspoon Pâté Seasoning I or II
¼ teaspoon thyme
1 bay leaf
2 hard-cooked eggs, peeled and chopped
Black pepper to taste
Salt to taste
½ cup crème fraîche
1½ cups melted Basic or Chicken Aspic

In a saucepan combine the chicken livers, bacon, onion, garlic, stock, brandy, pâté seasoning, thyme, and bay leaf. Cover the pan and cook over low heat for 15 to 20 minutes, stirring occasionally. Chill the mixture. Remove the bay leaf, stir in the eggs, and puree the mixture until smooth. Add pepper and salt. Test the seasonings and correct if necessary.

Fold in the crème fraîche. Spoon the farce into a well-buttered 6-cup mold and chill for at least 4 hours before serving. Decorate the top of the terrine with a garnish set in a layer of aspic.

Serving Suggestions
Serve the terrine in its mold, with plenty of French bread and a vegetable salad.

Swedish Liver Terrine

The Swedish version of liver terrine, called *leverpastej,* is enriched with cream and flavored with anchovies. The Danish prepare a similar dish.

YIELD: 1 terrine, about 3¼ pounds

1 pound trimmed calves liver, cut into strips
1 cup milk
1 pound fresh rindless pork belly or fatback, cut into strips
6 Swedish anchovy fillets, drained
2 tablespoons sautéed minced onion
5 eggs
2 tablespoons cream sherry or sweet vermouth
1½ tablespoons flour
1 cup heavy cream
1 cup light cream
1 teaspoon quatre épices
¼ teaspoon black pepper
½ teaspoon salt
1 pound fresh fatback, thinly sliced to line mold
1 bay leaf
2 whole cloves
3 black peppercorns

Soak the liver in the milk overnight. Drain and discard the milk. Combine the liver, pork belly, anchovies, and onion. Grind the meats twice through a food grinder fitted with a fine disk (about ⅛-inch holes). In a separate bowl, beat together the eggs, sherry, flour, cream, quatre épices, black pepper, and salt. Vigorously beat the egg mixture into the ground liver, about ¼ cup at a time. Test the seasonings and correct if necessary. Chill.

Line a 9- by 5- by 3-inch mold with fatback and pour the farce into the mold. Cover the farce with the remaining fatback and place the bay leaf, cloves, and peppercorns on top. Seal the mold with greased aluminum foil.

Bake in a water bath in a preheated 425°F oven for 1 to 1½ hours, or until cooked. Chill for at least 8 hours or overnight. Unmold when ready to serve.

Serving Suggestions
Garnish the terrine slices with a fresh sprig of thyme and a tablespoon of lingonberry preserves.

Variations
Substitute another kind of liver for the calves liver.

Eliminate the light cream and increase the amount of heavy cream to 2 cups.

SEAFOOD SPECIALTIES

Salmon Swirl Terrine

The rich creamy texture of this terrine enhances the delicate sweetness of fresh salmon. Accompanied by champagne, Salmon Swirl Terrine lends a simple elegance to any affair. See the color insert for a photograph of this terrine.

YIELD: 1 3-pound terrine (about twenty 3/8-inch slices)

Salmon Mousseline
1 pound salmon fillets
1/3 pound crustless bread
1 medium-size onion, thinly sliced
1 tablespoon unsalted butter
5/8 cup heavy cream
4 egg whites
2 cups heavy cream, whipped
1 teaspoon salt
1/2 teaspoon white pepper
1/4 teaspoon nutmeg
1 to 2 tablespoons white wine

Sole Mousseline
1/4 pound sole fillets
2 ounces crustless bread
1/2 small onion, thinly sliced
1 1/2 teaspoons unsalted butter
1 egg white
2 1/2 tablespoons heavy cream
1/4 cup heavy cream, whipped
1/4 teaspoon salt
1/8 teaspoon white pepper
Pinch of nutmeg
1 to 2 teaspoons white wine

1/2 pound spinach leaves, stems removed, washed
1/2 teaspoon unflavored gelatin
1 cup White Chaud-Froid to glaze

Prepare both the salmon and sole mousselines according to the procedures for Basic Seafood Mousseline or according to the alternate method, whichever you prefer.

Blanch the washed spinach leaves briefly in boiling water or steam them until they are pliable but still bright green in color. Immediately cool them in cold water and drain. Lay the spinach out flat on a dry, clean cloth or on paper towels. Overlapping the edges of the drained leaves, form the spinach into an 8- by 5-inch rectangle.

Spread the sole mousseline over the spinach leaves to form an even layer, then sprinkle the sole with gelatin. Roll the spinach and sole in a spiral fashion, like a jelly roll. Wrap the roll in plastic and place it in the freezer for 10 to 15 minutes, until it becomes slightly firm and holds its shape.

Grease a 6-cup mold (8½ by 4½ by 2½ inches). Fit the bottom of the mold with a piece of parchment or wax paper and grease the top of the paper. Layer the bottom of the lined mold with half the salmon mixture. Remove the spinach roll from the plastic wrap and center it in the mold on top of the salmon. Cover with the remaining salmon and seal the mold with greased aluminum foil.

Bake in a water bath in a preheated 350°F oven for about 1¼ hours, or until cooked. After baking, chill the terrine.

Note: If desired, glaze the terrine with chaud-froid, aspic, or with a mayonnaise aspic. If prepared a couple days in advance, leave the terrine in its mold and seal it in plastic wrap. Glaze it the day you serve it or the night before.

Serving Suggestions
Serve Salmon Swirl Terrine with Sherry Herb Sauce and a slice of lemon or a julienne of radish.

Variations
Flounder, pike, cod, or any nonoily white fish can substitute for the sole. Reduce the cost of the terrine by substituting white fish fillets for the salmon, and use the salmon for the smaller quantity of sole in the center roll.

Strips of Japanese kombu seaweed (softened in hot water for 20 to 30 minutes), romaine lettuce, or sorrel leaves can substitute for the spinach.

Swedish Salmon Pâté

The Swedes call this dish *laxpastej.*

YIELD: 1 pâté, about 6 pounds

2¼ pounds salmon fillets, finely ground
4 egg whites
3 tablespoons brandy, heated to evaporate alcohol and cooled
1½ teaspoons salt
½ teaspoon white pepper
¼ teaspoon mace
Pinch of cloves
1 quart heavy cream
¼ cup tomato puree
2 tablespoons chopped fresh dill
2 tablespoons chopped fresh chives
1½ cups drained smoked mussels, patted dry
1½ cups drained titi shrimp, patted dry
3½ pounds Pâté Pastry
Egg wash
3 cups Fish Aspic

Combine the ground salmon, egg whites, brandy, salt, pepper, mace, and cloves. In a food processor, puree the mixture in batches until smooth. Chill.

Slowly beat in the cream, a little at a time, until it is all incorporated. Test the seasonings and correct if necessary. Divide the mousseline in half. Into one half mix the tomato puree, dill, and chives. Fold the mussels and shrimp into the other.

Grease a 16-inch hinged pâté mold and line it with pastry. Spread half of the shrimp-mussel mousseline onto the bottom of the mold. Add a layer of half of the tomato-herb mousseline. Follow that with the remainder of the shrimp-mussel and then the tomato-herb mousseline. Fold over the dough edges and brush them with egg wash. Seal the pâté with a lid. Cut a steam hole in the center; decorate and egg wash the top.

Insert a foil chimney and bake in a preheated 425°F oven for 15 minutes. Lower the temperature to 325°F, bake for another 30 to 40 minutes, and refrigerate until chilled. Pour cooled, melted aspic into the steam hole until it reaches the top. Rechill and unmold when ready to serve.

Serving Suggestions
Serve with Remoulade Sauce.

Variations
Substitute a firm-fleshed, nonoily fish for the salmon.

Smoked Salmon Torte

You can prepare this torte up to 2 days in advance. Bake it a few minutes before serving.

YIELD: 1 10-inch torte (6 to 8 first-course servings)

1 pound smoked salmon fillets, thinly sliced
2 tablespoons olive oil
Juice of 1 lime
1 tablespoon Pernod
7 coriander seeds, crushed
1 scallion, chopped
2 sprigs fresh fennel leaves, chopped
Grated black pepper
1 pound Classic Puff Pastry, rolled out 1/8 inch thick
Egg wash

Marinate the salmon in the oil, lime juice, Pernod, coriander, scallion, fennel, and black pepper. Cover and refrigerate for 30 minutes.

Cut out two 10-inch circles of puff pastry. Place the base circle on a buttered baking sheet sprinkled with water. Egg wash the top. Remove the salmon slices from the marinade and arrange them on the pastry, leaving a

½-inch border of dough. Sprinkle the slices with any bits of seasonings or herbs from the marinade. Reserve the liquid. Cover the salmon with the other pastry circle and press the edges together to seal. Cover and chill the torte for at least 30 minutes.

Brush the top with egg wash and lightly score it with a curved radius design. Bake the torte in a preheated 350°F oven for 20 to 30 minutes. Lower the temperature to 225°F and bake for another 10 minutes.

Serving Suggestions
Whisk the reserved marinade liquid, plus additional chopped fennel leaves and scallions, into 1 cup of crème fraîche. Add more seasonings if required. Serve the warm torte with this spiced cream.

Harlequin Seafood Terrine

Due to the variations in texture, color, and shape, this terrine looks particularly attractive formed in an oval mold. It requires little or no garnish.

YIELD: 1 terrine, about 4 pounds

¾ pound yellowtail or pike, finely ground
⅓ cup Flour Panada
3 egg whites
2 shallots, minced
½ teaspoon white pepper
⅛ teaspoon mace
Salt to taste
1 cup heavy cream, whipped
⅔ pound salmon fillets, diced
½ pound sea scallops, quartered or halved
½ pound poached, shelled shrimp, diced
½ pound yellowtail or bass fillets, diced
¼ cup peas, blanched
¼ cup fresh sorrel leaves, julienned
1½ ounces black truffles or black olives, julienned
1 cup Fish Aspic to glaze

Combine the ground yellowtail, flour panada, egg whites, shallots, white pepper, mace, and salt. Puree the mixture in a food processor until smooth. Chill. Fold in the whipped cream. Test the seasonings and correct if necessary. Fold in the remaining ingredients except the aspic.

Grease an 8-cup mold and fill with farce. Seal the mold in greased aluminum foil.

Bake in a water bath in a preheated 350°F oven for about 1 hour, or until cooked. After baking, chill the mold. Unmold and glaze with aspic.

Serving Suggestions
Decorate the top with a tomato rose set among two or three fresh herb leaves.

Brioche Fish

You can prepare a variety of fillings for this recipe. Try an assortment of shellfish surrounded in mousseline, or perhaps a boned and stuffed whole fish. Serve small individual brioche fish as appetizers or one medium-size brioche fish as an entree.

YIELD: 1 brioche fish, about 4½ pounds (6 to 8 servings)

¼ pound flounder fillets, diced
1 small egg white
Pinch of cayenne
Pinch of nutmeg
Pinch of salt
½ cup heavy cream
2 tablespoons ⅜-inch cubed carrots, blanched
2 tablespoons ⅜-inch cubed broccoli stems, blanched
1 tablespoon chopped scallions
1 tablespoon chopped fresh coriander
2 to 2½ pounds Classic Brioche Dough
Egg wash
2 salmon fillets, about 1 pound each

Puree the diced flounder in a food processor until smooth. Add the egg white, cayenne, nutmeg, and salt. With the machine running, slowly pour in the cream. Remove the mixture from the processor and fold in the carrots, broccoli, scallions, and coriander.

Roll out the dough to ¼ inch thick. Cut out one fish shape (for the base) about 1 to 1½ inches larger than the width and length of the salmon fillets. Egg wash the base and place it on a greased baking sheet. Center a fillet on top of the base, matching the head and tail sections of the fish to the pastry. Spread mousseline over the fillet only. Place the second fillet on top. Lay the remaining dough over the filling and trim to ½ inch larger than the base. Press the edges together; fold the border under the fish, and egg wash to seal. Cut the excess dough into a mouth, eye, and fins and decorate.

Brush the pastry with egg wash. Use scissors or the wider edge of a pastry nib to cut scales into the dough. Take care not to pierce through to the fish. Place an aluminum foil chimney in the eye and bake in a preheated 425°F oven for 10 to 15 minutes. Lower the temperature to 350°F and continue to bake for another 40 to 50 minutes, or until cooked.

Serving Suggestions
Serve warm Brioche Fish with a coriander-flecked Lemon Mayonnaise.

Variations
Use Classic Puff Pastry or White Yeast Dough instead of brioche.

Tricolor Terrine

YIELD: 1 terrine, about 4 pounds

Farce
1½ pounds flounder, finely ground
4 eggs
¾ teaspoon white pepper
Salt to taste
2½ cups heavy cream, whipped

1 10-ounce package frozen spinach, thawed, squeezed dry, and chopped
2 tablespoons chopped fresh coriander
½ cup tomato puree
2 tablespoons julienned black olives
1 cup small shrimp, quickly blanched and peeled
½ pound flounder fillets, lightly pounded
1 cup Fish Aspic to glaze

Combine the ground flounder, eggs, white pepper, and salt. Puree the mixture in a food processor until smooth. Chill. Fold in the whipped cream. Test the seasonings and correct if necessary.

Puree the spinach with the coriander and reserve. Divide the farce into three parts. Mix the pureed spinach into one-third, the tomato puree into another, and the julienned olives into the last third.

Grease an 8-cup mold. Spoon the olive farce into the bottom of the mold. Add a layer of shrimp. Cover them with tomato farce. Add a layer of flounder fillets, and end with spinach farce. Seal the mold with greased aluminum foil.

Bake in a water bath in a preheated 350°F oven for 1 to 1¼ hours, or until firm but springy to the touch. After baking, chill the mold. Unmold; decorate the top and glaze with aspic.

Serving Suggestions
Accompany with Lemon Mayonnaise colored with tomato puree and sprinkled with freshly chopped coriander.

Variations
Substitute another firm, nonoily, white fish for the ground flounder.

Use another fish combination instead of small shrimp and flounder fillets to separate the layers of mousseline. You might try mussels and smoked eel.

Meat-Market Pâté.

(Left) *Liver Terrine.* (Right) *Pork and Veal Terrine with Shiitake and Pears.*

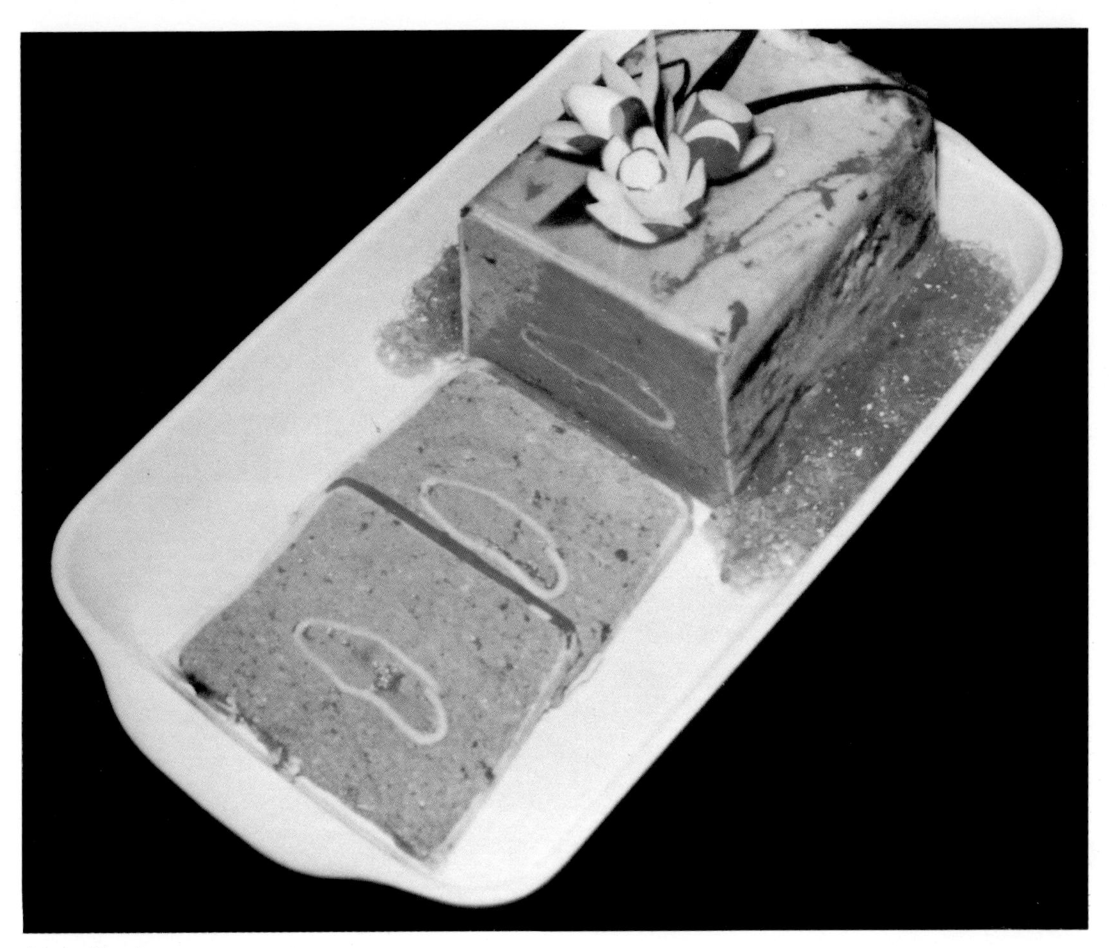

Liver Terrine.

Seafood Timbale with Titi Shrimp.

Salmon Swirl Terrine.

Winter Terrine.

Terrine of Garden Vegetables.

Mosaic Fruit Pâté.

Hot Gnocchi and Spinach Galantine.

Fish Terrine with Oysters and Periwinkles

YIELD: 1 mold, about 4 pounds

1 pound bass, finely ground
3 egg whites
3 tablespoons dry vermouth, heated to evaporate alcohol and cooled
½ teaspoon white pepper
2 tablespoons lemon juice
2 cups heavy cream
1½ cups smoked oysters
½ cup blanched, shelled periwinkles
⅓ cup red lumpfish caviar
2 cups Red Chaud-Froid to glaze

Combine the ground bass, egg whites, vermouth, white pepper, and lemon juice. Puree the mixture in a food processor until smooth. With the machine running, slowly pour in the cream. Test the seasonings and correct if necessary. Chill.

Separate 1 cup of the bass mousseline and mix it with the oysters and periwinkles. Mix the caviar into the remaining mousseline.

Grease a 6½-cup kugelhopf mold (8 by 4½ inches). Spoon all but 1 cup of the caviar mousseline into the mold. Add the oyster-periwinkle mix and top with the remaining cup of caviar mousseline. Seal the mold with greased aluminum foil.

Bake in a water bath in a preheated 350°F oven for about 30 to 40 minutes, or until cooked. After baking, chill the mold. Unmold and glaze with chaud-froid.

Serving Suggestions
Accompany the mold with finely julienned cucumber tossed in Horseradish Sauce, or serve Four-Pepper Mignonette Sauce on the side.

Variations
Substitute another firm, nonoily fish for the bass.

Substitute another shellfish combination for the oysters and periwinkles.

Perch and Peppercorn Terrine

YIELD: 1 terrine, about 4 pounds

Mousseline

1½ pounds perch fillets, cut into strips
⅓ pound crustless bread, cut into strips
1 onion, thinly sliced
1 tablespoon unsalted butter
¾ cup heavy cream
5 egg whites
3 cups heavy cream, whipped
1½ teaspoons salt
¾ teaspoon white pepper
⅜ teaspoon nutmeg
1½ to 3 tablespoons white wine

¾ to 1 pound large shrimp
15 to 18 sea scallops
½ pound thinly sliced smoked salmon
2 tablespoons green peppercorns, drained
1½ cups Fish Aspic to glaze

Prepare the perch mousseline according to the procedures for Basic Seafood Mousseline or according to the alternate method, whichever you prefer.

To straighten the shrimp, push a skewer lengthwise through each one, tail to cut end. Place the shrimp in boiling water and poach until the water returns to the boil (2 to 3 minutes). Cool the shrimp in a bowl of cold water. Drain, remove the skewers, shell and devein the shrimp. Chill.

Lay out the sliced salmon in a 12-inch long rectangle, overlapping the edges. Spread a very thin layer of perch mousseline onto the salmon. Set the scallops, like wheels on edge touching each other, along the length of the rectangle. Roll the salmon around the scallops to form a cylinder. Chill.

Fold the green peppercorns into the remaining mousseline. Grease a 10-cup mold (12 by 4½ by 4 inches). Spoon half the mousseline into the mold. Set the salmon-wrapped scallops lengthwise down the center of the mold, flanked on each side by a row of straightened shrimp. Gently press them in place. Cover with the remaining mousseline. Seal the mold with greased aluminum foil.

Bake in a water bath in a preheated 350°F oven for 1¼ to 1½ hours, or until cooked. After baking, chill the terrine. Unmold and glaze with aspic.

Serving Suggestions

For an extravagant garnish, cover the top of the terrine with a layer of cooked shrimp halves (sliced horizontally). Coat in aspic.

Variations

Substitute another firm, nonoily fish for the perch.

Eel Pâté

YIELD: 1 pâté, about 3 pounds

Teriyaki Sauce
1/4 cup sake
1/4 cup mirin (sweet Japanese cooking wine)
1/4 cup dark soy sauce
2 tablespoons honey or sugar
4 to 5 teaspoons cornstarch
2 tablespoons cold water

1 1/2 pounds smoked eel fillets
1/2 pound smoked trout or whiting fillets, diced
1 egg white
Pinch of cayenne
Pinch of nutmeg
1 cup heavy cream
1 1/2 pounds Short-Crust or Pâté Pastry, rolled out 3/16 inch thick
1/2 cup chopped scallions
Egg wash

In a saucepan, heat the sake, mirin, soy sauce, and honey. Make a paste of the cornstarch and water and stir it in to thicken. Pour the sauce over the eel fillets and marinate for 1 hour.

Puree the diced trout in a food processor until smooth. Add the egg white, cayenne, and nutmeg. With the machine running, slowly pour in the cream. Test the seasonings and correct if necessary. Chill.

Grease a 6-cup mold (8 1/2 by 4 1/2 by 2 1/2 inches) and line it with pastry dough. Starting and ending with the trout mousseline, assemble alternating layers of mousseline, smoked eel, and a sprinkling of scallions. When the pâté is filled, fold over the dough edges and brush them with egg wash. Seal the pâté with a pastry lid. Cut a steam hole in the center; decorate and egg wash the top.

Insert a foil chimney and bake in a preheated 425°F oven for 10 minutes. Lower the temperature to 350°F and bake for another 30 to 40 minutes. Chill.

Serving Suggestions
Serve with Watercress Sauce.

Hot Escargot Pâté

YIELD: 1 pâté, about 3 pounds

1 pound canned snails, halved (reserve the liquid)
1 quart Chicken Stock
½ cup white wine
⅓ cup chopped garlic
¼ cup chopped shallots
⅓ cup chopped fresh parsley
1 tablespoon lemon juice
½ pound boneless chicken, ground
½ teaspoon Poultry Seasoning
½ teaspoon salt
¼ teaspoon white pepper
1 egg
1 cup heavy cream, whipped
1½ pounds Pâté Pastry, rolled out 3/16 inch thick
Egg wash

In a saucepan, reduce the snail's liquid, chicken stock, and white wine to half. Add the garlic and shallots and continue to reduce until the liquid becomes thick and syrupy. Add the halved snails, parsley, and lemon juice. Allow to cool.

In a food processor, puree the chicken with the poultry seasoning, salt, and pepper until smooth. Add the egg and fold in the whipped cream. Fold the snail mixture into the farce. Test the seasonings and correct if necessary. Chill.

Grease a 6-cup mold and line it with pastry dough. Add the farce. Fold over the dough edges and brush them with egg wash. Seal the pâté with a lid. Cut a steam hole in the center; decorate and egg wash the top.

Insert a foil chimney and bake in a preheated 450°F oven for 15 minutes. Lower the temperature to 350°F and bake for another 30 to 40 minutes, or until cooked.

Serving Suggestions
Serve the pâté warm, garnished with a garlic-flavored Lemon Herb Butter Sauce.

Variations
Substitute pork, veal, or turkey for the chicken.

Scallop-Shell Pâtés

This exciting first course can be prepared ahead of time and kept refrigerated. Just pop the pâtés in the oven minutes before serving.

YIELD: 6 individual pâtés

1 cup Fish Stock
1¼ cups heavy cream
¼ teaspoon chopped fresh dill
White pepper to taste
1 pound Classic Puff Pastry, rolled out ⅛ inch thick
12 large sea scallops, halved horizontally
1½ teaspoons black or red caviar
Egg wash

Reduce the fish stock to 1 tablespoon. Add the cream and reduce to ¾ cup. Season with dill and pepper. Chill.

Using the edge of a large scallop shell as a guide, cut out six pastry lids ½ inch larger than the outline of the shell. Set six scallop shells on a baking sheet and arrange four scallop halves and ¼ teaspoon of caviar on each shell. Spoon 2 tablespoons of the dilled cream into each shell.

Brush the pastry lids with egg wash. Place the lids, egg side down, over the filled shells. Press the edges of the dough onto the outside of each shell to seal. Refrigerate.

Place the shells in the freezer for 10 minutes immediately before baking. Brush the lids with egg wash. With a knife, lightly score the pattern of a scallop shell on the top. Do not puncture the dough. Bake in a preheated 400°F oven for 10 minutes. Lower the temperature to 350°F and bake for another 10 to 12 minutes, until golden.

Serving Suggestions
Garnish with a lemon spiral and a sprig of dill or parsley.

Variations:
Substitute 12 large shrimp for the sea scallops.

Use 4-inch gratin dishes instead of the scallop shells.

Saffron Turban with Shellfish

This recipe was inspired by the Spanish dish *paella,* taking from it the saffron, seafood, pimiento, and peas.

YIELD: 1 turban, about 3½ pounds

¼ teaspoon crushed saffron threads
2½ cups heavy cream
1½ pounds sole fillets, finely ground
2 eggs
1½ teaspoons salt
½ teaspoon white pepper
¼ teaspoon allspice
¼ cup diced pimiento
¼ cup tiny peas, steamed
½ cup drained canned tiny mussels
½ cup drained canned titi shrimp
2 tablespoons chopped scallions
2 cups Fish Aspic to glaze

Heat the saffron in ½ cup of the heavy cream in order to release its color and flavor. Chill. Combine the ground sole, eggs, salt, pepper, and allspice. Puree the mixture in a food processor until smooth. With the machine running, slowly pour in the remaining heavy cream. Beat the chilled saffron cream into the sole mousseline. Test the seasonings and correct if necessary. Chill.

Mix 1 cup of the mousseline with the pimiento, peas, mussels, shrimp, and scallions. Grease an 8-cup ring mold. Spread two-thirds of the sole mousseline on the bottom and up the sides of the mold. Spoon the shellfish mixture into the trough of mousseline. Cover with the remaining mousseline. Seal the mold with greased aluminum foil.

Bake in a water bath in a preheated 350°F oven for about 1 hour, or until cooked. Chill. Unmold and glaze with aspic.

Serving Suggestions

Serve the unglazed turban warm, or chilled and glazed in aspic with a lemon- and saffron-flavored sour cream speckled with chopped scallions.

Variations:

Substitute another firm, nonoily fish for the sole.

Combine your own stuffing mix following the proportions in the recipe.

Smoked-Trout and Caviar Terrine

This terrine requires no baking; just assemble, chill, and serve. The asparagus spears form a square frame for the caviar center.

YIELD: 1 terrine, about 3 pounds

1 cup Chicken or Vegetable Stock
3 tablespoons (envelopes) unflavored gelatin
1/2 pound smoked trout fillets, 1-inch cubed
1/2 pound poached scallops
1 1/3 cups fish Velouté Sauce
1/4 teaspoon white pepper
Salt to taste
Pinch of nutmeg
1 1/2 cups heavy cream, whipped
2 cups melted Fish Aspic or White Chaud-Froid to line mold
25 8-inch asparagus spears (about 3/8-inch diameter), poached
1 to 1 1/2 cups red salmon caviar

Heat the stock and dissolve the gelatin in it. Cool. Combine the smoked trout, poached scallops, velouté sauce, pepper, salt, and nutmeg. Puree the mixture in a food processor until smooth. Mix the stock into the fish puree, and fold in a third of the whipped cream. Fold in the remaining whipped cream. Test the seasonings and correct if necessary.

Place a 6 1/2-cup mold (8 1/2 by 4 1/2 by 3 inches) in the freezer for 5 minutes. Add some cooled, melted aspic or chaud-froid and swirl it to line the mold. Place the mold in a basin of ice and water to set the aspic.

Spread two-thirds of the trout mousseline on the bottom and up the sides of the mold. Arrange the asparagus spears in a layer on the bottom (on top of the mousseline) and two-thirds of the distance up the sides. Cover the bottom and sides with mousseline to secure the asparagus in place. Form a groove down the center of the mousseline and fill it with caviar. Cover the caviar with a little more mousseline and set the remaining asparagus on top, parallel to the bottom layer. Cover with the remaining mousseline. Seal the mold in plastic wrap and refrigerate for 2 to 3 hours, until firm.

Before unmolding, chill the serving platter. Run a sharp, thin knife around the edge of the mold. Hold the mold in some warm (not hot) water for a moment. Be careful not to allow any water to seep over the rim into the mold. Place the chilled plate over the mold, and holding the two together, invert them. Position the mold where you want it on the plate. Gently shake to separate the mold from the terrine. Refrigerate. You can unmold the terrine several hours before serving.

Serving Suggestions
Serve with a slice of lime, extra caviar, and asparagus spears vinaigrette.

Variations
Replace the smoked trout and scallops with all trout, another smoked fish, or another poached fish.

Substitute another caviar, black or red, for the salmon caviar.

Jellied Lobster Mold

YIELD: 1 9- or 9½-inch ring mold

4 cups melted Fish, Vegetable, or Basic Aspic flavored with lemon
6 to 8 lobster tails, poached, chilled, and shelled
1 to 1½ bunches curly parsley, stems removed
1 pound small shrimp, poached, chilled, and shelled
1 small cauliflower, cut into florets and blanched

Place a 6- to 6½-cup ring mold in the freezer for 5 minutes. Remove and add some cooled, melted aspic and swirl it to line the mold. Set the mold in a basin of ice and water, swirling in more aspic until the insides are coated with a ¼-inch layer of aspic. Pour out the excess and chill the mold until the aspic coating sets.

Partially slit the underside of the lobster tails in order to loosen their curl enough to conform to the curve of the mold. Arrange the lobsters tails, slit side up, with their tips toward the outside of the mold. Set a few parsley tufts between the lobster tails. Spoon more liquid aspic over the lobster tails and parsley to keep them in place. Chill the mold in the ice basin to set the aspic. Pour a small amount of aspic into a side bowl. Dip each shrimp into the side bowl of aspic, then arrange them in the mold. Spoon in more aspic from the larger bowl and set in ice. Continue to layer all the shrimp in this way. Add a last layer of cauliflower florets. Cover the mold with plastic wrap and refrigerate for 2 to 3 hours, until firm.

Before unmolding, chill the serving platter. Run a sharp, thin knife around the edge of the mold. Hold the mold in some warm (not hot) water for a moment. Be careful not to allow any water to seep over the rim into the mold. Place the chilled platter over the mold and, holding the two together, invert them. Position the mold where you want it on the plate. Gently shake to separate the ring from the jellied mold. Refrigerate.

Serving Suggestions
Garnish with Sherry Herb Sauce.

Variations
Substitute any variety of fish and vegetables.

Substitute all vegetables or meat and vegetables in a lemon or meat aspic.

VEGETABLE HARVEST

Terrine of Garden Vegetables

This terrine captures the flavor and lightness of a cauliflower mousseline and contrasts it with a colorful array of fresh vegetables that retain their distinctive tastes and crispness. Though others appear similar, this recipe uses only vegetables—no chicken, ham, or fish to bind it. See the color insert for a photograph of this terrine.

YIELD: 1 3-pound terrine (about 15 ½-inch slices)

1½ pounds cauliflower, chopped
1 medium-size onion, thinly sliced
1 tablespoon unsalted butter
½ cup fresh corn kernels
1 carrot, scraped and ¼-inch julienned
1 medium-size yellow squash, ends trimmed and sliced lengthwise into 6 to 8 spears
1 medium-size zucchini, ends trimmed and sliced lengthwise into 6 to 8 spears
1 medium-size red pepper, seeded and ¼-inch julienned
2 ounces green beans, ends trimmed
3 eggs, lightly beaten
2 tablespoons chopped fresh dill
1 scallion, chopped
2 teaspoons salt
¼ teaspoon white pepper
¼ teaspoon nutmeg
2 tablespoons (envelopes) unflavored gelatin
1 cup heavy cream, well chilled
1 bunch broccoli florets, sliced in half
3 cups melted Vegetable Aspic to glaze

Steam the cauliflower until soft, then drain and cool in a colander. Sauté the sliced onion in the butter until limp and translucent but not browned. Meanwhile, steam each of the remaining vegetables separately until tender but still crisp. Drain these vegetables on a clean dry cloth or paper towels and chill.

Prepare the cauliflower mousseline using a food processor fitted with a metal blade. Grind the cauliflower and sautéed onion by frequently turning the machine on and off and scraping the vegetable from the sides of the bowl. Puree it until smooth. Combine the cauliflower puree, lightly beaten eggs, dill, scallion, and seasonings. Sprinkle the unflavored gelatin into the mixture and blend well. Test the seasonings and correct if necessary. Chill.

Whip the heavy cream until stiff. Gradually fold into the cauliflower mixture until thoroughly blended.

Grease a 6-cup mold (8½ by 4½ by 2½ inches). Fit the bottom of the mold with a piece of parchment or wax paper and also grease the top of the paper. Spread a layer of mousseline over the bottom. Arrange the yellow squash and corn on the mousseline. Continue with alternate layers of mousseline and vegetables except broccoli. Finish the terrine with a top layer of mousseline. Securely cover the mold with greased aluminum foil.

Bake in a water bath in a preheated 325°F oven for 1 to 1½ hours, or until done. Remove the terrine and let it cool on a wire rack. Chill thoroughly for several hours, preferably overnight. Unmold and decorate the top of the terrine with a layer of broccoli florets glazed in aspic.

If you prepare the terrine a day or two in advance, leave it in its mold and seal it in plastic wrap when cooled. Prepare the broccoli and decorate the terrine the night before or on the day you serve it.

Serving Suggestions

Serve the terrine with Tomato Herb Coulis.

Variations

Substitute any other vegetables or mushrooms for the cut vegetables in the recipe.

Cauliflower florets, alone or combined with broccoli florets, also can be used to decorate the terrine.

Substitute an assortment of Oriental vegetables for the cut vegetables listed to make an Oriental vegetable terrine. The following Oriental vegetables are possible choices:

- canned bamboo shoots, washed and blanched 2 minutes
- dried kampyō gourd, washed and boiled until softened
- canned baby corn ears, washed and blanched 1 minute
- canned lotus root, washed and blanched 2 minutes
- blanched snow peas
- dried shiitake mushrooms, softened
- fresh enoki mushrooms, washed
- pickled burdock (gobo), washed

Vegetable and Chicken Pâté

You can prepare this recipe using a cheese, seafood, or vegetable mousseline instead of chicken. Use whatever vegetables are in season to garnish the pâté.

YIELD: 1 pâté, about 4 pounds

3/4 pound boneless chicken cutlets, finely ground
2 egg whites
2 cups heavy cream
2 tablespoons chopped fresh borage
1/2 teaspoon chopped summer savory
Salt to taste
1/4 to 1/2 teaspoon white pepper
1 1/2 pounds Pâté Pastry, rolled out 3/16 inch thick
6 to 8 ounces okra, blanched and ends trimmed
3 large carrots, blanched and cut into strips
6 cooked artichoke hearts, cut into strips
1 large tomato, peeled, seeded, cut into strips
2 yellow squash, partly seeded, blanched, cut into strips
Egg wash

Puree the ground chicken and egg whites in a food processor until smooth. With the machine running, slowly pour in the cream. Fold in the borage, summer savory, and salt and pepper. Test the seasonings and correct if necessary. Chill.

Grease a 6-cup mold and line it with pastry dough. Starting and ending with the chicken mousseline, alternate layers of cut vegetables and mousseline. Try to arrange the okra in the center for a starburst effect. When the pâté is filled, fold over the dough edges and brush them with egg wash. Seal the pâté with a pastry lid. Cut a steam hole in the center; decorate and egg wash the top.

Insert a foil chimney and bake in a preheated 425°F oven for 10 minutes. Lower the temperature to 350°F and bake for another 30 to 40 minutes. Chill.

Serving Suggestions
Serve the pâté with julienned cucumbers and sun-dried tomatoes tossed with chopped borage and Vinaigrette Dressing.

Curried Cauliflower and Broccoli Terrine

YIELD: 1 3-pound terrine

2 pounds cauliflower
4 egg whites
2 teaspoons salt
1/4 teaspoon white pepper
1 cup heavy cream, whipped
1 to 1 1/2 bunches broccoli florets, steamed and cooled
2 1/2 cups melted Vegetable Aspic

Steam the cauliflower until very tender, then drain and cool it in a colander. Puree the cauliflower, egg whites, curry, salt, and pepper in a food processor until smooth. Beat in the whipped cream a little at a time. Test the seasonings and correct if necessary. Chill.

Grease a 6-cup mold (8 1/2 by 4 1/2 by 2 1/2 inches) and spoon in half the cauliflower mousseline. Arrange a cluster of broccoli florets down the center of the mousseline. Cover them with the remaining mousseline. Seal the mold with greased aluminum foil.

Bake in a water bath in a preheated 350°F oven for 1 hour. Chill the terrine. Unmold and decorate the cold terrine with a layer of the remaining broccoli florets. Glaze with cooled, melted aspic.

Note: If you prepare the terrine a day or two in advance, leave it in its mold and, once chilled, seal it in plastic wrap. Unmold and decorate the terrine the night before or on the day you serve it.

Serving Suggestions
Serve the terrine with Dal, a lentil dish of India.

Variations
Follow this basic recipe and substitute another choice of vegetables for the mousseline and garniture.

Warm Artichoke Pâté

YIELD: 1 pâté, about 3 pounds (6 to 8 servings)

3 slices bread, crusts removed and diced
1/4 cup milk
3 eggs
1/3 cup grated Parmesan or Romano cheese
1/4 teaspoon black pepper
1 1/2 cups ricotta or cottage cheese
1/2 cup shredded mozzarella cheese
12 ounces (2 6-ounce jars) of marinated artichoke hearts, drained and cut into wedges
1/2 cup prosciutto or ham, 1/2-inch cubed
1 finely diced onion, sautéed
1/2 cup sliced mushrooms, sautéed
2 tablespoons finely diced pimiento
1 pound Classic Puff Pastry, rolled out 1/4 inch thick
Egg wash

Soften the bread with the milk. In a food processor, puree the softened bread, eggs, Parmesan, and pepper until smooth. Add the ricotta and process until blended. Fold in the mozzarella, artichokes, prosciutto, onion, mushrooms, and pimiento. Test the seasonings and correct if necessary.

Grease an 8-inch springform mold and line it with pastry dough. Fill the lined mold with the artichoke-cheese mixture. Brush the edges of the dough with egg wash and cover the pâté with a pastry lid. Crimp the edges, trimming away any excess dough. Decorate and egg wash the top. With a fork, pierce the lid in several places to allow steam to escape.

Bake the pâté on the lower rack of a preheated 400°F oven for 40 to 50 minutes. Allow the pâté to sit for at least 15 minutes before serving or unmolding.

Serving Suggestions
Serve Warm Artichoke Pâté as a main course accompanied with soup and salad.

Spinach Terrine with Summer Squash and Carrots

YIELD: 1 terrine, about 3 pounds (10 to 12 servings)

2 pounds fresh spinach leaves, stems removed, washed, blanched, and drained, or 2 10-ounce packages frozen spinach, thawed and drained
1 cup cooked white beans (any variety)
2 eggs
½ teaspoon coriander
¼ teaspoon cumin
¼ teaspoon black pepper
Salt to taste
1 cup heavy cream
3 yellow squash, halved, seeded, and blanched
2 carrots, ¼-inch julienned and blanched
12 to 15 large cabbage or grape leaves, blanched
2 to 3 yellow squash, blanched and thinly sliced into rounds
1 cup melted Vegetable Aspic to glaze

Chop the spinach and puree it with the cooked white beans in a food processor. Add the eggs, coriander, cumin, pepper, and salt. Puree until smooth. With the machine running, slowly pour in the heavy cream. Test the seasonings and correct if necessary. Chill.

Spread the inside of each squash half with spinach mousseline. Arrange strips of carrots on the mousseline and cover with more mousseline. Fit the halves back together (more or less as if they were not cut).

Grease an 8-cup mold and line it with cabbage leaves. Spoon half of the spinach mousseline into the lined mold. Set the stuffed yellow squash down the center of the mousseline. Lightly press them in place, then cover with the remaining mousseline. Seal the mold with greased aluminum foil.

Bake in a water bath in a preheated 350°F oven for 45 minutes. Chill the terrine. Unmold and decorate the terrine with a layer of yellow squash rounds, slightly overlapping at their edges. Glaze with aspic.

Note: If prepared a day or two in advance, leave the terrine in its mold and, once chilled, seal it in plastic wrap. Unmold and decorate the night before or on the day you serve it.

Serving Suggestions
Serve the terrine with Caper Dill Sauce.

Variations
Make the spinach mousseline without the beans, following the proportions for another vegetable terrine recipe, such as Curried Cauliflower and Broccoli Terrine.

Winter Terrine

Most of the vegetable garniture for this terrine can be found in the root cellar all winter long. Its celeriac-potato base makes it an ideal winter terrine. See the color insert for a photograph of this terrine.

YIELD: 1 terrine, about 3 pounds (10 to 12 servings)

1 pound peeled and diced celeriac, cooked
3/4 pound potatoes, peeled, cooked, and diced
6 eggs
1 teaspoon salt
1/4 teaspoon white pepper
1/4 teaspoon allspice
1 1/2 tablespoons chopped fresh lovage
1 cup heavy cream, whipped
8 large cabbage or grape leaves, blanched
6 to 8 wedges cooked pumpkin or acorn squash
2 stalks of broccoli florets, crisply cooked
2 thin carrots, scraped and cooked
3 parsnips or small turnips, cooked and cut into wedges

Combine the celeriac, potatoes, eggs, salt, pepper, and allspice. Puree the mixture in a food processor until smooth. Remove the puree to a bowl and fold in the lovage and whipped cream. Test the seasonings and correct if necessary. Chill.

Grease a 6 1/2-cup mold (8 1/2 by 4 1/2 by 3 inches) and line it with cabbage leaves. Spread a quarter of the mousseline in the bottom of the lined mold. Arrange a layer of pumpkin wedges and cover them with another quarter of the mousseline. Center a row of carrots flanked on each side by a row of broccoli florets. Cover with more mousseline and add a layer of parsnip wedges. Add a final layer of mousseline. Cover with the remaining cabbage leaves. Seal the mold with greased aluminum foil.

Bake in a water bath in a preheated 325°F oven for 1 to 1 1/2 hours, or until cooked. After baking, chill the terrine.

Serving Suggestions
Serve with Tomato Chutney.

Variations
Substitute another vegetable, such as cauliflower, for the celeriac.

Use another assortment of vegetables as a garniture in the terrine.

Autumn Terrine of Wild Mushrooms

This is a terrine for autumn, the time of year when many varieties of fresh wild mushrooms are plentiful.

YIELD: 1 terrine, about 3 pounds

Mousseline
3/4 pound boneless veal or turkey, finely ground
1 1/4 cups fresh seasoned bread crumbs
2 egg whites
1/4 teaspoon white pepper
1/8 teaspoon ground cardamom
Salt to taste
1 cup heavy cream

3/4 cup shallots, minced
4 to 5 garlic cloves, pressed
2 tablespoons olive oil
2 tablespoons unsalted butter
3 pounds cleaned, fresh assorted mushrooms (such as field mushrooms, cepes, morels, shiitakes, chanterelles, oyster, or straw mushrooms)
3 tablespoons Benedictine
2 tablespoons brandy
1 1/4 cups White or Chicken Stock
2 tablespoons fresh chopped parsley
1 1/2 cups Brown Chaud-Froid or Basic Aspic to glaze
Mushrooms to garnish (optional)

Combine the ground veal, seasoned bread crumbs, egg whites, pepper, cardamom, and salt. Puree the mixture in a food processor until smooth. With the machine running, slowly pour in the heavy cream. Test the seasonings and correct if necessary. Chill.

In a large fry pan, sauté the shallots and garlic in the olive oil and butter. Add the mushrooms and stir fry a few minutes longer. Remove the mushrooms to a bowl, retaining their juice in the pan. Add the Benedictine, brandy, and stock to the pan and reduce the liquid to a thick glaze. Pour the glaze over the mushrooms and stir in the parsley.

Grease a 6-cup oval porcelain mold. Starting and ending with mousseline, alternate layers of mushrooms and mousseline. When the terrine is filled, seal the mold with greased aluminum foil.

Bake in a water bath in a preheated 350°F oven for 45 to 60 minutes. Chill the terrine. Glaze it with Brown Chaud-Froid or aspic. Place a cluster of fresh mushrooms on top for decoration.

Serving Suggestions
Serve with Gooseberry Almond Sauce.

Variations
Fold fresh truffles into the mousseline.

Instead of layering the terrine, mix the mousseline and sautéed mushrooms together and fill the mold.

Substitute a vegetable mousseline for the veal mousseline.

Tiny Cheese Pâtés

Basilica torta, the cheese recommended for this recipe, is imported from Milan. It consists of Robiola, Mascarpone, Parmesan, and Romano cheeses layered with fresh basil and pignoli nuts. Combine with sun-dried tomatoes for a true Italian delight.

YIELD: 4 first-course pâtés

2 pounds Classic Puff Pastry, rolled out 1/3 inch thick
3/4 to 1 pound basilica torta cheese, cut into 4 pieces
8 sun-dried tomatoes, julienned
Egg wash

Cut the puff pastry into eight 4-inch circles or squares. Brush four pieces with egg wash and, with a fork, prick them in several places. Grease a baking sheet and sprinkle it with water. Set the four pastry bases on the sheet, egg side up. Place a piece of cheese and two julienned sun-dried tomatoes on each base. Stretching the dough slightly, cover each base with a pastry lid and crimp the edges.

Refrigerate the pâtés for at least 15 minutes before baking. When ready to bake, brush the lids with egg wash and lightly score them in a pattern. Be careful not to puncture the dough.

Bake in a preheated 450°F oven for 5 minutes. Lower the temperature to 425°F and bake for another 10 to 15 minutes, until golden. Set the pâtés on a wire rack for 10 minutes before serving.

Serving Suggestions
Garnish the warm pâtés with marinated mushrooms set on a few sprigs of watercress.

Variations
Substitute another soft cheese for the basilica torta.

Substitute a couple of thin slices of pepperoni or prosciutto for the sun-dried tomatoes.

Cabbage Torte

(This torte is an adaptation of Florence Kosempa's recipe.)

YIELD: 1 4- to 4½-pound torte (6 to 8 servings)

3 to 4 tablespoons unsalted butter
2 onions, thinly sliced
1½ large heads Savoy cabbage, 3/8-inch julienned
Salt to taste
Black pepper to taste
1 recipe Whole-Wheat Pizza or Whole-Wheat Yeast Dough
Egg wash
1 tablespoon melted butter
Sugar

Melt the butter in a large, heavy fry pan. Add the onions and cabbage and sauté until they turn golden brown and begin to carmelize. Season and allow to cool.

Divide the dough in half. Roll out each half to ¼ to 3/8 inch thick. Place one piece on a greased baking sheet pan and brush it with egg wash. Spread the cabbage mixture, with its juices, over the dough, leaving a half-inch border. Cover with the remaining dough and press the edges together to seal. With a fork, pierce the lid in several places to allow steam to escape. Cover the torte with a damp dish towel and allow it to rise for about 30 minutes.

Remove the towel and bake in a preheated 375°F oven for about 45 minutes. Do not open the oven door during the first 25 minutes. After 25 minutes, brush the top with melted butter and generously sprinkle it with granulated sugar. Glaze the top with butter and sugar one or two more times. Allow the torte to sit for 15 to 20 minutes before serving.

Serving Suggestions
The warm torte makes a tasty brunch or dinner dish served with soup or salad and a jigger of zubrovka, a Polish vodka flavored with buffalo weed.

Eggplant Roll

Use this recipe as a basic method for preparing a variety of rolls. Choose among such fillings as layered cold cuts or cheeses, ratatouille, spinach and cheese, or sausage meat.

YIELD: 1 12-inch roll

1¼ pounds dough (White Yeast, Quick Brioche, or Pizza)
Egg wash
10 to 12 thin slices fried eggplant
¼ cup tomato sauce
2 tablespoons Parmesan cheese
1 tablespoon chopped fresh basil or parsley
Pinch of oregano

Roll out the dough into a rectangle, 9½ by 12½ inches, and egg wash its surface. Leaving a ½-inch border, arrange a layer of fried eggplant over it. Spread the tomato sauce over the eggplant and sprinkle with the Parmesan, basil, and oregano. Roll up the dough in a spiral fashion, like a jelly roll. Pinch the seam and edges together to seal. Place the roll, seam side down, on a greased baking sheet and cover it with a damp dish towel. Allow the dough to rise for 15 to 30 minutes.

Remove the towel, brush the roll with egg wash, and bake in a preheated 375°F oven for 25 minutes. Do not open the oven door during this time. Lower the temperature to 350°F and bake for another 20 to 30 minutes. Allow the roll to sit for 20 minutes before slicing.

Serving Suggestions
Serve Eggplant Roll warm, at room temperature, or slightly chilled. It can take the place of a sandwich at lunch, or it can accompany an entire meal.

Variations
Substitute puff pastry for the dough. If you use puff pastry, do not serve the roll chilled.

Vegetable Strudel

This recipe makes a tasty, do-ahead, hot appetizer.

YIELD: 1 10-inch strudel (about 6 servings)

3 tablespoons olive oil
1 small onion, minced
½ cup eggplant, ⅜-inch cubed
1 to 2 garlic cloves, minced
¾ cup ⅜-inch-cubed raw vegetables (carrot, celery, zucchini, yellow squash, green bell pepper, and red bell pepper)
2 tablespoons cooked chopped spinach
2 tablespoons sautéed sliced mushrooms
Juice of ½ lemon
3 tablespoons tomato puree
1 tablespoon chopped fresh parsley
1 tablespoon chopped fresh basil
Salt to taste
Pepper to taste
1 egg white
½ pound commercial filo or strudel dough, 12- by 18-inch leaves
¼ cup melted butter

In a large fry pan, heat the oil and sauté the onion, eggplant, and garlic. Add the carrot and celery, then the zucchini, yellow squash, and green and red bell pepper. When the vegetables are crisply cooked, stir in the spinach and mushrooms, lemon juice, tomato puree, parsley, basil, and salt and pepper. Let the mixture cool, then add the egg white.

Brush each strudel leaf with melted butter as you layer them on a pastry cloth or sheet of wax paper, one on top of the other. Shape the vegetable filling into a 10-inch cylinder along the 12-inch side of the dough, leaving a 1-inch border of strudel. Fold the dough borders over the filling. Using a pastry cloth or wax paper for support, loosely roll up the strudel. Place the strudel, seam side down, on a greased baking sheet, and brush the top with melted butter.

Bake the strudel in a preheated 350°F oven for about 30 minutes, or until golden brown.

Serving Suggestions
Serve the warm strudel with a lemon and tomato-flavored sour cream.

Variations
Substitute 1½ to 2 cups of your own vegetable filling.

Bake the filling in a thin layer of puff pastry (about 1 pound) rather than strudel dough.

SWEET DELIGHTS

Mosaic Fruit Pâté

This pâté requires no baking. Made with seasonal fruits, it jazzes up any birthday celebration. Serve it in place of cheesecake. See the color insert for a photograph of this pâté.

YIELD: 1 pâté, about 3 pounds (10 servings)

1 pound cream cheese
½ cup almond paste
1 tablespoon honey
1 teaspoon cinnamon
½ teaspoon almond extract
¼ teaspoon vanilla extract
Pinch of cloves
1 cup Mascarpone cheese or crème fraîche
1 8- by 4-inch loaf date-nut bread, sliced lengthwise ¼ inch thick
1½ cups small strawberries, hulled, rinsed, and dried
2 kiwis, pared and cut into 4 wedges each
2 ripe nectarines, cut into 4 wedges each
1½ cups seedless red grapes, stemmed, rinsed, dried
Confectioners' sugar

Mix the cream cheese, almond paste, honey, cinnamon, almond and vanilla extracts, and cloves together with an electric mixer. Mix in the Mascarpone cheese or crème fraîche until thoroughly blended. Refrigerate.

Lightly grease a 6-cup mold, 8½ by 4½ by 2½ inches, and line the bottom and longer sides with plastic wrap, leaving a 5-inch overhang on each side.

Trim the date-nut bread to fit into the bottom and sides of the mold and to extend about 1 inch above the mold.

Spread one-fifth of the cream cheese mixture in the bottom of the bread-lined mold. Arrange strawberries, stem side down, in three long rows over the filling. Carefully spread another one-fifth of the cream cheese over the berries, lightly pressing the mixture into all the spaces. Arrange three rows of kiwi and cover with another fifth of the cream cheese. Add four rows of nectarine wedges and again cover with one-fifth of the cream cheese. Finally, arrange grapes and cover with the remaining cream cheese mixture. Smooth the top. Place another layer of trimmed date-nut bread over all and lightly press it into the filling.

Wrap securely in plastic wrap and chill for 6 hours or overnight. It keeps, refrigerated, for about 3 days.

Before serving, unmold the pâté onto a platter and remove the plastic wrap. Place the pâté in the freezer for 20 to 30 minutes before slicing in order to firm up the cheese filling. Sprinkle the top with confectioners' sugar and, using a long, thin, sharp knife, slice the pâté into ½-inch portions.

Serving Suggestions
Serve with a dab of strawberry preserves, marmalade, or jam. Garnish with a fresh mint sprig and a whole berry or wedge of fruit.

Variations
You can substitute any fruit for the ones called for in the recipe. Remember, however, that berries tend to bleed when sliced. Seedless green grapes, raspberries, plums, apricots, peaches, pears, apples, papaya, figs, and pomegranate make tasty and colorful variations.

Pound cake, chocolate cake, banana cake, or any other firm cake baked in a loaf can be used in place of the date-nut bread. The cake should be frozen or stale so you can thinly slice it without breaking.

Banana Cream Terrine

YIELD: 1 terrine about 2½ pounds (8 to 12 servings)

8 ripe bananas, peeled and diced
1 pound Mascarpone cheese
¼ cup honey or sugar
4 eggs
2 tablespoons lemon juice
2 tablespoons crème de bananes liqueur

Puree the bananas and cheese in a food processor until smooth. Add the honey, eggs, lemon juice, and liqueur. Blend well.

Grease a 6-cup mold, 8½ by 4½ by 2½ inches, and fill it with the banana-cheese mixture. Seal the mold with greased aluminum foil.

Bake in a water bath in a preheated 350°F oven for 45 to 60 minutes, or until cooked. Chill.

Serving Suggestions
Serve the terrine with sliced fresh fruits or Spiced Brandied Peaches.

Variations
Substitute another fruit for the bananas and use a complementary liqueur.

Substitute cream cheese, farmer cheese, ricotta, or sour cream for the Mascarpone.

Almond Pear Torte

YIELD: 1 10-inch torte (8 to 10 servings)

7 ounces almond paste
4 tablespoons unsalted butter
1 to 2 tablespoons honey
1 egg
1½ teaspoons lemon juice
¾ teaspoon cinnamon
⅛ teaspoon nutmeg
¼ teaspoon almond extract
3 peeled Anjou pears, cored, sliced ⅛ inch thick
Acidulated water
2 pounds Classic or Quick Puff Pastry, rolled out ⅓ inch thick
Egg wash

Puree the almond paste, butter, honey, egg, lemon juice, cinnamon, nutmeg, and almond extract in a food processor. Dip the pear slices into acidulated water, then drain and dry.

Cut one 10-inch and one 11-inch circle of puff pastry. Sprinkle a buttered baking sheet with water and center the 10-inch pastry circle. Brush with egg wash and spread the almond mixture onto the dough, leaving a ½-inch border. Arrange the sliced pears in concentric circles on the almond spread. Lightly press the pears into the mix. Cover with the 11-inch pastry lid and gently press the edges together to seal. Cut a small steam hole in the center of the torte. With the dull side of a knife, slightly indent the edges of the pastry every inch and a half to form a scalloped edge. Refrigerate for at least 1 hour before baking.

Brush the lid with egg wash. With a sharp knife, lightly score the pastry top about 1⁄16 inch deep in a pinwheel pattern.

Bake in a preheated 425°F oven for 25 minutes. Do not open the oven during this time. Lower the temperature to 350°F and bake for another 15 to 20 minutes, until golden. Cool the torte on a wire rack before slicing.

Serving Suggestions
Serve the torte slightly warm or at room temperature with amaretto-flavored whipped cream.

Variations
Substitute apples for the pears.

Fresh Fruit Terrine

YIELD: 1 terrine, about 3 pounds (8 to 12 servings)

5 teaspoons unflavored gelatin
1/4 cup cold water
1 1/2 cups heavy cream
1/2 cup honey or sugar
1 teaspoon vanilla extract
2 1/2 cups plain yogurt
2 tablespoons chopped fresh mint
2 cups diced fresh fruit (such as apples, peaches, pears, apricots, grapes, and bananas)

Soften the gelatin in 1/4 cup cold water for 10 minutes. Heat the heavy cream, honey, and vanilla until the honey is dissolved. Stir in the softened gelatin and cool the mixture in a bowl for 15 to 20 minutes. Blend in the yogurt and chopped mint. When the gelatin mixture begins to thicken, fold in the diced fresh fruit.

Rinse a chilled 6-cup mold with cold water, but do not dry it. Spoon in the yogurt-fruit mixture. Cover the mold with plastic wrap and refrigerate for at least 3 hours, until firm.

Before unmolding, chill the serving platter. Run a sharp, thin knife around the edge of the mold. Hold the mold in some warm (not hot) water for a moment. Be careful not to allow any water to seep over the rim into the terrine. Place the chilled platter over the mold and, holding the two together, invert them. Position the mold where you want it on the platter. Gently shake to separate the mold from the terrine. Refrigerate.

Serving Suggestions
Serve with a fruit sauce or puree.

Apple and Nut Pâtés

YIELD: 4 individual pâtés

1/2 cup unsalted butter, softened
4 packed tablespoons soft brown sugar
2/3 cup walnuts, chopped
4 tablespoons white raisins
1 to 2 tablespoons cinnamon
2 tablespoons applejack brandy
1/8 teaspoon vanilla extract
4 large unpeeled Rome apples, cored to within 1/2 inch of bottom
2 pounds Short-Crust Pastry, rolled out 1/8 inch thick
Egg wash

Cream the butter and brown sugar together. Add the walnuts, raisins, cinnamon, applejack, and vanilla. Stuff the cored apples with the mixture. Chill.

Cut five 10-inch pastry circles. Center an apple on each circle. Cut five triangles from each circle to form a five-pointed star. Brush the points of the star with egg wash and fold them up over the apple to cover (fig. 2–10). Press the edges of the seams together to seal. From the trimmings, cut leaves and stems to decorate the apples. Score markings on the leaves.

Set the individual pâtés on a greased baking sheet and brush their crusts with egg wash. Bake in a preheated 375°F oven for about 40 minutes, or until golden.

Serving Suggestions
Serve the warm individual pâtés with crème fraîche or sour cream flavored with applejack and cinnamon.

Variations
Substitute pears for the apples, and pear william for the applejack.

2-10. Wrap the stuffed apple in the star-shaped pastry.

Cherry Pear Pâtés

During the summer, try a sweet Max Red Bartlett pear; at other times you cannot go wrong with the fragrant Comice, often referred to as "the queen of pears."

YIELD: 4 individual pâtés

2 tablespoons unsalted butter, softened
3 packed tablespoons soft brown sugar
2 tablespoons ground hazelnuts
Pinch of nutmeg
1 tablespoon kirsch
16 to 20 fresh cherries, pitted and cut in half
4 unpeeled pears, cored to within ½ inch of bottom
2 pounds Short-Crust Pastry, rolled out ⅛ inch thick
Egg wash

Cream the butter, sugar, and ground hazelnuts together. Add the nutmeg, kirsch, and cherries. Stuff the cored pears with the cherry mixture. Chill.

Cut five 10-inch pastry circles. Center a pear on each circle. Cut five triangles from each circle to form a five-pointed star. Brush the points of the star with egg wash, and fold them up over the pear to cover. Press the edges of the seams together to seal. From the trimmings cut leaves and stems to decorate the pears. Score markings on the leaves.

Set the individual pâtés on a greased baking sheet and brush their crusts with egg wash. Bake in a preheated 375°F oven for 30 to 40 minutes, or until golden.

Serving Suggestions
Serve with a Mascarpone cheese flavored with kirsch and nutmeg and garnish with fresh mint sprigs.

Variations
Substitute apples for the pears.

Vermont Maple Cheese Pâté

YIELD: 1 pâté, about 3 pounds (8 to 12 servings)

1 pound cream cheese, softened
⅓ cup packed, dark brown sugar
4 eggs
1 cup pure maple syrup
1 teaspoon maple extract
1 teaspoon vanilla extract
1½ cups coarsely chopped pecans
1½ pounds Short-Crust Pastry, rolled out 3/16 inch thick
Egg wash

Cream the cheese and brown sugar together. Add the eggs, maple syrup, and maple and vanilla extracts. Fold in the pecans.

Grease a 6-cup mold, 8½ by 4½ by 2½ inches, and line it with pastry dough. Fill the lined mold with the maple-cheese mixture. Brush the edges of the dough with egg wash and cover the pâté with a pastry lid. Crimp the edges, trimming away any excess dough. Decorate with maple leaf cutouts, and cut a small hole in the center of the lid for steam to escape. Egg wash the top.

Bake the pâté in a preheated 350°F oven for 45 to 60 minutes. Chill.

Serving Suggestions
Serve with fresh sliced figs, persimmons, or another fruit.

Pineapple Berry Terrine

YIELD: 1 terrine, about 3 pounds (8 to 12 servings)

1½ cups cooked or canned pineapple chunks
1½ cups fresh strawberries, halved
1½ cups fresh blueberries
1½ cups cooled, melted Fruit Aspic or lemon gelatin

Fill a chilled 6-cup mold with layers of strawberries, pineapple, and blueberries. Pour in the cooled, melted aspic. Cover the mold in plastic wrap and refrigerate for at least 3 hours, until firm.

Before unmolding, chill the serving platter. Run a sharp, thin knife around the edge of the mold. Hold the mold in some warm (not hot) water for a moment. Be careful not to allow any water to seep over the rim into the terrine. Place the chilled platter over the mold and, holding the two together, invert them. Position the mold where you want it on the platter. Gently shake to separate the mold from the terrine. Refrigerate.

Serving Suggestions
Garnish with Cointreau-flavored strawberry puree and a sprig of mint.

Summer Berry Delight

YIELD: 1 small pâté, about 2 pounds

1 tablespoon (envelope) unflavored gelatin
¼ cup water
1¾ pounds mixed fresh berries, hulled or pitted
¼ cup honey or sugar
Juice and grated zest of ½ lemon
1 4- by 4-inch loaf plain pound cake

Soften the gelatin in the water. Combine the berries, honey, lemon juice, and zest in a saucepan. Cover and slowly bring to a boil. Lower the heat and simmer for a minute. Reserve 1/4 cup of the berry juice in a separate bowl. Cool the berries to room temperature.

Meanwhile, slice the pound cake 1/4 inch thick. Grease a 4-cup rectangular mold and line the bottom and longer sides with a sheet of plastic wrap, leaving a 3-inch overhang on each side. Trim the pound cake to line the mold. Over a double boiler, dissolve the gelatin in its water. Stir the dissolved gelatin into the room-temperature berry mixture.

Spoon the berry mixture into the cake-lined mold. Cover the mixture with the remaining trimmed cake slices. Seal with the overhanging plastic wrap and chill for 6 hours or overnight.

Before serving, unmold the pâté onto a platter and remove the plastic wrap. Pour the reserved 1/4 cup berry juice over any portions of the cake not already colored with berry juice.

Serving Suggestions
Serve Summer Berry Delight with plain whipped cream.

SAVORY PIES

Steak and Shiitake Mushroom Pie

YIELD: 1 pie, about 5½ pounds (6 to 8 servings)

4 pounds boneless beef steak, cut into chunks
3 tablespoons bacon fat
1 pound pearl onions, peeled
2 tablespoons minced garlic
2 bay leaves
1 teaspoon thyme
1 teaspoon summer savory
3/4 cup tomato puree
1 quart Brown Stock
1½ ounces dried shiitake mushrooms, softened
5/8 cup burgundy wine
2 to 3 tablespoons roux
Salt to taste
Black pepper to taste
Egg wash
1 pound Short-Crust pastry, rolled out

Sauté the beef in the bacon fat. When well browned, remove the meat to a separate roasting pot and add a third of the onions. Sauté the remaining onions, garlic, bay leaves, thyme, and savory in the bacon fat. Add them to the meat, along with the tomato puree, stock, and mushrooms. Deglaze the pan with wine and add to the meat. Simmer, uncovered, until the beef becomes tender. If necessary, whisk in enough roux to thicken the sauce slightly. Season with salt and pepper.

Brush the rim of a 2½- to 3-quart casserole with egg wash. Cut a strip of dough and press it onto the rim. Spoon the beef stew into the casserole dish. Brush the rim of the dough with egg wash and cover the pie with a pastry lid. Crimp the edges, trimming away excess dough. Cut a steam hole in the center; decorate and egg wash the top.

Insert a foil chimney and bake in a preheated 375°F oven for 30 to 40 minutes, until golden brown.

Serving Suggestions

Serve the pie hot with sautéed string beans and warm garlic bread.

Variations

Substitute another kind of mushroom for the shiitakes.

Substitute puff pastry for the short crust.

Caraway Veal Pie

Make the pie in small soufflé dishes or crocks for individual-size portions.

YIELD: 1 pie, about 6 pounds (6 to 8 servings)

4 pounds boneless veal, cut into chunks
3 tablespoons bacon fat
14 ounces onion, thinly sliced
1½ teaspoons minced garlic
1 to 1½ teaspoons caraway seeds
1½ teaspoons sweet paprika
1 teaspoon thyme
1 bay leaf
4⅛ cups crushed peeled plum tomatoes, with juice
2⅔ cups White Stock
6 tablespoons white wine
2 to 4 tablespoons roux
Salt to taste
Black pepper to taste
2 tablespoons chopped fresh parsley
Egg wash
1 pound Short-Crust Pastry seasoned with caraway seeds, rolled out

Sauté the veal in the bacon fat. When well browned, remove the veal to a separate braising pot and add a third of the sliced onions. Sauté the remaining sliced onions, garlic, and seasonings in the bacon fat. Add them to the meat, along with the tomatoes and stock. Deglaze the pan with wine and add to the meat. Simmer, uncovered, until the veal becomes tender. If necessary, whisk in enough roux to thicken the sauce slightly. Season with salt and pepper and sprinkle with parsley.

Brush the rim of a 2½- to 3-quart casserole with egg wash. Cut a strip of dough and press it onto the rim. Spoon the veal stew into the casserole dish. Brush the rim of dough with egg wash and cover the pie with a pastry lid. Crimp the edges, trimming away excess dough. Cut a steam hole in the center; decorate and egg wash the top.

Insert a foil chimney, and bake in a preheated 400°F oven for 30 to 40 minutes, until golden brown.

Serving Suggestions
Serve the hot pie with a mixed vegetable salad.

Variations
Simmer some chopped vegetables, such as mushrooms, potatoes, carrots, or peas, with the meat.

Substitute puff pastry for the short crust.

Curried Lamb Pie

YIELD: 1 pie, about 5½ pounds (6 to 8 servings)

4 pounds boneless lamb shoulder or leg, cut into chunks
¼ to ⅓ cup curry powder
2 tablespoons flour
1 teaspoon cumin
1 teaspoon turmeric
1 teaspoon black pepper
Pinch of cloves
3 tablespoons olive oil
2 carrots, sliced
2 celery stalks, sliced
1 pound onions, sliced
3 garlic cloves, chopped
1 cup white wine
⅓ to ⅔ cup diced dried apples or mixed fruit
4 to 6 cups White or Chicken Stock
Salt to taste
Egg wash
1 pound Short-Crust Pastry, rolled out

Dredge the lamb chunks in a combination of curry powder, flour, cumin, turmeric, pepper, and cloves. Sauté the chunks a few at a time in hot olive oil. When well browned, remove the lamb and any extra seasoning mix to a braising pot. In the remaining oil, lightly sauté the carrots, celery, onions, and garlic. Add them to the meat. Deglaze the pan with the wine and add to the meat, along with the dried fruit and stock. Simmer, uncovered, until the lamb becomes tender. Season with salt.

Brush the rim of a 2½- to 3-quart casserole with egg wash. Cut a strip of dough and press it onto the rim. Spoon the lamb stew into the casserole dish. Brush the rim of the dough with egg wash and cover the pie with a pastry lid. Crimp the edges, trimming away excess dough. Cut a steam hole in the center; decorate and egg wash the top.

Insert a foil chimney and bake in a preheated 400°F oven for 30 to 40 minutes, until golden brown.

Serving Suggestions
Serve the hot pie with chutney, crusty warm bread, and a spinach salad. If served as a stew, accompany with rice pilaf and chutney.

Variations
Substitute puff pastry for the short crust.

Substitute beef or pork for the lamb.

Chicken and Vegetable Pie

This is a variation of the all-American chicken pot pie.

YIELD: 1 pie, about 5 pounds (6 to 8 servings)

4 carrots, cut into chunks
2 to 3 celery stalks, cut into chunks
1 large onion, finely diced
1 cup sliced mushrooms
2/3 cup peas, steamed
1/2 cup corn kernels
2 tablespoons olive oil
1/2 teaspoon thyme
1/4 teaspoon Poultry Seasoning
4 cups cooked chunks of chicken meat
3 cups chicken Velouté Sauce
Salt to taste
Black pepper to taste
3 tablespoons chopped fresh dill
Egg wash
1 pound Short-Crust Pastry, rolled out

Sauté the carrots, celery, onion, mushrooms, peas, and corn in the olive oil. Season with thyme and poultry seasoning. Add the chicken, velouté sauce, salt, and pepper. Mix well and sprinkle in the dill. Test the seasonings and correct if necessary.

Brush the rim of a 2½-quart casserole with egg wash. Cut a strip of dough and press it onto the rim. Spoon the chicken and vegetables into the casserole dish. Brush the rim of dough with egg wash and cover the pie with a pastry lid. Crimp the edges, trimming away excess dough. Cut a steam hole in the center; decorate and egg wash the top.

Insert a foil chimney and bake in a preheated 400°F oven for 30 to 40 minutes, until golden brown.

Serving Suggestions
Serve the hot pie with a crisp green salad.

Variations
Substitute puff pastry for the short crust.

Fishmonger Creole in Brioche

YIELD: 1 brioche, about 4 pounds (6 to 8 servings)

1/2 cup olive oil
2 cups chopped onions
3/4 cup chopped green bell peppers
3 to 4 garlic cloves, minced
18 jumbo shrimp, peeled and deveined (about 1 1/2 pounds)
1 pound crawfish tails, shelled
1/2 cup Cognac
1 1/2 cups heavy cream
1 16-ounce can crushed tomatoes, with juice
8 to 10 drops Tabasco sauce
1/2 teaspoon white pepper
1/2 teaspoon oregano
Salt to taste
1/2 cup chopped fresh parsley
1 large or 6 individual baked brioche, hollowed out

In hot olive oil, sauté the onions, green peppers, and garlic. Add the shrimp and crawfish. After 5 minutes add the Cognac and heavy cream. Reduce until thick. Stir in the tomatoes, Tabasco, white pepper, and oregano. Season with salt and sprinkle with parsley.

At the last moment, spoon the seafood filling into the hollowed-out brioche. Bake the stuffed brioche in a preheated 375°F oven until the filling is heated through and the brioche becomes hot and crisp.

Serving Suggestions
Serve with a side dish of okra or chayote.

Variations
Substitute other fish for the shrimp and crawfish.

Eliminate the brioche and make the creole in a casserole dish, as in the previous recipes, using short crust or puff pastry.

Pear and Stilton Pies

Serve these pies as a first course or as a dessert.

YIELD: 4 single-serving pies

4 peeled pears, cored and sliced
1/2 pound Stilton cheese, thinly sliced
3/4 pound puff pastry, rolled out 1/8 inch thick
Egg wash

In four 4-inch ramekins, arrange a sliced pear topped with 2 ounces sliced Stilton cheese. Cut out four 5½-inch pastry circles and brush the circles with egg wash. Place the lids, egg side down, on the filled dishes. Press the edges of the dough onto the outside of each dish. Refrigerate.

Place the shells in the freezer for 10 minutes immediately before baking. Brush the lids with egg wash and bake in a preheated 400°F oven for 10 minutes. Lower the temperature to 350°F and bake for another 10 to 12 minutes, until golden.

Serving Suggestions
Serve the pies hot, with a dusting of confectioners' sugar over their crusts.

Variations
Substitute apples for the pears.

Substitute another blue cheese for Stilton.

NOVELTIES

Pâtésticks

Pâtésticks are the answer to what to do with an extra bit of farce, cheese, dough, or leftovers. Each time you make a pâté or pie, roll up a bit of filling in the dough scraps from the crust. Freeze the pâtésticks and bake them when needed. They are good to keep on hand for snacks or hors d'oeuvre.

YIELD: 1 pâtéstick

1 ounce pastry dough
1½ to 2 tablespoons filling or a piece of luncheon meat or cheese
Egg wash
Sesame or poppy seeds

Roll out the dough into a rectangle, 3 by 5 inches. Place the filling in a strip along the 5-inch side of the dough. Dab the end edge with egg wash, fold over the sides, and roll up the filling. Swirl the pâtésticks in sesame seeds, gently pressing the seeds into the dough. At this point you can freeze the pâtésticks for later use. Place them on a baking sheet in the freezer. Once frozen, wrap them in plastic wrap or wax paper and then aluminum foil and store in the freezer.

Bake the pâtésticks on a greased baking sheet in a preheated 375°F oven until golden, or deep fry them for 3 to 5 minutes.

Serving Suggestions
Pâtésticks taste good hot from the oven or at room temperature. You may serve them with an appropriate dipping sauce or onion dip.

Patisseroles

Patisseroles result from turning a casserole into a pâté or terrine. You can convert any casserole that is more than half meat by following the proportions in the recipe for Marengo Patisserole. Use 2 pounds of casserole, usually serving four to six people, that contains about 1 to 1¼ pounds of boneless meat. Dice the casserole ingredients (meats and vegetables) into ½- to ¾-inch cubes. Check the flavor, since you may need to increase the seasonings after the additional ingredients are combined.

Marengo Patisserole

This pâté is made from veal marengo.

YIELD: 1 3½-pound pâté

2 pounds well-seasoned and cooked veal marengo, diced into ½- to ¾-inch cubes, chilled
1 pound untrimmed boneless pork butt, finely ground
1 egg
1 tablespoon flour
Black pepper to taste
Salt to taste
1½ pounds Short-Crust or Pâté Pastry
1 pound fresh fatback, thinly sliced to line mold
Egg wash
3½ cups melted Basic Aspic

Combine the veal marengo, ground pork, egg, flour, pepper, and salt. Mix well. Test the seasonings and adjust if necessary.

Grease a 6-cup mold (8½ by 4½ by 2½ inches). Line it with pastry dough and line the dough with fatback. Fill the lined mold with farce. Cover the farce with the remaining fatback. Fold over the dough edges and brush them with egg wash. Seal the pâté with a pastry lid. Cut out a steam hole; decorate and egg wash the top. Insert a foil chimney and bake in a preheated 350°F oven for 1 to 1½ hours.

Chill the patisserole and pour cooled, melted aspic into the steam holes until it reaches the top. Chill and unmold when ready to serve.

Serving Suggestions
Serve the patisserole either hot or cold, garnished with marinated mushrooms.

Variations
Substitute another cooked-meat casserole, such as chicken cacciatore, for the veal marengo.

To make a terrine (instead of a pâté), line an ungreased mold with fatback. Eliminate the dough and egg wash and bake in a water bath. Once cooked, weight the terrine for an hour with a 2-pound weight. Remove the weight, pour in melted aspic, and chill.

Follow the recipe for Marengo Patisserole, substituting lamb curry for the veal marengo. Garnish with softly whipped cream seasoned with a little pineapple puree and a grating of fresh ginger.

Gumbo Terrine

Friend and fellow chef Michael Vignapiano converted Paul Prudhomme's recipe for Chicken and Sausage Gumbo into this terrine.

YIELD: 1 terrine, about 2½ pounds

1¼ teaspoons black pepper
1¼ teaspoons white pepper
½ to 1 teaspoon cayenne
1 teaspoon garlic powder
2 teaspoons gumbo filé
1 teaspoon powdered mustard
¾ pound boneless chicken, light and dark meat
1 pound boneless pork butt
¼ pound fresh fatback
½ pound kielbasa
⅓ cup vegetable oil
¼ cup flour
¼ pound onions, thinly sliced
1 medium green bell pepper, thinly sliced
2 garlic cloves, chopped
½ cup chicken stock
Salt to taste
2 bay leaves
1 pound fresh fatback, thinly sliced to line mold
1½ cups melted Basic or Chicken Aspic

Mix the black and white pepper, cayenne, garlic powder, filé, and mustard together. Dice all the light chicken meat and half of the pork butt, fatback, and kielbasa into ⅝-inch cubes. Cut the remaining meats and fatback into strips and toss with two-thirds of the seasoning mixture. Grind the seasoned strips of meat and fat first through a medium-size grinding disk and then through the finest-size disk. Chill the ground mixture and the cubed fatback.

In a skillet, heat ⅓ cup oil and add the flour to make a roux. Taking care not to burn it, stir the mixture continuously over low heat until it turns chocolate brown. Set the roux aside to cool.

Sauté the diced meats in the remaining oil. Drain the meat and chill. Pour off most of the grease, then quickly sauté the onion, bell pepper, and garlic for 2 to 3 minutes. Add the chicken stock and boil for 1 minute. Stir in the roux and cook for another minute. Cool the mixture on a sheet pan in the refrigerator.

Mix the diced and ground meats and fat together. Puree the cooled vegetable mixture in a food processor until smooth, then stir it into the meat farce. Add remaining one-third of the seasoning mixture and the salt. Test the seasonings and correct if necessary.

Line a 6-cup mold with thinly sliced fatback and fill it with farce. Cover the farce with the remaining fatback and place the bay leaves on top. Seal the mold with greased aluminum foil.

Bake in a water bath in a preheated 350°F oven for about 1 hour. After baking, weight the terrine for 1 hour with a 2-pound weight. Remove the weight, pour in melted aspic, and chill. Serve in the mold.

Serving Suggestions
Serve the Gumbo Terrine with pickled watermelon rind.

Oriental Roll

The Japanese dish *futomaki* inspired this recipe.

YIELD: 1 roll (1 entree or 2 first courses)

1 sheet nori (dried and pressed seaweed sheets, about 8½ by 7½ inches)
⅔ cup firm fish mousseline, well chilled
1 thin cucumber spear, about 7¼ inches long
1 shiitake mushroom, softened and julienned
1 thin carrot spear, about 7¼ inches long
1 heaping tablespoon cooked chopped spinach
2 large shrimp, cooked and diced
1 thin yellow squash spear, about 7¼ inches long

Place the nori on a Japanese bamboo rolling mat or a sheet of wax paper. Spread mousseline onto the nori, leaving a ⅜-inch border along one 8½-inch side of the sheet. Starting about 1¼ inches from the opposite edge of the sheet (without the nori border), arrange parallel rows of the remaining ingredients. Moisten the ⅜-inch border of nori with water. Again, starting at the opposite end, use the mat or wax paper for support to roll up the ingredients, jelly-roll style (fig. 2-11). Adjust the shape, gently squeezing the paper-wrapped roll into a cylinder. Press the moistened border of nori to seal.

Chill for 3 to 5 minutes. When ready to serve, slice the roll in half and cut each half into four equal parts.

2-11. After layering the Oriental Roll ingredients onto the nori, roll them up like a jelly roll.

Serving Suggestions
Arrange the sliced Oriental Roll on a dish garnished with a clump of pickled sliced ginger root and a dab of mayonnaise flavored with wasabi (Japanese horseradish-like powder).

Variations
Substitute blanched spinach or lettuce leaves, formed into an 8½- by 7½-inch rectangle, for the nori.

Substitute meat or vegetable mousseline for the fish and change the fillings appropriately.

Choose from a variety of fillings such as the following:

- canned bamboo shoots, washed and blanched for 2 minutes
- canned lotus root, washed and blanched for 2 minutes
- Japanese gobō (pickled burdock root)
- Japanese kampyō gourd, washed and boiled to soften
- radish sprouts, scallions, celery, baby corn, avocado slices, other mushrooms such as enoki
- julienned zucchini or red and green bell peppers
- cooked peas, green beans, snow peas, broccoli florets, or sliced artichoke hearts
- cooked fish fillets, shellfish, meats, or cheeses

CHAPTER THREE

Timbales and Filled Pastries

TIMBALES

In bygone days, no royal menu was complete without a timbale. England's King Edward VII considered them one of his favorite dishes. They graced most formal menus and were popular at the old Ritz Hotel in New York. In earlier times, *timbales* referred to small, round, metal drinking cups. Some claim the word derives from the Arabic *thabal,* meaning "drum," which came to describe the decorative cylindrical pastry shell that held sweet or savory salpicons. Though still used to describe metal, earthenware, or porcelain bowls, the word more commonly conjures up tastes and images of exquisite culinary preparations.

CUSTARD TIMBALES

The consistency of a custard timbale lies somewhere between a quenelle and a soufflé. Made of meat, fish, vegetable, or fruit, they usually are formed in individual ramekins or dariole molds and baked in a water bath. As a rule of thumb, two large eggs will sufficiently bind one cup of ingredients. To ensure a smooth, creamy texture, make certain the water in the pan does not simmer or bubble. If necessary, lower the oven temperature toward the end of baking. The timbale is cooked when the top of the custard appears firm and its sides begin to shrink from the mold. A metal skewer inserted down through the center of the mixture will come out nearly clean.

Served hot, custard timbales can be prepared hours ahead and baked at the last minute. They can be kept warm for some time and even reheated. Leave the timbale molds in the water bath with the oven turned off; this will keep them warm for 30 to 45 minutes. To serve timbales, remove them from the oven and let them set for 15 to 20 minutes. Run a thin knife around the sides and unmold them immediately. They can be cooked a few days in advance and served chilled.

For variation and added surprise, timbales can be stuffed with a sauced filling of periwinkles, titi shrimp, morels, or raspberries. The secret will go undiscovered until the first forkful.

PASTRY TIMBALES

A pastry timbale consists of a salpicon (finely diced ingredients laced with sauce) either baked in or served in prebaked crusts or hollowed-out brioches. Classically, they are formed in round, high-sided molds, plain or fluted, and decorated with dough motifs. Pastry timbales also can be filled with forcemeat and cooked as a pâté. Regardless of how you fill them, serve timbales capped with their decorative lids. Savory timbales are usually served hot, but dessert timbales taste equally good at room temperature or slightly chilled.

SETTING THEM OUT

Shrimp timbales stuffed with crabmeat make a fine first course on special occasions. Simple dinners or luncheons could feature a pastry timbale of chicken with mushrooms, such as chanterelles, morels, or any other favorite. As a side dish, a broccoli or cauliflower custard dresses up even the simplest roast. Serve yam timbales, enriched with sweet Italian Mascarpone, as an accompaniment to a Thanksgiving Day turkey. Or, in answer to "What's for dessert?" present a refreshing pear and raspberry timbale.

BASICS OF MAKING A STUFFED TIMBALE

Half-cup ramekins called dariole molds are well-suited containers for timbales served as a first course. Allow two 4-ounce timbales or make individual 6- to 8-ounce timbales for each main-course serving. Traditional dariole molds are round or oval with straight sides, but custard cups, muffin tins, small brioche forms, or even heart-shaped molds can be used for variety. Bake large, family-style timbales in 1½- to 2-quart decorative forms, such as brioche or charlotte molds. Regardless of the shape of the container, gener-

3-1. Pipe a ½-inch mousseline shell into the mold.

ously (but evenly) grease the mold to enable easy removal of the cooked timbale.

Grease the insides of 4-ounce ramekins with butter or margarine. Using a pastry bag fitted with a no. 3 nib, pipe a ½-inch shell of mousseline on the bottom and up the sides of the mold (fig. 3-1). Make certain to leave no gaps or the filling will leak out.

Place the garniture (diced meat, fish, vegetable, fruit) in the center opening and add enough sauce to come slightly below the top of the mousseline (fig 3-2).

To seal the timbales, carefully and quickly pipe on a top layer of mousseline. Gently smooth the mousseline tops with a wet spatula (fig. 3-3). Be careful not to press the top down into the center or cause the sauce to squirt up through the mousseline.

3-2. Spoon the filling into the mousseline shell and add sauce.

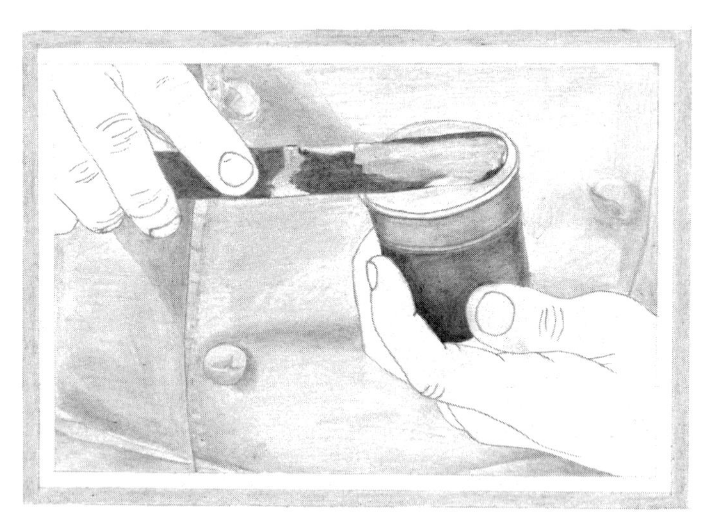

3-3. Pipe a top layer of mousseline onto the timbale and gently smooth it with a wet spatula.

Securely cover each ramekin with a well-greased piece of aluminum foil. Place the timbales in a water bath of almost boiling water (the water should come two-thirds up the sides of the ramekins) and bake at 350°F for the time required (usually 30 to 40 minutes).

When cooked, the mousseline will rise a little and feel firm but springy to the touch. If you wish to test it for doneness, insert a metal skewer into the side shell of the mousseline. Do not insert it through the center if there is a filling, or the sauce will leak out when served.

If you are serving the timbales warm, let them sit for 15 to 20 minutes before unmolding. Otherwise, chill the timbales thoroughly for several hours or overnight, then unmold. Left in their molds, individually sealed in plastic wrap and refrigerated, meat timbales keep for about 4 days, and seafood, vegetable, or dessert timbales keep for about 3 days.

The following rules of thumb may assist in planning new recipes:

- Use two eggs for each cup of liquid in a custard timbale.
- Since acids inhibit the solidifying properties of proteins, add more egg to a custard made with orange or lemon juice, wine, or vinegar.
- In starchy mixtures, such as those made with yams or sweet potatoes, use less egg.

BASICS OF MAKING A PASTRY TIMBALE

Two pounds of dough rolled 1/4 inch thick will line four 4-ounce oval dariole molds. To line four 7-ounce cylindrical molds, 2½ pounds of dough will be required.

Roll out the dough 1/4 inch thick. Using the opening of the mold, cut a cover and prick it in a few places with a fork. Decorate the cover with dough scraps. Lightly grease the mold and line it with dough.

For prebaked pastry shells, prick the dough along the bottom and sides of the mold. Fill it with pie weights or dried beans so the crust will not bubble. Bake both the mold and the cover on a cookie sheet at 475°F for 8 minutes. Remove the pie weights, brush the inside bottom and sides with egg, and continue baking for 4 or 5 minutes. Cool on a rack. Slip the cooled pastry shell from the mold. Fill it and serve.

If the filling is to be baked in the crust, do not prick the bottom and sides of the dough; leave a 3/8-inch dough overhang instead. Assemble the timbale as you would a small pâté. Using a pastry bag fitted with a no. 3 nib, pipe a 3/8-inch shell of mousseline against the bottom and sides of the dough. Make certain to leave no gaps for the filling to leak out. Spoon in the filling and smooth it as in "Basics of Making a Stuffed Timbale."

Fold the dough overhang onto the timbale mousseline, then brush it with egg. Fit the decorated dough cover on top and just barely press the edge of the top to the sides of the dough shell in order to seal the timbale. Bake the timbales on a cookie sheet at 350°F for the time required (usually 40 to 45 minutes). Egg wash the top crust for the last 10 minutes of baking. When cooked and golden in color, remove from the oven.

If you are serving the timbales warm, let them sit for 15 to 20 minutes before gently unmolding. Otherwise, chill the timbales thoroughly for several hours or overnight, then unmold.

EDIBLE TIMBALE MOLDS

You need not be limited to pastry crust as the only edible container for a timbale. Thin slices of meat or fish, as well as vegetables, fruits, and pasta, provide attractive alternatives in which to encase timbales.

MEATS AND FISH

Line the ramekin with alternating thin strips of meats, such as ham and turkey, then fill the timbale and bake or refrigerate.

Line the ramekin with alternating strips of fish, such as sole and salmon, then fill the timbale and bake or refrigerate. Instead of using two kinds of fillets, intersperse strips of crabmeat or shrimp between fillets. (Shell, clean, and score shrimp so they do not curl.)

VEGETABLES

Cut zucchini, yellow squash, eggplant, or carrots into 2-inch-long (or as long as required) strips, each about 1 inch wide and 1/8 inch thick. Blanch the vegetables and pat them dry. Line the ramekin bottom and sides with the vegetables (fig. 3-4). Wedges of red or yellow bell peppers alternating

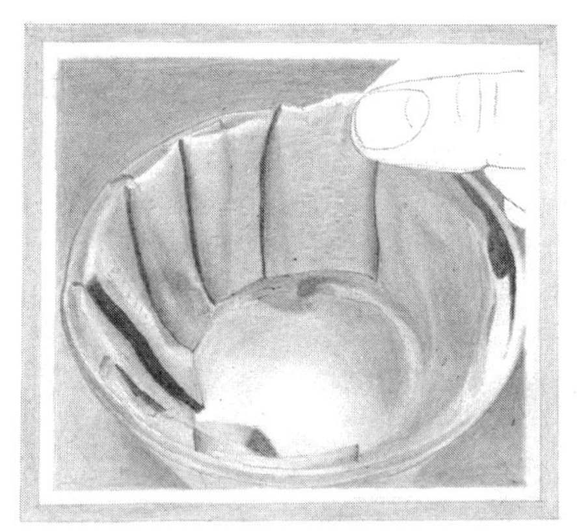

3-4. Use vegetables instead of mousseline to create a shell. Simply line the bottom and sides of a ramekin with leafy vegetables or with strips or wedges of squashes, carrots, or peppers.

with green beans or vegetable sticks look equally enticing. Spinach, lettuce, or cabbage leaves remain old favorites. For a new twist, line only part of the mold, with the leaf making an asymmetrical presentation. Fill the timbales and bake or refrigerate.

FRUITS

Arrange blanched fruit slices or sticks as you would vegetables. Another decorative touch is to line ramekins with aspic and berries, such as raspberries, then fill the mold with a gelatin-based mousse and refrigerate.

PASTA

Line ramekins with cooked ribbons of wide fettucini-like pasta, alternating white, green, and red pasta if desired. Fill the timbale and bake or refrigerate.

BASICS OF MAKING ASPIC-LINED TIMBALES

Some timbales require no baking. The cooked ingredients are simply combined with gelatin and chilled. The final presentation is enhanced by first lining the molds with aspic, mayonnaise-aspic, or chaud-froid. Spoon in the mousseline to set and chill. Because of the opacity of mayonnaise-aspic or chaud-froid, the garnish must be added after the timbale is unmolded.

Chill the molds, then ladle cooled, melted aspic into them. Chill the aspic-filled molds in a large bowl of ice cubes and water (fig. 3-5). The ice water should come up to just under the rim of the timbale. The aspic will gel and adhere to the sides of the mold.

Once the mold is lined with ⅛-inch layer of aspic (less if a second layer of aspic is to be added), pour the excess back into the bowl of melted aspic.

3-5. Chill the aspic-filled molds in ice.

At this point you can add a large amount of chopped herbs to the excess melted aspic. Add a second, thinner layer of herbed aspic for decoration.

Or set a garnish such as an herb leaf or a vegetable cutout in the bottom of the aspic-lined mold. Add another tablespoon of aspic or just enough to hold the garnish in place (fig. 3-6). Refrigerate to set aspic.

Fill the aspic-lined molds with mousseline, and refrigerate until the mousseline chills and sets, usually at least 4 to 6 hours.

Before unmolding the timbales, chill the serving plates. Run a sharp, thin knife around the edge of each mold. Hold the mold for a moment in warm (not hot) water. Take care not to allow any water to seep over the rim into the timbale. Quickly dry the outside of the mold. Place a chilled plate over the mold and, holding the two together, invert them. Position the

3-6. Set garnish into the bottom of an aspic-lined mold.

timbale where you want it on the plate. (It is easier to do on a plate that has been rinsed with cold water.) Gently shake to separate the mold from the timbale. Refrigerate. You may unmold the timbales several hours before serving.

Chicken and Chanterelle Pastry Timbale

YIELD: 4 4-ounce timbales

Mousseline
1/2 pound chicken fillets, finely ground
2 shallots, minced
1 egg
1/8 teaspoon white pepper
Pinch of nutmeg
Salt to taste
1/4 cup heavy cream

Sauce
2/3 cup light or heavy cream
2/3 cup rich Brown Stock
2 tablespoons tomato puree
2 to 4 tablespoons Frangelico liqueur
2 teaspoons chopped fresh tarragon
2 teaspoons chopped chives
2 teaspoons lemon juice
1/2 teaspoon white pepper
1/2 teaspoon cinnamon
Salt to taste

2 pounds Short-Crust Pastry, rolled out 1/4 inch thick
Egg wash
4 tablespoons small, whole chanterelles (fresh or reconstituted) for the filling

Combine all the ingredients for the mousseline except the heavy cream and puree in a food processor until smooth. With the machine running, slowly pour in the heavy cream. Refrigerate. Julienne the chanterelles and mix them together with all the ingredients for the sauce.

Follow the directions in "Basics of Making a Pastry Timbale." Bake the filling in the crust. Reserve any extra sauce to serve on the side. Bake the timbales on a baking sheet in a preheated 350°F oven for 30 to 40 minutes.

Serving Suggestions
These timbales taste best hot from the oven or at room temperature. Place a whole chanterelle with a tarragon sprig on each plate for garnish.

Variations
Substitute any lean meat for the chicken.

Substitute any mushrooms for the chanterelles.

Substitute 1/3 cup Meat Glaze mixed with 1/3 cup water for the Brown Stock.

Smoked Turkey and Cranberry Timbale

Turkey with cranberries is as American as burgers with french fries. This recipe offers a new twist on a national favorite.

YIELD: 8 4-ounce timbales

1 tablespoon (envelope) unflavored gelatin
1/4 cup Chicken or White Stock or cold water
1 1/2 cups pureed smoked turkey
1/4 cup chopped scallions
1/2 teaspoon Poultry Seasoning
1/4 teaspoon nutmeg
Dash of dry sherry
2 egg whites, whipped until stiff but not dry
1/2 cup heavy cream, whipped
2 cups melted Chicken or Basic Aspic to line molds
1/2 cup cranberry relish, jelly, or sauce

Soften the gelatin in the water or stock for 5 minutes. Over low heat, dissolve the gelatin in the liquid, then let it cool to room temperature. Combine the pureed smoked turkey, scallions, Poultry Seasoning, nutmeg, sherry, and gelatin liquid. Stir in one-fifth of the whipped egg whites. Fold in the whipped cream, then the remaining egg whites.

Line eight 4-ounce timbales with aspic. Spoon the turkey mixture into molds, sealing a tablespoon of cranberry relish in the center of each timbale. Chill for at least 6 hours. Unmold when ready to serve.

Serving Suggestions
Decorate the timbale tops with a parsley leaf and two cranberry halves.

Variations
Substitute smoked chicken or plain cooked turkey or chicken for the smoked turkey.

Duck and Red-Currant Pastry Timbale

YIELD: 4 4-ounce timbales

Mousseline
1/2 pound lean duck fillets, finely ground
2 shallots, minced
1 egg
1/4 cup Flour Panada
1/4 teaspoon black pepper
1/8 teaspoon allspice
Salt to taste
1/4 cup heavy cream

Sauce
2 tablespoons red-currant jelly
3/4 cup rich Brown Stock
2 to 4 tablespoons cassis
1/3 cup light or heavy cream
2 tablespoons orange juice
2 teaspoons chopped scallions
1/4 teaspoon black pepper
Salt to taste

2 pounds Pâté Pastry, rolled out 1/4 inch thick
Egg wash
4 tablespoons fresh red currants

Combine all the ingredients for the mousseline except the heavy cream and puree in a food processor until smooth. With the machine running, slowly pour in the heavy cream. Refrigerate.

Melt the red-currant jelly in the meat stock and cassis. Cool to room temperature, then blend in the remaining ingredients for the sauce. Refrigerate.

Follow the directions in "Basics of Making a Pastry Timbale." Bake the filling in the crust. Reserve any extra sauce to serve on the side. Bake the timbales on a baking sheet in a preheated 350°F oven for 30 to 40 minutes.

Serving Suggestions
These timbales taste best hot from the oven. Place a scallion flower on each plate for garnish.

Variations
Substitute 1/3 cup Meat Glaze mixed with 1/3 cup water for the Brown Stock.

Ham Timbale

Made from leftover ham, these timbales taste and look as sumptuous as the original meal from which they came.

YIELD: 6 4-ounce timbales

1 tablespoon (envelope) unflavored gelatin
2 tablespoons cold water
2 tablespoons cold pineapple juice (canned or preboiled, not fresh)
1½ cups pureed lean smoked ham
1 teaspoon Dijon-style mustard
1 teaspoon prepared horseradish
⅛ teaspoon mace
2 egg whites, whipped until stiff but not dry
½ cup heavy cream, whipped
2 cups melted Basic Aspic to line molds

Soften the gelatin in the water and pineapple juice for 5 minutes. Over low heat, dissolve the gelatin in the liquid, then let it cool to room temperature. Combine the pureed ham, mustard, horseradish, mace, and gelatin liquid. Chill the mixture until it just starts to set. Stir in one-fifth of the whipped egg whites. Fold in the whipped cream, then the remaining egg whites.

Line six 4-ounce ramekins with aspic. Spoon the mousseline into the molds and chill for at least 6 hours. Unmold when ready to serve.

Serving Suggestions
Garnish the timbales with fresh pineapple and a dab of Mustard Horseradish Cream.

Variations
Substitute cooked lean tongue or turkey for the ham.

Add ¼ to ½ cup minced ham or cooked tiny green peas for garniture.

Liver Timbale with Poached Quail Eggs

A center of soft poached egg makes a tasty, rich sauce for this liver timbale.

YIELD: 8 4-ounce timbales

1 tablespoon (envelope) unflavored gelatin
¼ cup Chicken Stock or cold water
1½ cups liverwurst puree or liver mousse
1 teaspoon Dijon-style mustard
Dash of Madeira
2 egg whites, whipped until stiff but not dry
½ cup heavy cream, whipped
2 cups melted Chicken or Basic Aspic to line molds
8 quail eggs, poached

Soften the gelatin in the water or stock for 5 minutes. Over low heat, dissolve the gelatin in the liquid, then let it cool to room temperature. Combine the liverwurst, mustard, Madeira, and gelatin liquid. Stir in one-fifth of the whipped egg whites. Fold in the whipped cream, then the remaining egg whites.

Line eight 4-ounce timbales with aspic. Spoon the liver mixture into the molds, sealing one poached egg in the center of each timbale. Chill for at least 6 hours. Unmold when ready to serve.

Serving Suggestions
Sprinkle with chopped fresh herbs.

Variations
Substitute pureed liver rillette, smooth chopped-liver spread, or leftover liver terrine for the liverwurst.

Steak Tartare Timbale with Peewee Egg

This makes an interesting presentation for steak tartare. Grease some 4-ounce ramekins and line them with oiled plastic wrap. Firmly press the steak tartare mixture into the lined mold, sealing a whole, raw, peewee egg yolk in the center of each timbale. Chill for a couple hours. Unmold when ready to serve by gently holding the plastic wrap down while at the same time lifting the ramekin off. Discard the plastic.

Accompany the timbale with the traditional steak tartare garnish of chopped capers, onions, and parsley.

Variations
Substitute *chee keufteh,* an Armenian version of steak tartare made with lamb. Season lean, ground lamb with cumin, cayenne, black pepper, and allspice. Mix the seasoned lamb with fine bulgur (softened in water and squeezed dry) in the proportion of ½ pound lean lamb to 1 cup softened bulgur. Add chopped green bell pepper, scallions, and tomatoes to the assortment of garnishes served on the side.

Form timbales in smaller molds and use a raw quail egg yolk in the center.

Sole Timbale with Baby Clams and Caviar

The combination of clams and caviar satisfies the peasant and aristocrat in each of us. The small bean clam proliferates on the Pacific coast, while the Coquina abounds on the Atlantic and Mediterranean shores. These clams measure at most 3/4 inch long. Small smoked clams also can be used.

YIELD: 4 6-ounce timbales

Mousseline
1/2 pound sole fillets, finely ground
1 egg white
1/2 cup Flour Panada
1 to 2 tablespoons tomato paste or puree
1/8 teaspoon white pepper
1/8 teaspoon salt
Pinch of nutmeg
3/4 cup heavy cream, whipped

1 pound sole fillets (about 4 fillets, 4 ounces each), lightly flattened
4 teaspoons baby clams
2 teaspoons caviar

Combine all the ingredients for the mousseline except the heavy cream and puree in a food processor until smooth. Fold in the whipped cream. Refrigerate.

Grease four 6-ounce custard cups or ramekins. Line the molds with the fillets, skinned side out. Follow the directions in "Basics of Making a Stuffed Timbale." Fold any ends of fillet over the top of the mousseline. Bake the timbales in a water bath in a preheated 350°F oven for about 30 minutes, until the mousseline rises a little and feels firm but springy to the touch.

Serving Suggestions
Glaze chilled timbales with aspic. Serve hot or cold. Accompany the timbales with a lime- and herb-seasoned crème fraîche and garnish with a fresh herb sprig.

Variations
Substitute monkfish or any nonoily fish for the ground sole.

Substitute trout or other fish fillets for the flattened sole.

Seafood Timbale with Titi Shrimp

Seafood timbales are truly elegant fare. Serve them as the first course of a formal dinner, as a luncheon or brunch entree, or on a hot or cold buffet. These timbales make any occasion memorable. See the color insert for a photograph of this timbale.

YIELD: 10 4-ounce timbales

Mousseline
1 pound sole fillets
1/3 pound crustless bread
1 medium-size onion, thinly sliced
1 tablespoon unsalted butter
4 large egg whites
5/8 cup heavy cream
1 teaspoon salt
1/2 teaspoon white pepper
1/4 teaspoon nutmeg
1 to 2 tablespoons white wine
2 cups heavy cream, whipped

Sauce
2/3 cup mayonnaise
2/3 cup Fish Stock or clam juice
2 tablespoons tomato puree or paste
2 teaspoons lemon juice
1 teaspoon nutmeg
1 teaspoon dry mustard
1 teaspoon chopped fresh dill
1 teaspoon chopped fresh parsley
1/2 teaspoon white pepper

1/2 pound titi shrimp (approximately 60)

Reserve 10 shrimp for garnish. Prepare the mousseline according to the procedures for Basic Seafood Mousseline or according to the alternate method, whichever you prefer.

Follow the directions in "Basics of Making a Stuffed Timbale." Bake the timbales in a water bath in a preheated 350°F oven for about 30 minutes, until the mousseline rises a little and feels firm but springy to the touch.

Serving Suggestions
Glaze the chilled timbales with Mayonnaise Chaud-Froid or Aspic. Served hot or cold, each timbale may be garnished with a shrimp and a sprig of dill on top.

Variations:
Substitute fillets of flounder, pike, cod, or any nonoily white fish for the sole.

Smoked Trout Timbale

This recipe also works well as a spread or as a fancy-shaped 4-cup mold.

YIELD: 8 4-ounce timbales

1⅓ tablespoons (envelopes) unflavored gelatin
¼ cup Fish Stock or cold water
1 pound smoked trout, skinned, boned, and diced
⅓ cup chopped fresh dill
2 tablespoons grated fresh horseradish or drained prepared horseradish
3 tablespoons lemon juice
¼ teaspoon white pepper
¼ teaspoon nutmeg
1 cup heavy cream, whipped
2 cups melted Fish Aspic to line molds

Soften the gelatin in the stock or water for 5 minutes. Over low heat, dissolve the gelatin in the liquid, then cool it to room temperature. Puree the trout in a food processor until smooth. Add the remaining ingredients except the heavy cream and aspic. In a large bowl, blend the gelatin with the trout mixture and fold in the whipped heavy cream.

Line the molds with aspic. Spoon the mousseline into the molds and chill for at least 6 hours. Unmold when ready to serve.

Serving Suggestions
Sprinkle with chopped herbs and accompany with Lemon Mayonnaise.

Smoked Salmon Timbale with Cape Scallops and Truffles

Small cape scallops are harvested in the shallow waters off the New England coastline. They range in size from 450 to 850 per gallon and vary from white, light tan, to pinkish in color. Genuine Cape Cod scallops, however, are always creamy white. Similar-sized calico scallops, obtained along the continental shelf from Florida to the Carolinas, are not considered to be as sweet tasting.

YIELD: 6 4-ounce timbales

Mousseline
½ pound smoked salmon, skinned, boned, and diced
2 shallots, minced and sautéed in butter
2 eggs
1 tablespoon tomato puree or paste
¼ teaspoon white pepper
¾ cup heavy cream, whipped

Sauce
¼ cup heavy cream
¼ cup Fish Stock or clam juice
2 teaspoons chopped fresh dill
2 teaspoons lemon juice

6 ounces cape scallops
1 tablespoon finely diced black truffles

Puree the salmon and shallots in a food processor until smooth. Add the eggs, tomato puree, and pepper. In a large bowl, fold the whipped cream into the salmon mixture. Mix together all the ingredients for the sauce.

Follow the directions in "Basics of Making a Stuffed Timbale." Bake the timbales in a water bath in a preheated 350°F oven for 20 to 30 minutes, until the mousseline rises a little and feels firm but springy to the touch.

Serving Suggestions
Glaze the chilled timbales with White or Mayonnaise Chaud-Froid or Aspic. Serve hot or cold and decorate each timbale with a poached cape scallop topped with a piece of truffle.

Variations
Substitute another smoked fish for the salmon.

Dice sea scallops or fish fillets to replace the bay scallops.

Julienne black olives to replace the truffles.

Shrimp Timbale with Crabmeat

YIELD: 8 4-ounce timbales

1½ tablespoons (envelopes) unflavored gelatin
¼ cup Fish Stock or cold water
1½ cups pureed cooked shrimp
1 cup diced cooked crabmeat
1 tablespoon chopped fresh parsley
1 to 2 teaspoons Dijon-style mustard
¼ teaspoon nutmeg
2 egg whites, whipped until stiff but not dry
½ cup heavy cream, whipped
2 cups melted Fish Aspic to line molds

Soften the gelatin in the stock or water for 5 minutes. Over low heat, dissolve the gelatin in the liquid, then let it cool to room temperature. Add the remaining ingredients except the heavy cream and egg whites. Chill the mixture until it just starts to set. Stir in one-fifth of the whipped egg whites. Fold in the whipped cream, then the remaining egg whites.

Line the molds with aspic. Spoon in the mousseline and chill for at least 6 hours. Unmold when ready to serve.

Serving Suggestions
Garnish the tops with a cooked shrimp and a parsley sprig. Accompany with Mustard Sauce.

Scallop Timbale with Periwinkles

YIELD: 6 4-ounce timbales

Mousseline
1½ cups pureed cooked scallops
1 egg white
1 tablespoon white wine
¼ teaspoon white pepper
⅛ teaspoon nutmeg
Salt to taste
½ cup heavy cream, whipped
1 egg white, whipped until stiff but not dry

Sauce
⅓ cup heavy cream
⅓ cup Fish Stock or clam juice
2 tablespoons lime or lemon juice
2 tablespoons minced red bell pepper or pimiento
1 teaspoon chopped fresh coriander
1 teaspoon chopped fresh parsley
½ teaspoon Dijon-style mustard
¼ teaspoon white pepper

⅓ pound steamed, shelled periwinkles

Reserve 12 periwinkles for garnish. Combine the ingredients for the mousseline except the heavy cream and egg white. Fold in the whipped heavy cream, then the whipped egg white. Refrigerate. Mix together all the ingredients for the sauce. Refrigerate.

Follow the directions in "Basics of Making a Stuffed Timbale." Bake the timbales in a water bath in a preheated 350°F oven for 30 to 40 minutes, until the mousseline rises a little and feels firm but springy to the touch.

Serving Suggestions
Glaze chilled timbales with White or Mayonnaise Chaud-Froid or Fish Aspic. Serve hot or cold and garnish each timbale with two periwinkles and a coriander leaf on top.

Variations
Substitute any nonoily white fish for the scallops.

Substitute smoked periwinkles or fresh or smoked baby clams for the periwinkles.

Nova and Cream-Cheese Timbale

Instead of the usual cream cheese and lox on a bagel, try this timbale for Sunday brunch.

YIELD: 4 4-ounce timbales

1½ cups cream cheese, softened
¼ cup blue cheese or Gorgonzola, softened
2 tablespoons minced red onion
2 tablespoons chopped fresh herbs (such as parsley, dill, basil, chives)
1 to 1½ pounds Nova Scotia smoked salmon fillets

Blend the cream cheese and blue cheese together. Mix in the minced red onion and chopped herbs. Grease four 4-ounce ramekins and line them with plastic wrap, allowing at least an inch overhang. Line the bottom and sides with Nova fillets, leaving the ends to hang over the rim. Spoon the cheese mixture into the mold, then fold the fillet ends over the top of the mixture. Wrap in plastic and chill.

Unmold the timbale when ready to serve by gently holding the plastic wrap down and at the same time lifting the ramekin off. Discard the plastic.

Serving Suggestions
Garnish the plate with onion rings, sliced tomato, and an herb sprig. Serve with spicy, cold Bloody Marys and golden, toasted bagels.

Variations
Substitute another smoked fish or cooked and sliced meat for the Nova fillets.

Substitute any cheese spread or gelatin-based mousseline (of meat, fish, or vegetable) for the cheese mixture.

Mushroom Medley Timbale in Pastry

Few food combinations are more seductive than mushrooms in cream, and autumn is the season for mushroom harvests. Select an assortment of fresh wild and cultivated mushrooms or reconstitute a variety of dried ones for this recipe.

YIELD: 4 4-ounce timbales

1½ cups mixed mushrooms (such as field, cepes, morels, and shiitakes), small ones kept whole and large ones diced
1 garlic clove, minced
2 tablespoons lemon juice
4 tablespoons unsalted butter
¾ cup heavy cream
White pepper to taste
Pinch of salt
1 teaspoon chopped fresh tarragon
¾ teaspoon arrowroot
2 to 4 tablespoons Madeira
4 prebaked pastry shells

In a skillet over medium heat, sauté the mushrooms and garlic, with the lemon juice in butter until cooked. Add the heavy cream and reduce the liquid to a little over half a cup. Season with pepper, salt, and tarragon. Dissolve the arrowroot in the Madeira and stir it into the mushroom mixture to thicken the sauce.

Spoon the mushrooms into warmed, prebaked pastry shells and serve immediately, before the pastry gets soggy.

Serving Suggestions
Serve the timbale as a first course or as an accompaniment to poultry, veal, or fish.

Broccoli and Cauliflower Timbale

YIELD: 6 4-ounce timbales

1¼ cups pureed cooked broccoli
3 eggs, lightly beaten
¾ cup heavy cream
2 tablespoons chopped scallions
¼ teaspoon nutmeg
¼ teaspoon white pepper
Salt to taste
⅔ cup tiny cauliflower florets, steamed, drained, and dusted in flour

In a bowl, combine all the ingredients except the cauliflower. Test the seasonings and correct if necessary. Fold in the cauliflower florets.

Grease six 4-ounce ramekins. Spoon in the mixture and cover with greased aluminum foil. Bake the timbales in a water bath in a preheated 350°F oven for about 30 minutes, until the mousseline rises a little and feels firm but springy to the touch.

Serving Suggestions
Glaze chilled timbales with Classic, White, or Mayonnaise Chaud-Froid or aspic. Served hot or cold, these timbales make a decorative accompaniment to any meal.

Variations
Eliminate the cauliflower and add ⅔ cup more broccoli puree.

For curried timbales, add 1 to 2 teaspoons curry powder, depending on your taste.

Reverse the recipe by using cauliflower puree and broccoli florets.

Make a layered timbale using ¾ cup broccoli puree (instead of 1 cup) and ¾ cup cauliflower puree (instead of ½ cup florets).

For a basic custard timbale, substitute a cup of vegetable puree, such as beets, turnips, parsnips, squash, peas, or brussels sprouts, for the broccoli. In place of cauliflower florets, use any diced vegetable or eliminate the garniture completely.

Spinach and Cheese Timbale

This makes a good breakfast or brunch item. Serve it in place of an omelette.

YIELD: 6 4-ounce timbales

1½ pounds spinach leaves, steamed and squeezed dry
4 eggs, lightly beaten
¾ cup heavy cream
½ cup crumbled or shredded cheese (such as Monterey Jack, mozzarella, cheddar, or goat cheese)
2 tablespoons chopped chives or scallions
Pinch of allspice
White pepper to taste
Salt to taste

Combine all the ingredients. Test the seasonings and correct if necessary.

Spoon the mixture into six greased 4-ounce ramekins and securely cover with a well-greased piece of aluminum foil. Bake the timbales in a water bath in a preheated 350°F oven for 30 to 40 minutes, until the timbale rises a little and feels firm but springy to the touch.

Serving Suggestions
Serve the timbales hot or at room temperature. A bit of tomato sauce nicely offsets this dish.

Variations
Substitute any leafy green vegetable for the spinach. Or, 1½ 10-ounce packages of frozen spinach can be used.

Carrot Timbale with Peas and Corn

YIELD: 6 4-ounce ramekins

1¼ cups pureed cooked carrot
3 eggs, lightly beaten
¾ cup heavy cream
2 tablespoons chopped fresh dill
¼ teaspoon cinnamon
⅛ teaspoon white pepper
Salt to taste
¾ cup mixed peas and corn kernels, steamed, drained, and dusted in flour

In a bowl, combine all the ingredients except the peas and corn. Test the seasonings and correct if necessary. Fold in the peas and corn kernels.

Grease six 4-ounce ramekins. Spoon in the mixture and cover with greased aluminum foil. Bake the timbales in a water bath in a preheated 350°F oven for about 30 minutes, until the mousseline rises a little and feels firm but springy to the touch.

Serving Suggestions
Glaze chilled timbales with White or Mayonnaise Chaud-Froid or Mayonnaise Aspic.

Open-Faced Breakfast Timbales

YIELD: 6 2¾-inch timbales

1½ cups coarsely ground seasoned bread crumbs
¼ teaspoon black pepper
1 tablespoon chopped fresh parsley
¼ cup cold unsalted butter, cut into small pieces
1 egg white, beaten until foamy
6 large eggs
6 tablespoons sautéed chopped spinach
Grated cheese
Chopped chives (or another herb such as dill)

Combine the bread crumbs, pepper, and parsley in a bowl. Cut in the pieces of butter until the mixture becomes coarse and crumbly. Mix the crumb mixture into the beaten egg white.

Grease a six-muffin tin. Press the crumb mixture against the bottom and sides of each muffin cup, forming a ⅛-inch shell. Bake the shells at 375°F for 8 minutes.

Set the whole eggs, still in their shells, in 140°F water for 10 minutes to warm. Meanwhile, place a tablespoon of spinach in each prebaked crust. Crack a warmed egg into each partially filled timbale. Bake the timbales for 6 minutes. Midway through the cooking time, sprinkle each one with grated cheese and chopped chives. Unmold almost immediately.

Serving Suggestions
Serve each timbale, egg side up, with your favorite sausage, bacon, or grilled ham.

Variations
Substitute sautéed mushrooms, onions, or diced ham and cheese for the chopped spinach.

Yam Timbale with Mascarpone and Cinnamon

This timbale can be served as a side dish. Garnished, it makes an attractive first course or lightly sweetened dessert.

YIELD: 8 4-ounce timbales

1 egg
1½ teaspoons (envelopes) unflavored gelatin
¼ cup maple syrup
1½ cups pureed cooked yams or sweet potatoes
1⅛ teaspoons cinnamon
¼ teaspoon ginger
¼ teaspoon allspice
1 pound Mascarpone cheese

Beat the eggs until they become thick and light yellow in color. Meanwhile, soften the gelatin in the maple syrup for about 5 minutes. Over low heat, dissolve the gelatin in the syrup, then slightly cool it.

Beat the syrup-gelatin into the eggs. Stir in the yam puree, cinnamon, ginger, and allspice. Thoroughly fold in the Mascarpone.

Spoon the mousseline into eight greased 4-ounce ramekins and chill for at least 6 hours. Unmold when ready to serve.

Serving Suggestions

Garnish the timbales with a candied flower and fresh mint leaves.

Serve the timbales with a dollop of fruit-swirled Mascarpone (pureed fruit swirled into the Mascarpone) or whipped cream.

Variations

Substitute 3/4 to 1 cup heavy cream, whipped to measure 2 cups, for the 1 pound Mascarpone cheese.

Substitute pumpkin puree for the yam.

Pumpkin Timbale with Candied Chestnuts

YIELD: 6 4-ounce timbales

1 1/4 cups cooked or canned pumpkin puree
3 eggs, lightly beaten
3/4 cup heavy cream
2 tablespoons honey
1 to 2 tablespoons molasses
1 teaspoon vanilla extract
1/2 to 3/4 teaspoon cinnamon
1/4 to 1/2 teaspoon ginger
1/4 teaspoon cloves
Pinch of ground cardamom
1/2 cup chopped candied chestnuts, dusted in flour

In a bowl, combine all the ingredients except the candied chestnuts. Test the seasonings and correct if necessary. Fold in the chopped candied chestnuts.

Spoon the mixture into six greased 4-ounce ramekins and cover with greased aluminum foil. Bake the timbales in a water bath in a preheated 350°F oven for 30 to 40 minutes, until the mousseline rises a little and feels firm but springy to the touch.

Serving Suggestions

Drizzle cranberry sauce over the hot timbales. Glaze chilled timbales with White Chaud-Froid or Vegetable Aspic. Served hot or cold, these timbales make a decorative accompaniment to any meal. You might even consider pumpkin timbales for dessert.

Variations
Substitute candied walnuts for the chestnuts.

Substitute pureed yams, sweet potatoes, or acorn squash for the pumpkin puree.

Pear and Raspberry Timbale

Serve framboise as an after-dinner drink with these timbales. Each bottle of framboise, a French eau de vie, captures all the flavor and fragrance of the forty pounds of raspberries that went into making it.

YIELD: 6 4-ounce ramekins

2 tablespoons (envelopes) unflavored gelatin
1/4 cup pear or orange juice
1 cup pear puree
1 to 2 tablespoons honey
1 tablespoon lemon juice
3/4 teaspoon vanilla extract
1/4 teaspoon almond extract
1/8 teaspoon allspice
1 1/2 egg whites, whipped until stiff but not dry
1/2 cup raspberries, hulled

Soften the gelatin in the fruit juice for about 5 minutes. Over low heat, dissolve the gelatin in the juice, then cool it to room temperature.

In a bowl, combine all the ingredients except the egg whites and raspberries. Chill. When the mixture begins to set, beat in 1/4 cup of the whipped egg whites, then fold in the remaining egg whites and the raspberries.

Grease six 4-ounce ramekins. Spoon in the mousseline and chill for at least 6 hours. Unmold when ready to serve.

Serving Suggestions
Serve the chilled timbales with Berry Sauce. Garnish each timbale with a pear wedge, two raspberries, and a mint sprig.

Peach Timbale

A tasty filling also for thimble-size chocolate cups.

YIELD: 6 4-ounce ramekins

2 tablespoons (envelopes) unflavored gelatin
1/4 cup peach or orange juice
1 cup peach puree
1 to 2 tablespoons honey
1 tablespoon lemon juice
3/4 teaspoon vanilla
1/8 teaspoon mace
1 1/2 egg whites, whipped until stiff but not dry

Soften the gelatin in the fruit juice for about 5 minutes. Over low heat, dissolve the gelatin in the juice, then cool it to room temperature.

In a bowl, combine all the ingredients except the egg whites. Chill. When the mixture begins to set, beat in 1/4 cup of the whipped egg whites, then fold in the remainder.

Spoon the mousseline into six 4-ounce ramekins and chill for at least 6 hours. Unmold when ready to serve.

Serving Suggestions
Serve the chilled timbales with Peach Brandy Sauce. Garnish with a peach wedge and mint sprig.

Variations
Form the timbales in thimble-size chocolate cups.

Substitute another fruit puree, such as apricot, melon, pear, or strawberry, for the peach puree.

Banana Timbale with Mandarin Oranges

YIELD: 10 4-ounce timbales

2 1/3 tablespoons (envelopes) unflavored gelatin
1/2 cup coconut milk
3 large, ripe bananas, pureed
1 tablespoon lemon juice
1 tablespoon crème de bananes
1/4 cup honey
1 teaspoon vanilla extract
1/4 teaspoon cinnamon
1 cup heavy cream, whipped
1/2 cup Mandarin oranges, halved

Soften the gelatin in the coconut milk for about 5 minutes. Over low heat, dissolve the gelatin in the juice, then cool it to room temperature.

In a bowl, food processor, or mixer, blend together all the ingredients except the cream and the oranges. Fold in the whipped heavy cream and the Mandarin oranges.

Spoon the mousseline into ten greased 4-ounce ramekins and chill for at least 6 hours. Unmold when ready to serve.

Serving Suggestions
Serve the chilled timbales with Berry Sauce and garnish each plate with a banana slice, an orange wedge, and a mint sprig.

Variations
Substitute canned or cooked pineapple juice or orange juice for the coconut milk.

Substitute pomegranate kernels, mango, pineapple, or papaya pieces for the Mandarin oranges.

Persimmon Timbale

YIELD: 10 4-ounce timbales

1¼ cups persimmon puree
1 teaspoon lemon juice
½ cup honey
3 eggs, lightly beaten
¾ cup buttermilk or ⅜ cup sour cream mixed with ⅜ cup milk
2 tablespoons heavy cream
¾ cup all-purpose flour
½ teaspoon baking powder
¾ teaspoon cinnamon
⅛ teaspoon allspice
½ teaspoon baking soda

In a large bowl, mix together the persimmon puree, lemon juice, honey, eggs, buttermilk, and heavy cream. Combine the remaining dry ingredients and gradually beat them into the puree.

Grease ten 4-ounce ramekins and spoon in the mousseline. Bake the timbales in a preheated 350°F oven for about 30 minutes, until the mousseline rises a little and the edges brown. Let the timbales set for at least 15 minutes before unmolding. They will contract slightly, making a denser mousseline.

Serving Suggestions
Serve the timbales warm or at room temperature with a napping of warm Persimmon Sauce.

FILLED PASTRIES

Large vol-au-vent and small bouchée shells, made from puff pastry, are cousins of the pastry timbale. These delicate, flaky crusts, often called patty shells, are prebaked and filled with any of the cooked salpicons served in pastry timbales. Of the vol-au-vent, the great French chef Antonin Carême once said, "This entree is pretty and good without doubt," and "It is eaten with pleasure for its extreme delicacy and lightness."

Bouchées are individual vol-au-vents. Very tiny bouchées, barely mouthfuls, make perfect hors d'oeuvre. According to *The New Larousse Gastronomique*, Queen Marie Leczinska, the wife of Louis XV, was noted for her fondness of food, especially vol-au-vents. She is credited with having invented the bouchée in order to enjoy these miniatures at whim.

BASICS OF MAKING PUFF PASTRY SHELLS

Vol-au-vent and bouchée shells are made from puff pastry dough. Always work puff pastry in a cool room and on a cool surface such as marble. When rolling out the dough, roll in all directions—top to bottom, left to right—or the pastry will rise unevenly and become misshapen when baked. You can layer two sheets of dough together with egg wash or water and a light roll of the rolling pin. This forms a thicker, higher-rising pastry shell. To shape the shell, cut the dough with a sharp knife or pastry cutter. Assemble it and allow it to rest for 15 to 30 minutes in the refrigerator before baking. When glazing the dough with egg wash, be careful not to drip egg down the sides or it will seal the side layers together, inhibiting the dough from rising. Sprinkle an ungreased baking sheet with water; as the water vaporizes in the hot oven, it encourages the dough to rise. Do not open the oven door for the first 5 minutes of baking or the steam may condense and cause the pastry to fall.

Two pounds of puff pastry dough, rolled ⅓ inch thick, will make one 8½-inch or two 6-inch vol-au-vents; four 4-inch patty circles or squares with lids; or seven 3-inch or fifteen 2-inch bouchées with lids.

Once baked and tightly wrapped in aluminum foil, these flaky, buttery, pastry containers keep for 2 to 4 weeks if frozen or stored in a dry place. Reheat unfilled shells for 10 minutes in a preheated 350°F to 400°F oven.

TRADITIONAL METHOD

Use 2 pounds of Classic Puff Pastry.

YIELD: 4 4-inch patty shells with lids

Roll out the dough ⅓ inch thick. Using a sharp knife or pastry cutter (so as not to pinch the pastry layers together), cut out eight circles or squares. To make the tops, cut the center out of four of these circles or squares, leaving a ½-inch border all around. (Leave a 1¼-inch border on large vol-au-vent shells.) Reserve the centers as lids. Brush the tops of the pastry borders with egg wash.

Sprinkle an ungreased baking sheet with water. Arrange the solid pastry bases on the sheet and brush them with egg wash. Set the egg-washed side of the pastry borders on top of the bases and lightly press them in place. Use the back of a knife to flute or indent the sides. With a fork, prick the bases several times to prevent air bubbles.

To ensure even rising, snugly fit an aluminum foil collar (folded over two or three times), into the center of the pastry (fig. 3-7). Arrange the reserved lids on the baking sheet. Refrigerate the patties and lids for at least 15 minutes before baking. Brush the tops of the borders and lids with egg wash. Score the lids with a fork or add dough cutouts for a decorative finish.

3-7. To ensure even rising, fit aluminum foil collars into the patty shells.

Bake the shells for 5 minutes in a preheated 475°F oven. Lower the temperature to 425°F and continue to bake for 10 to 15 minutes more (20 to 25 minutes for larger shells), until golden. Bake the lids separately for 5 minutes at 475°F and then about 10 minutes more at 425°F. Remove the foil collars immediately and pick out any uncooked layers of dough from the centers of the bases. If necessary, set the patties in a preheated 200°F oven for another 15 minutes to dry out the insides. Fill and serve.

MODERN METHOD FOR LARGE PATTY SHELLS

Use 2 pounds of Classic or Quick Puff Pastry or even Short-Crust Pastry for the shell.

YIELD: 1 12-inch patty shell

Roll out the dough 3⁄16 inch thick. Using a sharp knife or pastry cutter (so as not to pinch the pastry layers together), cut out one 12-inch circle for the base. Set the pastry base on an ungreased baking sheet sprinkled with water. Place a softly packed 5-inch-diameter ball of aluminum foil on the center of the base and brush the dough border with egg wash.

Roll the dough left from cutting the circle and gently cover the foil ball with it (fig. 3-8). Lightly press the borders together to seal. Following the outline of the base, cut away any excess dough. Brush the shell with egg wash and decorate it using scraps of dough.

Add a 2- to 2½-inch strip of fresh dough on top of the border. Flute, notch, or scallop the edges, and score around the top where the lid will be (fig. 3-9). Refrigerate the patty shell for at least 30 minutes before baking. Brush the decorated shell with egg wash and bake for 30 to 35 minutes in a preheated 425°F oven, until golden.

After the shell cools for about 10 minutes, cut off the lid along the scored line. Carefully remove the aluminum foil ball and pick out any uncooked layers of dough from the center (fig. 3-10). If necessary, set the shell in a preheated 200°F oven for another 15 minutes to dry out the insides. Fill and serve.

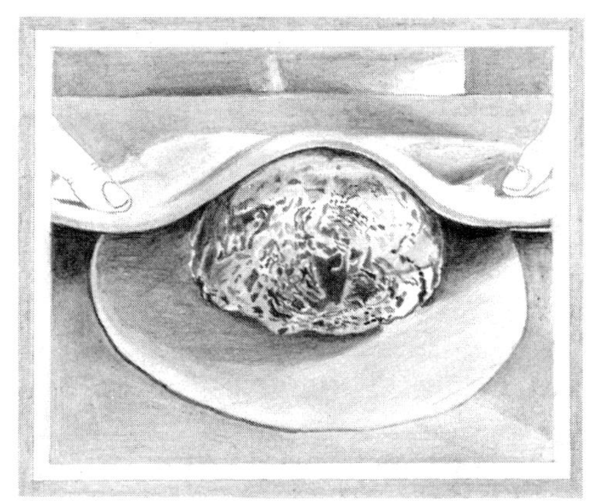

3-8. Gently cover the foil ball inside the vol-au-vent with dough.

3-9. Scallop the edges and score around the top where lid will be.

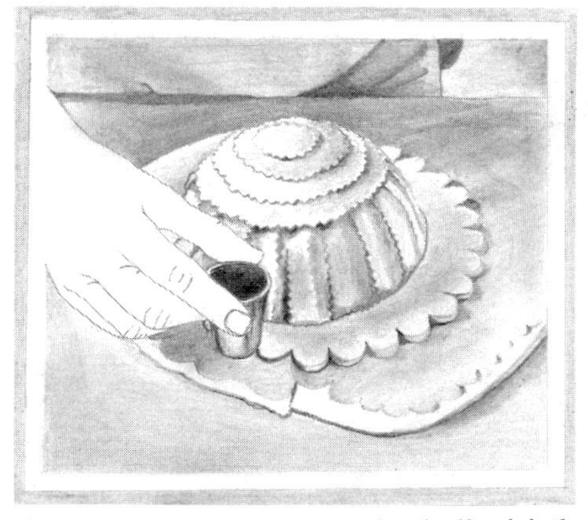

3-10. Carefully remove the ball of foil.

Lobster and Prawn Vol-au-Vent

When serving a vol-au-vent, slice up all the portions first, then remove each portion to serve.

YIELD: 1 12-inch vol-au-vent (6 to 8 servings)

1 pound large prawn or shrimp, shelled and deveined
1 pound lobster meat chunks
3/4 cup unsalted butter
1/3 cup minced shallots
1 1/2 tablespoons flour
1 3/4 cups Fish or Chicken Stock
1/2 teaspoon salt
1/8 teaspoon cayenne
1/8 teaspoon allspice or nutmeg
1 1/4 cups heavy cream
1 egg yolk
2 tablespoons chopped fresh tarragon
1 tablespoon chopped fresh dill
12 or more morels, soaked, cleaned, and split
1 12-inch prebaked puff pastry shell

Lightly sauté the prawns and lobster in butter. Remove and reserve until later. Add the shallots to the remaining butter. When the shallots become soft and translucent, add the flour and cook it a bit longer as you would a roux. Stir in the stock and simmer until it reduces to 1 cup. Add the salt, cayenne, allspice, and cream. Simmer until thickened. Add the egg yolk to bind, taking care not to curdle it. Mix in the remaining ingredients and the reserved shellfish. Gently heat the filling through but make sure it does not boil.

Ladle the shellfish mixture into a warm puff pastry shell and serve immediately.

Serving Suggestions

Serve the vol-au-vent with finger-size carrots and green asparagus tips or tiny peas.

Variations

Use mushrooms instead of morels.

Add 2 tablespoons tomato sauce for color and flavor.

Substitute chunks of monkfish, crabmeat, or scallops for the lobsters and prawns.

The filling can be used for six to eight individual patty shells instead of one large pastry shell.

Bouchées of Crab with Shrimp Mousse

For a cocktail party, arrange an hors d'oeuvre platter of these bouchées.

YIELD: 20 2-inch bouchées (4 first-course servings)

½ cup pureed cooked shrimp
⅛ cup crème fraîche or sour cream
20 2-inch bouchée shells, prebaked
½ pound pasteurized lump crabmeat
3 tablespoons red or black caviar
Snipped fresh chives for garnish

Blend the shrimp puree and crème fraîche to make a mousse. Place about a teaspoon of mousse in each bouchée. Top with a piece of crabmeat and a dot of caviar. Sprinkle with fresh chives.

Serving Suggestions
Set five bouchées on a mirror of sauce made from crème fraîche and mustard. Sprinkle with chives. If serving the bouchées on an hors d'oeuvre platter, serve the sauce on the side.

Variations
Substitute any cooked fish or poultry puree for the shrimp puree.

Substitute shrimp, scallops, clams, or vegetables for the cooked crabmeat.

For dessert bouchées, substitute a fruit mousse for the shrimp mousse and diced fresh fruit for the crabmeat. Sprinkle with chopped fresh mint.

Scallop and Vegetable Bouchées

Do not stuff the bouchée shells until ready to serve or they will get soggy.

YIELD: 4 4-inch bouchées

1½ cups cooked scallops or seviche
½ cup broccoli florets, blanched
2 tablespoons finely diced red bell pepper
2 tablespoons finely diced yellow bell pepper or yellow squash
2 tablespoons julienned shiitake mushrooms
⅓ cup olive oil
2 tablespoons lime juice
1 garlic clove, pressed
2 tablespoons chopped fresh scallions
1 tablespoon chopped fresh parsley
1 tablespoon toasted sesame seeds
Black pepper to taste
4 prebaked bouchée shells, each about 4 to 5 inches

Toss all the ingredients for the filling together and test the seasonings. Stuff the bouchée shells when ready to serve.

Serving Suggestions
The filling may be served chilled, at room temperature, or slightly warm. Serve with Lime Vinaigrette Dressing on the side.

Variations
Substitute any cooked fish or meat for the scallops.

Bread Surprise

Hollowed-out loaves of round Italian, long French, rye, or pumpernickel bread make crusty shells for an endless array of fillings. Layer round loaves with an assortment of cold cuts, cheese, vegetables, fish, purees, and salads. Stuff long, cylindrical loaves with a mixture of a soft salad (such as egg salad) speckled with a colorful finely diced garniture of olives, pickles, pimientos, meats, or cheese. Chill the stuffed bread for several hours, until the filling sets, or bake it until warm and firm. You also can make individual Bread Surprises in small round or oblong rolls.

Slice off and reserve the top of a round loaf. Cut around the inside of the loaf, leaving a ½-inch crust along the sides and bottom. Pull out the dough from the center. Or cut off the ends of a cylindrical loaf and, using a long, narrow knife, work from both ends to cut out and remove the dough from the center, leaving a ¼-inch crust. Coat the inside of either loaf with softened butter, mayonnaise, or cheese spread to prevent the bread from becoming soggy. Chill for 10 minutes to firm up the spread.

Line the cavity of the round loaf with thin slices of cold cuts or cheese. Spread a vegetable mixture over the bottom. Continue to layer the meats, vegetables, and cheese until the cavity is stuffed nearly to the top. Fold the overhanging ends of the sliced cold cuts or cheese across the top of the fillings and replace the bread's lid. Or use a long-handled spoon to stuff the hollowed-out cylindrical loaf solidly with chopped liver, tuna salad, or another salad or spread (fig. 3-11).

Either wrap the loaf in foil and chill for several hours to set the stuffing before serving or bake it until heated through. To heat, place the loaf on a baking sheet. Brush the crust with vegetable oil and bake in a preheated 375°F oven for about 20 minutes. To serve, cut the round loaf into wedges or the cylindrical loaf into ½-inch slices.

Once wrapped in foil and refrigerated, the stuffed loaf will keep for 2 or 3 days.

3-11. Stuff the loaves by layering meat, vegetable, and cheese fillings into the hollow of a round loaf or by scooping a spread into the cavity of a cylindrical loaf.

Rye Pasties

Pasties is pronounced "pass-tees." Cornish miners immigrated to America during the Industrial Revolution to pioneer the West and settle in Grass Valley, California, the site of the Sierra Nevada gold rush. With them came the Cornish pasty, which traditionally contained potatoes, meat, onions, seasonings, and sometimes turnips or carrots. Today pasties are made with any number of different fillings—even vegetarian.

YIELD: about 14 pasties

1¼ pounds Rye Dough, rolled out ⅛ inch thick
½ pound boneless beef chuck, ¼-inch cubed
1 peeled baking potato, ⅛-inch cubed
½ cup ⅛-inch cubed carrots or turnips
1 onion, finely diced
2 to 4 tablespoons chopped fresh parsley
½ teaspoon salt
¼ to ½ teaspoon black pepper
¼ teaspoon crumbled dried sage
Egg wash

Cut fourteen 5-inch circles from the dough, making certain to use up any scraps.

Combine the remaining ingredients except the egg wash and mix well.

Spoon about 3 tablespoons of the mixture onto half of each dough circle, allowing a ¼-inch border. Moisten the dough border with egg wash. Fold the dough in half to cover the filling and crimp the edges to seal.

Keeping them covered with a damp cloth, set the pasties on a baking sheet to rise for 45 minutes. Brush the pasties with egg wash and bake them in a preheated 425°F oven for 10 minutes. Reduce the heat to 375°F and continue to bake for about 45 minutes more, until golden.

Freeze the baked pasties on a baking sheet, then individually wrap them in foil. Prepared in this way, they keep for up to a month in the freezer. To reheat frozen pasties, unwrap and bake at 325°F for 30 to 40 minutes, until thawed and heated.

Serving Suggestions

Pasties may be served piping hot from the oven, at room temperature, or cold.

Variations

Any other dough or pastry crust substitutes for the rye dough.

Substitute pork, ham, or turkey for the beef.

Make the pasties with a favorite fish, fruit, or vegetable filling.

Tempting Turnovers

Like pasties, turnovers lend themselves to all manner of fillings. Do not hesitate to try other combinations and invent new ones such as apple-cheddar or pumpkin-pecan.

YIELD: 6 turnovers

1 pound Classic or Quick Puff Pastry
1 tablespoon vegetable oil
¾ pound lean ground beef or pork
1 small onion, finely diced
1 medium tomato, peeled, seeded, diced
1 garlic clove, minced
¾ cup tomato sauce
2 tablespoons raisins
1 teaspoon Chili Spice
½ teaspoon salt
¼ teaspoon cumin
Cayenne to taste
Egg wash

Divide the dough into six equal portions and roll out each into a 6-inch square. Meanwhile, sauté the ground meat in oil; add the onion, tomato, and garlic. Stir in the remaining ingredients except the egg wash, and simmer for about 5 minutes. Cool the meat mixture before stuffing the pastry.

Spoon the meat mixture a little off center onto each pastry square, leaving a ½-inch border. Moisten the dough border with egg wash. Fold the dough in half to cover the filling and form a triangle. Crimp the edges to seal and cut two short slits in the top for steam to escape. Brush the turnovers with egg wash and bake on a baking sheet for 10 minutes at 400°F. Reduce the temperature to 350°F and continue baking for 20 to 30 minutes more, until golden.

Note: Both baked and unbaked turnovers keep for up to a month in the freezer if they are individually frozen and then wrapped tightly in foil. Thaw unbaked turnovers for 30 minutes and then bake as usual. Thaw baked turnovers for 5 minutes and reheat at 375°F for about 30 minutes.

Serving Suggestions
Serve hot turnovers with a wedge of cheese and a vegetable salad or sweet-and-sour vegetables.

Variations
Substitute a thawed package of frozen patty shells for puff pastry. Roll out each shell to over 7 inches. Stuff and bake.

Apple-cheddar: Add shredded cheddar cheese to apple pie filling and bake as turnovers. Serve with hard sauce.

Pumpkin-pecan: Stuff turnovers with pumpkin or sweet potato pie filling and chopped pecans. Dust with confectioners' sugar when ready to serve.

Crescents and Horns

Pastry crescents and horns roll up into savory hors d'oeuvre or canapés. Finely diced chicken, tuna, egg, or ham and cheese salads, as well as leftover cooked sausage meat, pâté, rillette, mousse, or spinach and feta, make tempting stuffings. For a New Year's Eve gala, pass around prebaked pastry horns filled with sour cream and caviar and dusted with sieved hard-cooked egg yolks.

YIELD: 24 crescents or horns

1 pound Short-Crust Pastry or Quick Puff Pastry
¾ cup cooked filling, finely diced or pureed
Egg wash

Roll the dough into a rectangle, 12 by 16 inches. Cut the rolled dough into 4-inch-wide squares, then cut diagonally across each square to form two triangles.

3-12. Place a teaspoon of filling in the centers of the triangles, brush with egg wash, and then roll up crescents.

For crescents, place about a teaspoon of filling at the base (longest side) of each triangle. Using a pastry brush, moisten the edges with egg wash, then roll the dough around the filling (fig. 3-12). Pinch the edges and curve the stuffed pastry into a crescent. Brush the stuffed crescents with egg wash and bake on a well-greased baking sheet in a preheated 375°F oven for about 30 minutes.

For horns, shape the dough triangles into horns. Stuff each horn with a teaspoon of filling and bake for about 20 minutes as you would the crescents. Or stuff a bit of foil into the horns and prebake them for 10 to 12 minutes. Once cooled, remove the foil and stuff.

Serving Suggestions

Serve the crescents and horns hot or at room temperature. Set out a dipping sauce with them.

CHAPTER FOUR

Galantines, Ballotines, and Stuffed Meats

GALANTINES AND BALLOTINES

Chilled and glistening in aspic, galantines contain flavorful stuffings often abstractly patterned with fruits, nuts, vegetables, or truffles. The term *galantine* probably derives from the Old French word *géline* or *galine*, meaning chicken. Originally, it was a poultry dish, but by the close of the seventeenth century, cooks also prepared galantines of various meats and fish. During the mid-eighteenth century, the word referred to "a particular way of dressing a pig." Our contemporary definition of galantine—a cold dish of boned, stuffed, and poached meat or fish—was adopted in France by the turn of the eighteenth century.

The terms *ballotine* and *galantine* frequently are confused. Both are similarly prepared, but they are cooked and served differently. A ballotine also consists of boneless meat, poultry, or fish stuffed and rolled into a *ballot*, or bundle. Unlike galantines, they are baked or braised in their skins and served hot as entrees. Some food connoisseurs insist the meat is not stuffed, while others claim it to be stuffed into a leg cut of meat and none other.

Classically, full-sized capons are used for galantines. Any poultry, game bird, fish, or cut of meat such as lamb shoulder or pork or veal breast can be used. Do not choose fowl, however; the prolonged cooking it requires destroys the flavor, texture, and appearance of the dish.

CRAFTING AND COOKING

The preparation of birds and fish requires careful boning. Keep the blade of the knife close to the bone so as not to pierce the skin. The skin-covered flesh forms an edible container, sealing in layers of forcemeat and garnitures. Most pâté or terrine fillings work well for galantines. Garnitures may include strips of smoked meat or fish, fat, liver, pistachios, wild mushrooms, pimientos, diced vegetables, apricots, raisins, julienned truffles, or black olives. An 8-pound capon will hold about 4 pounds of farce, and each pound of farce equals approximately 1 cup.

Roll up the galantine with the skin overlapping slightly or sew it closed. On occasions when you have ingredients for a stuffing but no bird or whole fish on hand, wrap the farce in caul fat, sliced fatback, or heat-resistant plastic wrap instead. Or securely wrap the galantine in muslin or cheesecloth and poach it in a rich, gelatinous stock. The exchange of flavors between the galantine and the stock enhances both. To ensure succulent results, slowly simmer over gentle heat. The stock should never boil or bubble. At temperatures over 180°F, the protein in meat or fish becomes tough and sinewy and will disintegrate before it tenderizes. Only long, slow simmering or stewing will sufficiently break down the protein, soften the connective tissue, and result in a moist, tender galantine.

Once cooked, allow the galantine to cool in the poaching liquid. When cooled, remove it, squeeze out the extra stock, and weight it. Galantines keep for several days, refrigerated.

Clarify the poaching stock. This stock, enriched with a squeeze of lemon and a splash of Madeira, port, or sherry, makes a good-tasting aspic. If the jelly is too soft, melt it and add 1 tablespoon (envelope) of unflavored gelatin to 2 cups of liquid.

SETTING THEM OUT

Glaze the galantine with aspic or chaud-froid and serve it with its natural jelly as you would a pâté or terrine. A simple decoration is appropriate, but avoid the antiquated and garish custom of painting pastoral or nude pictures on the breasts of capons. The simplest presentation is the most exquisite. Once served, the galantine reveals its colorful mosaic of texture—decorative and delicious.

BASICS OF BONING FOR A GALANTINE

Carefully bone poultry or game birds from the back, trying not to puncture the skin. Should you puncture it accidentally, remove a piece of skin from the leg or wing and patch it in from underneath the skin. You can use other cuts of meat, such as pork loin or veal breast. Simply bone the meat, cutting

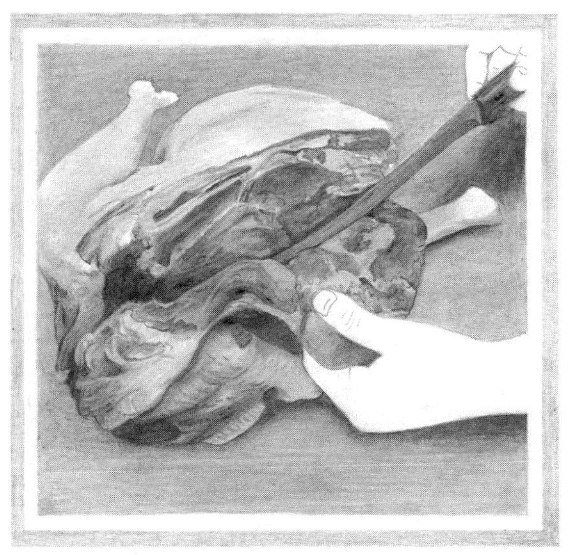

4-1. With the chicken breast down, slit down the backbone from the neck to the tail. Cut the meat away from the bones and remove the carcass.

a pocket for stuffing, or slice the loin into ½-inch-thick, single, flattened pieces.

To bone poultry, remove the wings above the first joint and also remove about ½ to 1 inch of the drumstick tips.

Place the bird on its breast. Cut a slit (down to the backbone) beginning at the neck and ending at the tail. Holding the knife blade against the bone, cut the carcass away from the skin and flesh (fig. 4-1).

Bend the wings to expose the joint that attaches the wing to the shoulder. Pop the joint and cut between the ball and the socket to separate the two. Separate the drumstick and thigh bones in the same manner.

The carcass remains attached at the collarbone and breastbone. Snap the wishbone, then cut along the edge of the breastbone to free the carcass. Take care not to lacerate the skin, as there is no meat between the breastbone and the skin. Remove the collarbone.

Hold the inside joint of the wing. Cut and scrape the flesh down off the bone, then pull out the bone. Remove the other wing and both drumsticks in the same manner (fig. 4-2). Pull the skin and flesh from the boned wings and drumsticks onto the inside of the meat.

Remove the tendons and sinews from the flesh; trim and discard any excess loose fat. Separate the fillets from the breast and slice off some of the thick meat near the thighs and wings. Distribute this meat evenly over areas of the skin that have little or no flesh. Lay the boned poultry out flat and marinate as required. Marinate the skins for up to two days if desired.

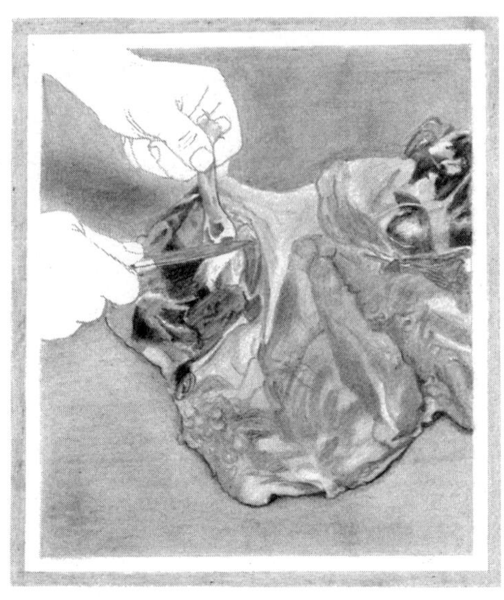

4-2. Cut and scrape the flesh down off the wing and drumstick bones, then pull out the bone.

ALTERNATE METHOD OF BONING FOR A GALANTINE

Use this method of boning poultry or game birds when you want the wings or drumsticks to remain attached to the galantine. This method does not alter the flavor of the galantine; it only changes the presentation.

Follow the first step in "Basics of Boning for a Galantine" but leave the wing or drumstick bones intact and remove only the carcass. Marinate the skins for up to two days if desired or as required.

BASICS OF ASSEMBLING AND COOKING A GALANTINE

Traditionally, galantines always were sewn closed, but it is sufficient to overlap the unseamed edges and securely encase the galantine in cloth. A cheesecloth or muslin wrapping will allow an exchange of flavors between the stock and the galantine, enriching both. For an even richer stock, chop the carcass into pieces and roast the bones in a 350°F oven until browned. Add them to the stock, along with carrots, onions, celery, leeks, and an herb bouquet.

In order to poach a galantine in plain water instead of stock, wrap it in heat-resistant plastic wrap. This impermeable plastic casing prevents (or at least minimizes) the savory juices of the galantine from escaping or from being diluted in the plain water during poaching.

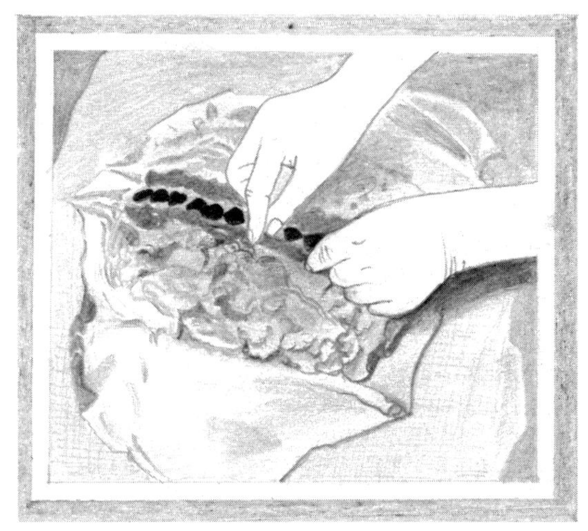

4-3. Spread farce over the meat and then add a layer or two of garniture.

Lay the boned meat out flat on a cloth or heat-resistant plastic wrap. Spread the farce over the meat, leaving a ¾-inch border, and add one or more layers of garniture—strips of meat, vegetables, nuts (fig. 4-3). Or mix a diced garniture into the farce and simply spoon the farce down the center of the meat, neck to tail.

Using the cloth or plastic wrap for support, lift one side of the poultry over the center (fig. 4-4). Lift the other side and fold it to overlap the first center edge slightly, making a cylinder. Tuck in the extra skin at each end to close the roll.

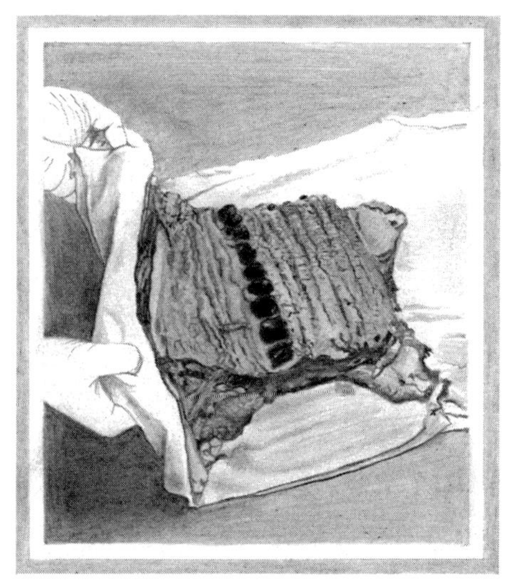

4-4. Roll up the galantine, using the cloth to support it.

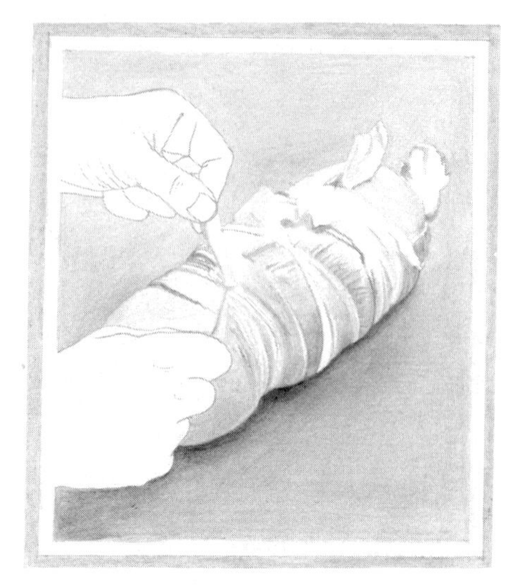

4-5. Wrap galantine in cloth, twist the ends, and tie with string.

Roll the galantine in the cloth or plastic wrap; twist the ends and tie them with string. If using cloth, securely tie two or three 18-inch strips of cloth (equally spaced) around the galantine to hold it closed (fig. 4-5). For plastic wrapping, use string.

Bring the stock or water to a boil in a covered pot fitted with an optional rack on the bottom. Add the galantine and return the stock to the boiling point. Lower the heat, cover, and simmer at about 175°F to 180°F for 1¼ to 2 hours (depending on the recipe), until the galantine feels firm. On average, poach a galantine 15 to 20 minutes per pound.

Allow the galantine to cool in its stock until lukewarm. When cooled, remove it from the liquid, squeeze out the extra stock, and set the roll on a platter or tray. Secure a board on top of the galantine by tying it to the platter with string (fig. 4-6). Chill for 8 hours or overnight. For a denser roll, place a 2- to 2½-pound weight on the board and chill overnight. Refrigerated, most galantines keep for several days. (Weighting the galantine with a board or weight is optional.)

Alternatively, once the galantine cools, squeeze out any extra stock and remove the galantine from the cloth. In order to keep the roll evenly shaped, tightly rewrap it in a clean cloth and return it to the cooled stock. Place a board or flat dish inside the pot (on top of the galantine in the stock) and weight it. Chill for 8 hours or overnight. Remove the weighted galantine from the stock. Refrigerated, it keeps for several days.

If desired, clarify the stock and use it to make an aspic. Allow 1 tablespoon (envelope) of unflavored gelatin for 2 cups of stock.

4-6. Tie a clean board to the top of the galantine with string to weight it.

ALTERNATE METHOD OF ASSEMBLING AND COOKING A GALANTINE

Use this method of assembling galantines when the wing or drumstick bones remain attached.

Stuff the poultry or game bird as described in "Basics of Assembling and Cooking a Galantine." Instead of overlapping the edges, sew the back slit closed and truss the bird. Wrap the galantine in cloth, as the bones could puncture plastic wrap. Follow the remaining steps in "Basics of Assembling and Cooking a Galantine."

BASICS OF BONING A ROUND FISH

The skeletons of most round fish, except shad, consist of a simple backbone and ribs. Once these are removed, the fish can be stuffed and poached while still maintaining its shape.

Completely scale and gut the fish and remove the dorsal fin and bones. Cut off the pectoral fins by slicing forward, and trim the tail.

Slit the belly open down to the tail. Hold the fish open and, beginning at the tail end, slice under the ribs to the backbone, angling the knife blade away from the flesh against the bones (fig. 4-7).

Hold the ribs aside and slide the knife along each side of the backbone without cutting through the skin. Loosen the skeleton and cut the backbone at each end. Remove the skeleton (fig. 4-8). Cut out any ribs still remaining.

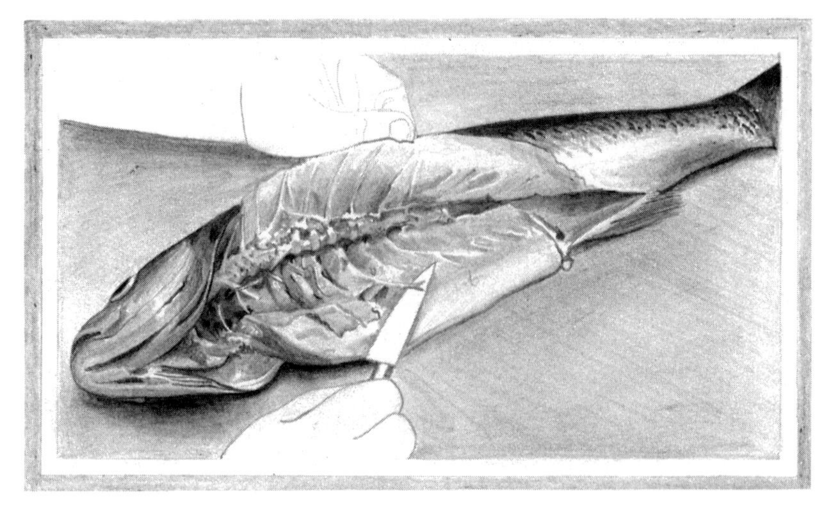

4-7. From the tail end, slice under the ribs to the backbone of the fish, angling the knife away from the flesh.

CANADIAN METHOD OF TIMING FISH

Use this method for timing the cooking of whole fish, steaks, and fillets or stuffed whole fish or fillets. The timing remains the same for baking, braising, broiling, frying, poaching, sautéing, or steaming.

Lay the fish on its side and measure it at the thickest point. Cook fresh fish for 10 minutes per inch of thickness. Do not thaw frozen fish, but cook it for 20 minutes per inch of thickness. A 1½-inch-thick fish will cook in 15 minutes, while the same size frozen, unthawed fish takes 30 minutes.

4-8. Remove the fish skeleton.

Beef and Vegetable Ballotine

This recipe is a version of the Argentine dish *matambre,* made of stuffed and rolled flank steak. The taste of coriander gives an unexpected flavor.

YIELD: 1 ballotine, about 5½ pounds (8 to 10 servings)

Marinade
½ cup red wine vinegar
¼ cup red wine
5 garlic cloves, minced
1 teaspoon thyme
½ teaspoon chopped fresh rosemary
1 bay leaf

2 2½-pound flank steaks, butterflied, flattened, and trimmed of fat
½ pound fresh escarole or spinach, washed and stems removed
5 whole carrots, cooked (about 7 inches long)
4 hard-cooked eggs, cut into 8 wedges each
1 large onion, sliced into ⅛-inch-thick rings
¼ cup chopped fresh parsley
2 tablespoons chopped fresh coriander
¼ to ½ teaspoon red pepper flakes
1 tablespoon coarse or kosher salt
3 to 4 cups Brown or White Stock
1 to 2 cups water

Marinate the steaks in the refrigerator for 6 to 24 hours, turning them occasionally.

Lay out the steaks, cut side up, overlapping 2 inches at one side. Pound the overlapping seam together. Spread the escarole or spinach over the meat, leaving a 1-inch border. In alternating rows, lay the carrots and eggs across the grain of the meat. Add a layer of onion rings, then sprinkle the parsley, coriander, red pepper flakes, and salt over all.

Roll the stuffed meat, jelly-roll style with the grain of the meat, to form a cylinder. Tie string around the ballotine at 1-inch intervals.

Set the ballotine in a 12-quart casserole with the stock. Add water to come ⅓ of the way up the sides of the roll. Cover tightly and bake in a preheated 375°F oven for about 1 hour. When cooked, remove the ballotine from the oven and let it rest in a warm place for 10 minutes before carving. Cut away the string before serving.

Serving Suggestions
Serve the ballotine hot or weight and chill it as you would a galantine.

Variations
Substitute a 5- to 5½-pound lamb shoulder or boned and butterflied pork.

Stuffed Steaks Poached in Tomato Sauce

This is a version of the traditional Italian dish *braciole.* Slice 3⁄4-inch-thick beef steaks from the center cut of a top or bottom round and flatten the steaks with a meat mallet.

YIELD: 6 stuffed steaks

6 braciola steaks (about 1 1⁄2 pounds), pounded thin
1 egg, lightly beaten
6 thin slices prosciutto, salami, or ham (about 1⁄4 pound)
1⁄4 to 1⁄3 cup grated Parmesan or Romano cheese
2 tablespoons seasoned bread crumbs
2 tablespoons chopped fresh parsley
Pinch of oregano
Grated black pepper
Pinch of garlic powder
2 tablespoons pignoli nuts
Oil for sautéing
3 to 4 cups tomato sauce

Lay the steaks out flat and brush them with the lightly beaten egg. Layer each steak with a slice of prosciutto and sprinkle with cheese, bread crumbs, parsley, oregano, black pepper, garlic powder, and pignoli nuts.

Roll up each steak, jelly-roll style, and close the ends with toothpicks or tie with string. Sauté the stuffed steaks in oil until just browned on all sides. Remove them from the pan and drain on paper towels.

Slowly simmer the stuffed steaks in tomato sauce for 45 minutes to 1 hour, until very tender. Remove the toothpicks or string before serving.

Serving Suggestions
Serve the warm stuffed steaks and tomato sauce with pasta or risotto. They also go well accompanied by vegetables, mushrooms, or artichokes and a salad.

Variations
Substitute pork, veal, or turkey for the beef steaks.

Substitute thinly sliced Fontina or provolone cheese for the Parmesan.

Add a thin layer of marinated artichoke heart wedges or puree to the filling.

Poach the stuffed steaks in a rich stock or soup instead of tomato sauce.

Duck Galantine with Apricots

YIELD: 1 galantine, about 3¾ pounds

Marinade
½ cup Cognac or brandy
2 tablespoons chopped fresh parsley
2 large shallots, chopped
1 bay leaf, broken in half
½ teaspoon thyme
Grated black pepper

Farce
1¼ pounds pork, grind half and dice half
¾ pound veal, grind half and dice half
½ cup diced dried apricots
⅓ cup julienned, softened shiitake mushrooms
1 garlic clove, minced
½ teaspoon Pâté Seasoning II
Salt to taste
Black pepper to taste
Pinch each of basil, nutmeg, clove, and cayenne

1 5-pound duck, boned for a galantine, with drumsticks attached
2 to 3 quarts rich, gelatinous Brown Stock (enough to cover galantine)
Herb bouquet
2 cups melted Basic Aspic or White or Brown Chaud-Froid to glaze

Combine the ingredients for the marinade and marinate the duck in the refrigerator for 6 hours or overnight, turning it at least once.

Remove the duck from the marinade. Over medium-high heat, reduce the marinade until the parsley and shallots are moist. Mix together the reduced marinade and the ingredients for the farce. Test the seasonings and correct if necessary.

Follow the directions in "Alternate Method of Assembling and Cooking a Galantine." Poach the duck in the stock with an herb bouquet for 1½ to 2 hours, until the galantine feels firm. Remove the galantine when it has cooled to lukewarm and weight it if desired. Chill.

Glaze the chilled galantine with aspic or chaud-froid and decorate.

Serving Suggestions
Serve each slice of galantine with fresh aspic and a sprig of curly parsley or a Belgian endive leaf. Add a dab of apricot puree spiked with sherry and a bit of honey.

Variations
Substitute another poultry or a game bird for the duck.

Substitute other dried fruits (for example, dried apples, pineapple, papaya, or pears) for the apricots or add a sprinkling of chopped nuts.

Quail Ballotine

Squab or Cornish hens can be stuffed with this same rice filling.

YIELD: 4 individual ballotines (4 first-course servings)

Farce
1/2 cup cooked wild rice
1/4 cup sautéed mushrooms
2 tablespoons finely diced red bell pepper or pimiento
1 tablespoon chopped black walnuts
1 tablespoon chopped fresh parsley
1 shallot, minced
1 garlic clove, minced
Black pepper to taste
Salt to taste
2 tablespoons Frangelico liqueur
1 egg lightly beaten

4 quail, boned for a galantine, with drumsticks attached
4 bacon strips

Mix together the ingredients for the farce. Test the seasonings and correct if necessary.

Follow the directions in "Alternate Method of Assembling and Cooking a Galantine." Cut the bacon strips in half. Arrange two bacon halves in an X on the breast of each quail. They will keep the delicate skin from burning while continuously basting the bird.

Bake the ballotines in a preheated 450°F oven for 10 to 12 minutes, or until cooked. Remove the string and serve hot or chilled.

Serving Suggestions
Set each quail on a crisp potato nest lined with a bed of finely julienned and cooked vegetables, such as yellow and green squash. Puree red raspberries with a dash of white wine vinegar for a condiment.

Turkey Galantine with Spiced Chestnuts

YIELD: 1 galantine, about 7 pounds (about 11 servings)

1 4-pound turkey breast half with skin or 1 12- to 15-pound turkey
10 ounces shelled chestnuts, cooked

Marinade
1/4 cup Cognac or brandy
1/4 cup Grand Marnier or other orange liqueur
2 shallots, minced
1 garlic clove, minced
Zest of 1/2 orange
1 tablespoon blackstrap molasses
1/4 teaspoon cinnamon
Black pepper to taste

Farce
Meat from the turkey, half ground and half cut into 1/2-inch-wide strips
2 pounds fatty pork or sausage meat, ground
2 eggs
1/4 cup minced shallots or onion
1 tablespoon chopped fresh parsley
1 1/3 tablespoons Pâté Seasoning III
Salt to taste
Black pepper to taste

3 to 4 quarts rich, gelatinous Chicken or White Stock (enough to cover galantine)
Herb bouquet
2 cups melted Chicken Aspic or Classic Chaud-Froid to glaze

If you use a whole turkey, follow the directions in "Basics of Boning for a Galantine," but also remove all or most of the meat from the skin, trying not to puncture the skin. For the turkey breast, simply remove all the meat from the skin. Grind or cut the meat for the farce as required. Marinate the skin, the 1/2-inch turkey strips, and the chestnuts for 4 hours or overnight in the refrigerator, turning them at least once.

Remove the turkey from the marinade. Over medium-high heat, reduce the marinade until it just moistens the shallots and garlic. Meanwhile, mix together all the ingredients for the farce except the marinated turkey strips and chestnuts, and add the reduced marinade to the mixture. Test the seasonings and correct if necessary.

Follow the directions in "Basics of Assembling and Cooking a Galantine." Poach the turkey in the stock with an herb bouquet for about 1 1/2 hours, or until the galantine feels firm. Remove the galantine when it has cooled to lukewarm and weight it if desired. Chill. Refrigerated, the galantine keeps for about 4 days.

Glaze the chilled galantine with aspic or chaud-froid and decorate.

Serving Suggestions
Serve each slice of galantine with fresh aspic and Cumberland Sauce or Orange Cranberry Relish on the side.

Variations
If you have enough turkey meat for a farce but no skin, substitute about 1 pound of fatback for the skin. Slice it thin and lay it out (overlapping the edges) to form a rectangular casing for the farce.

Use strips of ham or tongue with or instead of the turkey strips.

Substitute two 5½ pound chickens for the turkey.

Stuffed Capon or Chicken Galantine

This galantine consists of all lean meats, making it a lower-fat, lower-cholesterol dish.

YIELD: 1 galantine, about 5½ pounds

2 pounds boneless lean pork, finely ground
2½ cups seasoned bread crumbs
1 onion, finely diced
2 garlic cloves, minced
3 egg whites
1¼ teaspoons black pepper
¾ teaspoon Poultry Seasoning
Salt to taste
½ cup Madeira or sweet vermouth
⅓ cup finely diced black olives
1½ cups finely chopped cooked spinach
½ teaspoon nutmeg
1 5- to 6-pound capon or chicken, boned for a galantine
½ cup pimiento strips
3 to 4 slices ham, ¼ inch thick
2 to 3 quarts rich, gelatinous Brown Stock (enough to cover galantine)
Herb bouquet
2 cups melted Basic Aspic or Brown Chaud-Froid to glaze

Mix together the ground pork, seasoned bread crumbs, onion, garlic, 2 egg whites, black pepper, Poultry Seasoning, salt, and Madeira. Test the seasonings and correct if necessary. Divide the mixture in half and mix the diced olives into one half. Reserve both. Separately mix together the spinach, 1 egg white, and nutmeg and reserve.

Follow the directions in "Basics of Assembling and Cooking a Galantine." Spread the plain pork farce over the capon. Press a layer of pimiento strips down into the farce and smooth over the top with a wet spatula. Add a layer of ham slices, followed by the olive-pork farce. Form the spinach mixture into a cylinder and place it down the center of the farce. Continue following the basic method. Poach the capon in the stock with an herb bouquet for about 1½ hours, or until the galantine feels firm. Remove the galantine when it has cooled to lukewarm and weight it if desired. Chill. Refrigerated, the galantine keeps for about 4 days.

Glaze the chilled galantine with aspic or chaud-froid and decorate.

Serving Suggestions
Serve the galantine with Tomato Chutney.

Variations
Substitute julienned black truffle for the black olives.

Capon Ballotine

This ballotine also tastes good cooked in a covered clay baking pot on a bed of diced vegetables with a little stock. Baking in clay eliminates the need for basting.

YIELD: 1 ballotine, about 6½ pounds

Farce
1 pound chicken livers, diced and lightly sautéed
½ pound smoked ham, diced
1½ cups diced provolone (or other firm cheese)
1 cup sautéed, chopped mushrooms
1¾ cups seasoned bread crumbs
½ cup Chicken Stock
1 onion, minced
1 garlic clove, minced
2 eggs
¼ cup chopped fresh basil
¼ cup chopped fresh parsley
½ teaspoon oregano
½ teaspoon black pepper
Salt to taste

1 6-pound capon, boned for a galantine, with drumsticks attached

Mix the ingredients together for the farce. Test the seasonings and correct if necessary.

Follow the directions in "Alternate Method of Assembling and Cooking a Galantine." Bake the ballotine in a preheated 425°F oven for 15 minutes. Lower the temperature to 350°F and bake for another 1½ to 1¾ hours, basting the bird every 20 minutes. If the bird starts to brown too fast, cover it with an aluminum foil tent. When cooked, remove the ballotine from the oven and let the capon rest in a warm place for 15 to 20 minutes before carving. Remove the string before serving.

Serving Suggestions
Serve the ballotine hot with Mustard Herb Sauce. Chilled leftovers go well with the same sauce.

Galantine of Striped Bass with Salmon and Asparagus

This is the answer to a summer buffet. The assertive flavor of the striped bass melds beautifully with the subtler flavor of salmon. Slice the cooked galantine as you would fish steaks, but leave the slices arranged as a whole fish.

YIELD: 1 galantine, about 6½ pounds (8 to 10 servings)

1 6- to 8-pound striped bass
1¼ pounds salmon fillets, diced
3 egg whites
½ teaspoon salt
½ teaspoon white pepper
½ teaspoon nutmeg
1 cup heavy cream
9 asparagus, cooked but crisp
1 tablespoon (envelope) unflavored gelatin
Fish Stock or Court Bouillon to cover
3 cups melted Fish Aspic to glaze

Scale and bone the bass through the belly, leaving the head and tail intact.

Keep all the ingredients cold and prepare a salmon mousseline in two batches. Grind the salmon in a food processor. Add the egg whites, salt, pepper, and nutmeg. With the machine running, gradually pour in the heavy cream and process until smooth. Test the seasonings and correct if necessary. Chill.

Lay the bass out on a cloth. Dry the inside of the fish and sprinkle it with gelatin. Spread half the salmon mousseline inside the fish, leaving a ½-inch border at the belly. Place the asparagus down the center and cover them with the remaining mousseline. Close the fish and press the edges together. Wrap the stuffed fish in cloth; twist the ends and tie them with string. Securely, but not tightly, tie four cloth strips around the fish to hold it closed.

Bring the stock to a boil. Add the galantine, cover it with wax paper, and simmer at 175°F to 180°F, until firm. Turn the fish over halfway through the cooking time. Use the Canadian timing method (10 minutes per inch of fish measured at the thickest point) to determine how long to poach the bass. Or poach it in a preheated 450°F oven for the same length of time. After cooking, lift the fish out of the stock and promptly remove the cloth strips so they will not leave marks around the fish. Cool the galantine on a platter. Chill. Refrigerated, it keeps for about 2 days.

Slice the chilled galantine and glaze the slices, head, and tail with aspic.

Serving Suggestions
Reassemble the fish on a platter and serve the galantine with sliced fresh lemon and an herbed mayonnaise.

Variations
If you do not have a large enough pan in which to poach the fish, cut the bass in half crosswise and poach each half separately.

You can double the recipe and use a 12- to 16-pound bass.

Substitute any seasonal fish for the bass.

Substitute flounder, pike, halibut, or other fish for the salmon.

Sole and Gravad Lax Galantines

Gravad lax is a traditional Scandinavian salt- and sugar-marinated salmon. In the old days, kings and princes on angling expeditions lodged at the Lindström Hotel on the Laerdal River in Norway, where they customarily breakfasted on *gravad lax* with aquavit chasers. A method of making *gravad lax* follows this recipe.

YIELD: 4 individual galantines

4 sole fillets, 8 to 10 ounces each
4 gravad lax slices, 4 ounces each
Fresh dill sprigs
Fish Stock or Court Bouillon to cover

Lay the sole fillets out flat, with the bone side down. Place a slice of *gravad lax* on each fillet and place a few sprigs of dill at the beginning of each roll, so that the dill eventually becomes the center. Roll the fish in a spiral fashion, like a jelly roll. Secure the end with a toothpick.

Bring the stock to a boil. Add the individual galantines, cover, and simmer at 175°F to 180°F, until firm. Turn the rolls over halfway through the cooking time. Use the Canadian timing method (10 minutes per inch of fish measured at the thickest point) to determine how long to poach the galantines. Or poach them in a preheated oven at 450°F for the same length of time. After cooking, lift the rolls out of the stock and cool the galantines on a platter. Chill. Refrigerated, they keep for about 2 days.

Serving Suggestions
Slice and serve the galantines hot or cold with Piquant Mustard Dill Sauce. Serve each galantine as an individual main course or set the slices on a platter and pass them around as hors d'oeuvre.

Variations
Substitute other fish fillets for the sole.

Substitute fresh or smoked salmon for the *gravad lax.*

Gravad Lax

The proportion of salt to sugar can vary. The Swedes prefer two parts sugar to one part salt. While some recipes call for equal parts sugar and salt, others call for more salt than sugar.

2 pounds salmon, center cut if possible
½ cup sugar
¼ cup salt
3 teaspoons crushed white peppercorns
1 bunch fresh dill sprigs, coarsely cut

Scale and bone the salmon, leaving the skin attached, and split it in half. Wipe the fish dry but do not rinse it. Mix the sugar, salt, and peppercorns together and lightly rub the seasonings into the bone sides of the fish. Arrange one salmon half, skin side down, on a tray and cover it with dill sprigs. Place the other salmon half on top, skin side up, so that the large end of the upper half is over the small end of the bottom half. Cover the salmon with a weighted plate and refrigerate for 24 to 48 hours, turning the fish over a few times. Remove the plate and weight, then cover with parchment paper.

Note: Refrigerated, the *gravad lax* will keep for at least 1 week and up to 2 weeks, depending on the freshness of the fish and the efficiency of the refrigerator.

Serving Suggestions
Thinly slice the salmon on a diagonal, cutting away from the skin.

Baby Salmon Galantines

YIELD: 4 individual galantines

4 baby salmon, 8 to 10 ounces each
1/2 pound fish fillets (such as sole, trout, pike, or whiting), diced
1 egg white
1/4 teaspoon salt
1/4 teaspoon white pepper
Pinch of nutmeg
1/2 cup heavy cream
1 tablespoon chopped fresh Fine Herbs
Fish Stock or Court Bouillon to cover

Scale and bone each salmon through the belly, leaving the head and tail intact.

Grind the fish fillets in a food processor. Add the egg white, salt, pepper, and nutmeg. With the machine running, slowly pour in the heavy cream and process until smooth. Mix in the fine herbs. Test the seasonings and correct if necessary. Chill.

Lay each fish out on a piece of cloth. Dry the insides of the fish and spoon the mousseline into a pastry bag filled with a plain tube. Pipe the mousseline into the salmon and press the edges together. Wrap each salmon in cloth; twist the ends and tie them with string.

Bring the stock to a boil. Add the galantines, cover them with wax paper, and simmer at 175°F to 180°F, until firm. Turn the fish over halfway through the cooking time. Use the Canadian timing method (10 minutes per inch of fish measured at the thickest point) to determine how long to poach the salmon. Or poach them in a preheated 450°F oven for the same length of time. After cooking, lift the galantines out of the stock and cool them on a platter. Chill. Refrigerated, they keep for about 2 days.

Serving Suggestions

Salmon galantines can be served warm with a fish Velouté Sauce or chilled with Horseradish Sauce. For a fancier presentation, remove the skin from the top side of each salmon. Glaze and decorate if served chilled or sprinkle with chopped herbs if hot.

Variations

Substitute rainbow or brook trout for the salmon.

Rainbow Trout and Scallop Galantines

YIELD: 2 2½-inch round galantines, or about 3 pounds (8 to 10 servings)

1½ pounds fresh rainbow trout fillets, diced
½ pound smoked trout fillets
3 egg whites
¾ teaspoon white pepper
¾ teaspoon salt
Pinch of mace
1⅓ cups heavy cream
1 to 1½ cups minced fresh herbs (such as chives, dill, parsley, and tarragon)
½ pound Cape scallops or diced sea scallops
½ cup red caviar
Court Bouillon or water to cover

Grind the fresh and smoked trout fillets in a food processor. Add 2 egg whites, pepper, salt, and mace. With the machine running, slowly pour in the heavy cream and process until smooth. Test the seasonings and correct if necessary. Chill.

Mix the scallops, caviar, and remaining egg white together and chill. Spread the trout mousseline onto two 12- by 20-inch sheets of heat-resistant plastic wrap that have been lightly greased, leaving a border of plastic. Divide the minced herbs and sprinkle evenly over each rectangle of mousseline. Divide the scallop-caviar mixture in half, and place the scallops along one of the long sides of each rectangle, eventually to become the center. Using the plastic wrap for support, lift the end of the mousseline with the scallops, and roll in a spiral fashion, like a jelly roll. Wrap the galantine in the plastic wrap; twist the ends and tie them with string.

Bring the court bouillon or water to a boil. Add the galantines, cover, and simmer at 175°F to 180°F, until firm. Turn the rolls over halfway through the cooking time. Use the Canadian timing method (10 minutes per inch of fish measured at the thickest point) to determine how long to poach the galantines. Or poach them in a preheated 450°F oven for the same length of time. After cooking, lift the rolls out of the stock and cool the galantines on a platter. Chill. Refrigerated, they keep for about 2 days.

Serving Suggestions
Serve the chilled galantines with a dab of Lemon Mayonnaise, a round of fresh lemon, and a dill sprig. If served warm, accompany with Lemon Herb Butter Sauce.

Variations
Eliminate the smoked trout and use all fresh fillets.

Eliminate the scallop-caviar center.

Substitute salmon or any nonoily fish for the trout, such as flounder, or halibut.

Add 1 or 2 tablespoons tomato paste to the mousse.

Hot Gnocchi and Spinach Galantine

I adapted this recipe from a dish that chef Arnold Fanger served when we worked together at the Market Bar and Dining Room in the World Trade Center. Quick and simple to make, this galantine freezes well and is good to have on hand for an impressive impromptu dinner. See the color insert for a photograph of this galantine.

YIELD: about 26 ½-inch slices

1 pound spinach, washed
1 medium-size onion, minced
2 tablespoons unsalted butter
¼ teaspoon black pepper
⅛ teaspoon nutmeg
1 whole egg
½ cup grated Parmesan cheese
2½ pounds Potato Gnocchi Dough
Chicken or Vegetable Stock or water to cover

Remove the stems from the spinach. Steam or blanch the leaves until limp but still bright green in color. Squeeze out the excess water and chop the spinach. Sauté the minced onion in butter, add the pepper and nutmeg, and stir in the chopped spinach. Let the mixture cool. In a bowl, combine the spinach, egg, and ½ cup Parmesan.

Roll out the dough or form it by hand into a rectangle measuring 9 by 13 inches. If you do not have a pot wide enough to hold a 13-inch-long galantine, make two rolls instead of one. Place the dough on cheesecloth. Shape the spinach mixture into a 12-inch-long roll down the center of the gnocchi dough. Leave a ½-inch dough border at each end. Using the cloth as support, lift one side of the dough over the filling. Lift the other side and fold it to overlap slightly, making a cylinder. Smooth the seam where the dough overlaps and pinch the ends closed. Roll the galantine in the cheesecloth. Twist the ends of the cloth and tightly tie them closed with string. Wrap two cloth strips around the bundle (dividing the galantine into thirds), and tie them loosely so as not to cut into the dough.

Bring the stock or water to the boiling point in a fish poacher or other covered pot. Place the roll in the pot; lower the heat and cover. The galantine will float. Simmer it for 15 minutes on one side. Turn it over and simmer for 10 to 15 minutes more. When cooked, the roll will expand slightly and feel firm.

Remove the galantine from the stock and set it on a platter for 10 to 15 minutes before unwrapping or slicing it. If you are preparing the galantine in advance, allow it to cool on the platter. Unwrap and cut the roll into ½-inch slices. Reassembled and covered in plastic wrap, the galantine will keep, refrigerated, for 2 or 3 days.

Note: To freeze the galantine, wrap the slices individually. They keep for at least 1 month when frozen. Defrost as many slices as you need and reheat them by steaming for 5 to 10 minutes immediately before serving.

Serving Suggestions
Serve the Hot Gnocchi and Spinach Galantine with a Bordelaise or marinara sauce or with room-temperature Tomato Concasse. Line the plate with sauce and place the galantine slices on top. Onto each slice, grate about 1 teaspoon of Parmesan cheese, then melt the cheese with a splash of hot, melted brown butter or place the dish under a broiler until the cheese melts. Sprinkle with chopped fresh parsley or basil.

Serve two slices as an appetizer or five slices as an entree.

Variations
If you use frozen spinach (two 10-ounce packages), simply defrost the spinach and eliminate the blanching.

Substitute low-fat cottage cheese, farmer cheese, or Sapsago cheese for the Parmesan.

Eggplant and Cheese Galantine

It is important to use fresh pasta, not dried, in this recipe.

YIELD: 2 galantines (4 main-course servings or 6 to 8 first-course servings)

8 ounces cream cheese, softened
1/2 cup ricotta or small-curd cottage cheese
1/3 cup grated Parmesan cheese
1 whole egg
1/2 cup finely diced smoked ham (optional)
2 tablespoons minced scallions
2 tablespoons minced fresh parsley
1/4 teaspoon nutmeg
Black pepper to taste
4 12- by 4-inch sheets fresh spinach pasta (or 2 12- by 8-inch sheets)
6 1/16-inch-thick slices medium-size eggplant, fried and drained
Clear Vegetable Stock or water to cover

Blend the cream cheese, ricotta, Parmesan, and egg until smooth. Stir in the ham, scallions, parsley, nutmeg, and pepper. Chill.

Moisten the long edge of one pasta sheet with a little water. Lay the edge of the second sheet over the moistened area, overlapping the edges by 1/2 inch. Press the overlapped edges together so they adhere. Join the remaining two sheets in the same way. (This procedure is not required if using two 12- by 8-inch sheets.)

Lay the two sheets of joined pasta out flat. Spread half the cheese mixture over the pasta, leaving a 1/2-inch border, then cover the mixture with a layer of fried eggplant slices. Roll the layered pasta in a spiral fashion, like a jelly roll. Wrap the galantine in cloth; twist the ends and tie them with string.

Bring the stock to a boil. Add the galantines, cover, and simmer at 175°F to 180°F for 10 to 15 minutes on each side. Remove the galantines and set them on a platter for 10 to 15 minutes before unwrapping or cutting into ½-inch slices.

If you are preparing the galantines in advance, allow them to cool, then unwrap and slice. Reassembled and covered in plastic wrap, they keep refrigerated, for about 3 days. Reheat the slices by steaming them for 5 to 10 minutes before serving.

Serving Suggestions
Serve the galantines warm or at room temperature on a thin mirror of tomato sauce. Garnish with basil leaves and a tomato rose.

Variations
Substitute fried zucchini slices or smoked ham slices for the eggplant.

Stuffed White Eggplant

These white eggplants are stuffed with basically a ratatouille made from their pulp, but any cornucopia of vegetables or meat makes a good stuffing. They can be served as a first course, a side dish, or as a brunch entree.

YIELD: 5 individual eggplants

5 round white eggplants, 6 to 8 ounces each
Acidulated water
¼ cup unsalted butter
¼ cup oil
1¼ cups finely diced onions (about 2 medium)
4 garlic cloves, minced
1 zucchini, cut into ¼-inch cubes
1 1-pound can plum tomatoes, drained and crushed
Juice of ½ lemon
White pepper to taste
Salt to taste
2 tablespoons chopped fresh basil
1 cup tomato juice or Chicken Stock

Slice off the stems of the eggplants to use as caps or covers. Remove the pulp of the eggplants, leaving ⅜- to ½-inch shells. Dip the hollowed-out eggplant shells and caps into acidulated water to prevent them from discoloring. Dice the pulp into ¼-inch cubes and reserve. Steam the eggplant shells and caps for 7 to 10 minutes to tenderize them but not to cook thoroughly.

Sauté the onions and garlic in the butter and oil. Add the zucchini and the diced eggplant pulp. After a few minutes add the crushed plum tomatoes, lemon juice, pepper, and salt. Sauté the mixture until the vegetables are just cooked but still crisp. Remove from the heat and stir in the basil. Spoon the stuffing into the eggplants and cover with the caps.

Set the eggplants in a baking dish containing the tomato juice or stock. Cover with aluminum foil and bake in a preheated 350°F oven for about 30 minutes, or until tender.

Serving Suggestions

Simply serve each stuffed eggplant on a plate lined with radicchio, mustard greens, or green lettuce leaves. The dish tastes good hot from the oven or cooled to room temperature.

Variations

Instead of ratatouille, stuff the eggplants with caponata, the Sicilian version of ratatouille. Its delicate sweet-and-sour flavor is enhanced when served at room temperature or slightly chilled.

Completely cook the eggplant shells and marinate them in Vinaigrette Dressing overnight. Steam a medley of vegetables, such as eggplant pulp, squash, carrots, celery, onion, peas, or beans, and also marinate them in Vinaigrette Dressing overnight. Stuff the eggplants and set them out when ready to serve.

Small Plum Galantines

In Germany and Switzerland these galantines or dumplings become a favorite summer treat, especially when Italian blue plums are in season. Although Europeans sometimes use a cheese or noodle dough to encase the plums, the cheese filling is a new variation.

Pitted fresh plums freeze well to keep for winter use; freezing also tenderizes the fruit.

YIELD: 12 small galantines

1 recipe Sweet-Potato Gnocchi Dough
12 small blue Italian plums, pitted
3 to 4 tablespoons fruttosella alla pera (semi-soft, sweet Italian cheese), goat cheese, or another semi-soft cheese
Cinnamon sugar
Unsalted butter
Bread crumbs

Roll out the dough to at least 1/4 inch thick and cut it into twelve equal squares. Place a bit of cheese in the center of the plum where the pit was removed. Reshape the plum to look whole and dredge it in cinnamon sugar. Wrap each plum in a dough square, pinching the ends together and smoothing the surface with your hands.

Drop a few galantines at a time into boiling water, then lower the heat to a simmer. Poach them, uncovered, for 10 to 15 minutes. Spoon out each galantine and drain in a colander. Sauté the drained galantines in butter with bread crumbs until golden. Sprinkle with cinnamon sugar.

Serving Suggestions
Serve with *café au lait* and perhaps some cheese on the side. These dumplings also make a delightful side dish to meats.

Variations
Cherry Galantines: Follow the recipe for Small Plum Galantines, substituting three or four fresh or frozen bing cherries for each plum. Eliminate the cheese center.

Apricot Galantines: Follow the recipe for Small Plum Galantines, substituting fresh or frozen apricots for the plums. Do not use dried apricots.

STUFFED MEATS

Roast Beef Stuffed with Parsley and Garlic

The mouth-watering roast adds elegance to the otherwise standard fare of meat and potatoes. The cooking time given makes a tender, moist roast—browned on the outside, rosy and juicy on the inside, with a fragrant herb center.

YIELD: 1 4½-pound roast (10 to 12 servings)

1 4½-pound roast, eye round or seamed eye round
2 cups chopped fresh parsley
1 cup seasoned bread crumbs
¼ to ⅓ cup chopped garlic (according to taste)
½ cup olive oil
2 tablespoons pignoli nuts
½ teaspoon salt
¼ teaspoon black pepper

With a long, thin knife, cut a lengthwise slit through the center of the roast to stuff. Mix the remaining ingredients together. Using the handle end of a long wooden spoon, stuff the filling into the roast. Rub any remaining crumbs from the filling over the outside of the roast.

Set the stuffed roast on a rack in a roasting pan with about a cup of water. Roast in a preheated 450°F oven for 20 to 30 minutes, until browned.

Lower the temperature to 300°F to 325°F and continue to cook for about 1 hour, or until done. Remove the roast from the oven and allow it to rest in a warm place for 10 to 15 minutes before carving. Remove any string before serving.

Serving Suggestions
Thinly slice the stuffed roast beef and serve it immediately with the pan juice gravy, baked or roasted potatoes, a fresh green vegetable, and tossed salad. This roast also tastes good the next day served chilled on a sandwich or set out on a platter.

Stuffed Pork Trotter

Zampone is the Italian name for this dish. In Italy, during the Christmas season, it often is served alone as a main course or together with other meats in a *gran bollito misto.* Stuff a whole pork leg in the same manner by increasing the amount of farce.

YIELD: 1 pork trotter, about 3 pounds

1 pork trotter (foot), about 2 pounds
½ pound boneless pork, ground
½ pound boneless veal, turkey, or chicken, ground
½ pound smoked ham, diced
¼ pound fresh fatback, ground
1 onion, finely chopped
4 garlic cloves, minced
3 tablespoons coarsely chopped pistachio nuts
¼ cup chopped fresh parsley
1 tablespoon Pâté Seasoning IV
Salt to taste
Black pepper to taste
Brown Stock or water to cover

Boil some salted water. Hold just the toe end of the trotter in boiling water for 2 to 3 minutes. Push the foot nails off the trotter as you cool it under cold running water. Scrape off any bristles at the same time. Make a lengthwise cut through the skin down to the bone. Using a small, sharp knife, slowly separate the skin from the bones and meat. Cut through the joint at the foot end to remove the bone. Trim any bits of meat from the bone and add them to the stuffing. The bone contains lots of gelatin and can be used to make stock. Sew up the lengthwise cut to make a pocket.

Mix the remaining ingredients together except the stock. Test the seasonings and correct if necessary. Stuff the farce into the trotter, then sew the end closed and secure it with a knot. For a richer taste, refrigerate the trotter for 1 to 2 days to mature it before cooking.

Prick the stuffed trotter in several places, then poach it in stock or water for 3 to 3½ hours. If chilling, first allow the trotter to cool in its stock. Remove the thread before serving.

Serving Suggestions
Serve Stuffed Pork Trotter hot with garlicky, herb-flecked mashed potatoes or cold with pungent mustard and a lentil salad. A trotter also makes a fine first course or hors d'oeuvre.

Variations
Stuff the trotter with a favorite farce or sausage mixture.

After the trotter has been poached and cooled, bake it in a brioche dough as you would sausage in crust.

Stuffed pork trotter tastes good and keeps longer smoked.

Gorgonzola-Stuffed Breast of Veal

The combination of meats, greens, pimiento, and Gorgonzola cheese gives this recipe its distinctive flavor. Have the butcher bone and butterfly the breast and use the bones for a rack on which to roast the veal.

YIELD: about 5 pounds (6 to 8 servings)

3/4 pound boneless lean pork, finely ground
3/4 pound boneless lean beef, finely ground
1/2 to 3/4 pound Gorgonzola or other blue cheese, crumbled
1/2 pound each of cooked Swiss chard and kale, chopped
3/4 cup bread crumbs
2/3 cup diced pimientos
1 teaspoon black pepper
1 teaspoon salt
1/2 teaspoon thyme
1/2 teaspoon nutmeg
1 5-pound breast of veal, boned and butterflied

Mix together all the ingredients except the veal. Test the seasonings and correct if necessary. Spread the stuffing over the veal, leaving a 1-inch border, and roll it, jelly roll style, or form the stuffing into a cylinder in the center of the butterflied breast and wrap the sides of the veal around it. Tie string around the stuffed breast at 1-inch intervals.

Set the stuffed veal on the bones in a large roasting pan and cover with aluminum foil. Roast in a preheated 400°F oven for 30 minutes. Add water to the pan and reduce the temperature to 350°F. Cover and braise for another 1½ to 2 hours, removing the cover during the last 15 minutes. After cooking, remove the veal from the oven and let it rest in a warm place for about 10 minutes before carving. Cut away the string before serving.

Meanwhile, remove the bones and skim the fat from the pan juices. Strain and season the juice to make a sauce. Reduce if necessary to thicken.

Serving Suggestions
Serve hot Gorgonzola-Stuffed Breast of Veal with the sauce made from its pan juices. Add a dash of port or sherry to the sauce for added flavor. If served cold, chill the sauce into aspic.

Variations
Substitute spinach for the Swiss chard and kale.

Stuffed Turkey Breast

YIELD: about 4½ pounds (12 servings)

1 3- to 4-pound turkey breast half, boned, with skin attached
½ pound cooked spinach, chopped
⅓ pound ham, prosciutto, or smoked ham, ground
¼ pound Swiss cheese, ground
1½ cups grated Parmesan cheese
⅓ cup seasoned bread crumbs
1 onion, finely diced
¼ cup chopped fresh parsley
1 to 2 tablespoons minced garlic
1 egg
Vegetable oil

With a long, thin knife, cut a lengthwise slit through the center of the breast to stuff. Carefully remove the skin from the breast and reserve.

Mix the remaining ingredients together except the oil. Using the handle end of a long wooden spoon, stuff the filling into the breast. Place the reserved skin over the *boned* side of the breast and tie the turkey with string at 1-inch intervals. Rub oil and any remaining crumbs of stuffing over the outside of the breast.

Preheat the oven to 450°F. Set the stuffed turkey on a rack in a pan with about a cup of water. Place the turkey in the oven and lower the temperature to 325° to 350°F. Roast the stuffed breast for 1¼ to 1½ hours, or until done. Baste the meat occasionally. Remove the turkey from the oven and allow it to rest in a warm place for 10 to 15 minutes before carving. Cut away the string before serving.

Serving Suggestions
Slice Stuffed Turkey Breast and serve it hot as you would any poultry dish. The turkey is equally good served chilled or at room temperature.

Variations
Stuff the turkey with a favorite pork sausage or pâté farce.

Stuffed Turkey or Goose Neck

Remove the neck from a whole turkey or goose by cutting it just below the beak and again at where it meets the breast. The farmers of southwestern France prepared stuffed goose necks as confit. It provides another meat item that can be preserved by potting. It also can be poached in stock and eaten fresh or smoked.

YIELD: 1 stuffed neck, (2 to 3 main-course servings)

1 turkey or goose neck
1 turkey or goose liver, finely diced
1 cup meat scraps, such as pork, veal, ham, finely diced or ground
¼ cup seasoned bread crumbs or cooked wild rice
2 tablespoons chopped truffles or shiitake mushrooms
1 onion, finely diced
2 garlic cloves, minced
2 tablespoons coarsely chopped pistachio nuts
2 eggs, lightly beaten
Dash of applejack
1 tablespoon chopped fresh parsley
1 teaspoon chopped fresh sage
Salt to taste
Black pepper to taste
Stock or soup for poaching

Gently peel the skin off the neck using a small, sharp knife to loosen any membrane. Trim any bits of meat from the bone and add them to the stuffing. The bone can be used to make stock.

Mix the remaining ingredients together except stock. Test the seasonings and correct if necessary. Tie or sew closed one end of the neck skin. Using a spoon, stuff the filling into the neck. Tie or sew the other end closed.

Slowly poach the stuffed neck in stock or soup for 20 to 30 minutes, or roast it in goose fat (basting it frequently) for the same amount of time. Remove the string before serving.

Serving Suggestions
Serve the stuffed neck hot or cold with Braised Red-Cabbage Relish, a garlic-flavored potato salad, and lettuce. It also makes a good addition to cassoulet. Or thinly slice the neck to set out on an hors d'oeuvre platter.

Variations
Stuff the neck with a favorite stuffing, farce, or mousseline.

Double-Stuffed Capon

The boned capon is stuffed in the inner cavity and also under the skin. This method ensures succulent, flavorful results. Even the breast meat stays moist and well seasoned, retaining a crisp roasted skin.

YIELD: 1 capon, about 6½ pounds

Farce
12 ounces ricotta or dry-curd cottage cheese
1¾ cups seasoned bread crumbs
1 cup grated Parmesan or Romano cheese
1 pound pork sausage, casings removed
2 to 3 eggs
1 pound zucchini and/or yellow squash, finely julienned and lightly sautéed
½ pound mushrooms, sliced and sautéed
1 onion, minced
¼ cup chopped fresh parsley
2 tablespoons chopped or 1 teaspoon dried fresh marjoram or oregano

1 5- to 6-pound capon, boned for a galantine, with drumsticks attached
Vegetable oil
1 cup Chicken Stock or water

Mix together the ingredients for the farce. Test the seasonings and correct if necessary.

Loosen the skin from the capon by sliding your hand between it and the meat (fig. 4-9). The skin will remain attached to the body at the backbone, the tips of the drumsticks, and the center of the breast.

Using a handful at a time, stuff the farce under the skin, starting with the drumsticks and then the breasts. Turn the capon over and stuff and truss the inner cavity following the "Alternate Method of Assembling and Cooking a Galantine." Rub the outside skin with oil, and mold the stuffing to follow the original shape of the bird as much as possible.

Set the capon on a rack in a pan with the cup of stock. Bake in a preheated 425°F oven for 15 minutes. Lower the temperature to 350°F and bake for 1½ to 1¾ hours, basting the bird every 20 minutes. If the bird starts to brown too fast, cover it with an aluminum foil tent. After cooking, remove from the oven and let the capon rest in a warm place for 10 to 15 minutes before carving. Cut away the string before serving.

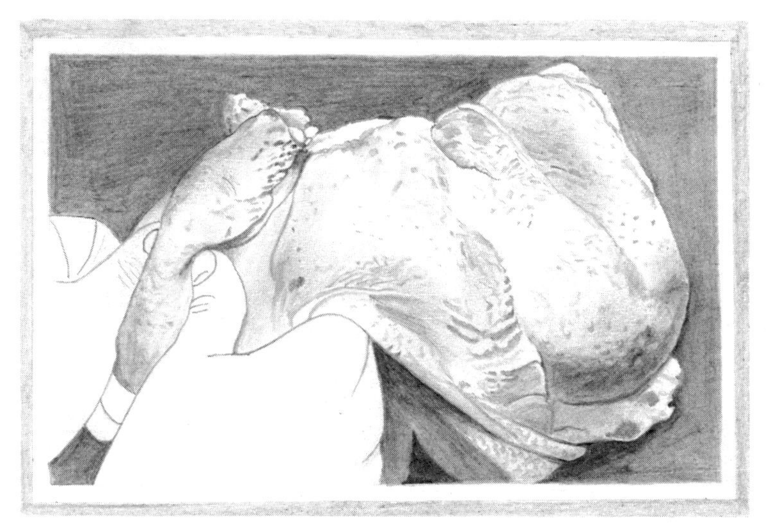

4-9. Loosen the capon skin.

Serving Suggestions
Serve Double-Stuffed Capon hot or chilled with roasted red peppers, broccoli, and salad.

Variations
Substitute chicken, turkey, or game hens for the capon.

Substitute a favorite stuffing for the one given in the recipe or use two different stuffings—one under the skin and another in the inner cavity—for instance, a vegetable and a cheese filling or a rice and a meat filling.

Savory Stuffed Chicken Breasts

YIELD: about 4 main-course servings

4 boned chicken breast halves (about 1½ pounds)
½ pound spinach leaves, washed, steamed, and chopped
½ cup ricotta or low-fat cottage cheese
2 tablespoons finely diced prosciutto or ham
2 tablespoons finely diced mozzarella cheese
1 egg
1 small garlic clove, minced
⅛ teaspoon black pepper
Flour
1 egg, lightly beaten
Seasoned bread crumbs
Unsalted butter

Slit the chicken breast halves to make a pocket for stuffing. Mix together the spinach, ricotta, prosciutto, mozzarella, 1 egg, garlic, and pepper. Stuff the filling into the pockets of the chicken breasts.

Dredge the chicken breasts in flour; dip them into the lightly beaten egg and then the bread crumbs. Sauté the stuffed breasts in butter until browned and cooked.

Serving Suggestions
Serve Savory Stuffed Chicken Breasts hot with a cheese or Mornay sauce or chilled with fresh lemon.

Mock Chicken Hams in Pastry

These chicken legs are stuffed, wrapped in pastry, scored, and shaped to look like miniature bone-in hams. They are especially good for a hot buffet.

YIELD: 4 first-course servings

½ cup smoked ham, ⅛-inch cubed
½ cup Monterey Jack or Swiss cheese, ⅛-inch cubed
2 tablespoons chopped fresh parsley
1 plum tomato, peeled, seeded, and ⅛-inch cubed
1 hard-cooked egg, grated or mashed through a sieve
Black pepper to taste
4 whole chicken legs (6 to 8 ounces each), thigh bone removed but drumstick intact
Oil
1 pound Short-Crust Pastry
Egg wash

Mix together the ham, cheese, parsley, tomato, egg, and pepper. Stuff each chicken leg with the filling, and close it with a toothpick.

In oil, sauté the stuffed legs on all sides for about 20 minutes, or until nearly cooked. Drain on paper towels and remove the toothpicks. Roll out the pastry dough ¼ inch thick and cut it into four pieces. Wrap each chicken leg in the dough, leaving the tip of the bone exposed. Pinch the ends of the dough together underneath. Lightly brush the pastry with egg wash and bake the chicken hams on a greased baking sheet for 15 to 20 minutes, until the pastry turns golden.

Serving Suggestions
Serve Mock Chicken Hams for brunch, as first course to a dinner, or on a hot buffet accompanied with Persimmon Sauce and lemon-flavored rice pilaf.

CHAPTER FIVE

Sausages, Boudins, Confits, and Rillettes

SAUSAGES

Carefully guarded secret recipes, often passed down from charcutiers, chefs, and families, elevate sausage making into an art. Some commercial brands of sausage, loaded with fillers and spiked with additives and preservatives, have tarnished the reputation of this basic food. Spicy, hearty, easily prepared and preserved, homemade sausage still remains at the heart of many culinary heritages—an international tradition. It gives farmers another means of using odds and ends of meats from animals butchered in early spring or late fall. Meat from a pig's neck, for instance, contains the finest fat and adds a moist, velvety smoothness to sausage. For the urban cook, a visit to the butcher provides meat for making an unlimited variety of sausages in a limited amount of time.

Derived from the Latin word *salsus*, meaning "salted," sausage was originally dry-salted for preservation. Ginger and pepper heavily seasoned the final dish in order to conceal the salty taste. Although the Germans claim to have invented sausages, the first recorded sausage makers were Roman. Earlier, primitive people encased an animal's viscera in its paunch and baked it over a fire. North American Indians made pemmican—sun-dried, lean buffalo or venison meat, pounded with fat, mixed with vegetables and cranberries, stuffed in hide skins, and sealed with tallow.

Sausage making represents a vital country art with national and regional distinctions in ingredients, shapes, and techniques. Italians, known for their fresh and dried sausage, inspired American versions of bologna and salami. German and Swiss immigrants who settled in the Midwest contributed bratwurst, frankfurters, and Milwaukee cervelat and knockwurst. The Poles and Russians brought kielbasa, a widely available spicy beef and pork sausage made fresh or smoked. Creole-Acadian boudins and andouilles (large tripe sausages) were influenced by the French, as were the less commonly found crépinettes. Maryland sausage differs from most East Coast preparations, and Pennsylvania boasts numerous local varieties of fresh or lightly smoked sausage of beef and pork. American summer sausage, dried and smoked, is noted for its characteristic pungent flavor. Sausage recipes vary in different regions and are as individual as the person making them.

Sausage consists of minced pork, poultry, veal, lamb, rabbit, or game. Seasonings include herbs, spices, onions, garlic, sweet peppers, chilies, grains, vegetables, liquors, and truffles. Use one part fat to two, three, or four parts lean meat, depending on the recipe and your preference. You can use most pâté farces for sausage too. Sausage may be precooked, cooked fresh, frozen, potted in fat like a confit, cured, air dried, or smoked. Refrigerated and wrapped in plastic or foil, most fresh sausage keeps for several days.

CRAFTING AND COOKING

The procedure for making sausage is quick, simple, and requires no fancy equipment. Combine all the ingredients, chop or grind the meat and fat to the desired consistency, then either stuff the filling into casings or caul fat or form it into patties. If you use a grinder fitted with a sausage attachment, the ingredients can be ground and stuffed at the same time. What could be simpler? You can also use a hand sausage stuffer, a ¾-inch wide-mouthed funnel, or a pastry bag with a large, plain tube.

Pork and lamb casings, stuffed to about 1 inch in diameter, make good size sausages for frying, broiling, or grilling. For poached sausages, 1½ to 2 inches thick, beef casings are more appropriate. Since casings tear easily, buy double the length you need. Estimate about 1 yard of casings per pound of farce. Pack the excess casings in kosher or coarse salt and refrigerate or freeze. They will keep indefinitely. Prior to stuffing, soak the skins in acidulated water for 30 minutes, or until soft and elastic, then rinse the casings by running cold water through them. If you fill the skins too tightly, they will burst when cooked (despite pricking with a fork). You can cook the sausages at once or hang them in a cool, dry place overnight or up to two days until the flavor matures.

Sausages also can be prepared in a poke—a cloth sack. Sew a 3- by 12-inch bag out of unbleached muslin or sackcloth. Dampen the bag, fill it with sausage meat, and securely tie the opening closed. Coat the poke in paraffin to seal out the air or wrap it in foil and freeze. It will keep for several months. Unlike other sausages, pokes need not be hung to dry.

Sausages can be poached, steamed, braised, or fried. However you cook them, use moderate heat; too high a temperature will cause the casings to burst.

SETTING THEM OUT

Sausage is integral to a cassoulet and is commonly found in a *bollito misto* or pot-au-feu. A natural with Apple Herb Sauerkraut, a hot potato salad, or Lentils with Sorrel and Red Onions, sausages are also a pleasant accompaniment to Italian polenta, French ratatouille, or Basque pipérade. Fried onions, freshly grated horseradish, or a julienne of celeriac or Jerusalem artichoke tossed in a spicy mustard dressing complement the taste of sausage. For an alfresco meal, serve sausage as an alternative to pâté. Rub the sausage with olive oil and grill them over hot wood coals until crisp and brown, or wrap them in foil and bake them among burning embers.

BASICS OF MAKING LINK SAUSAGE

If you do not have a meat grinder with a sausage attachment, grind the meat in a food processor or chop it by hand. Use a hand sausage stuffer, a 3/4-inch wide-mouthed funnel, or a pastry bag fitted with a large plain tube to stuff the casings. Before grinding, chill the sliced (or diced if using a food processor) meat and fat to about 30°F to 32°F, or until it feels firm and slightly stiff but not frozen. Not only does chilling inhibit bacterial growth, but the firm meat will be cut rather than crushed, hence retaining its flavorful juices. A coarse meat sausage is ground once and stuffed. For a finer-textured sausage, first pass the meat through a larger grinding disk (3/8-inch holes), then through a smaller disk (3/16-inch holes) into the casings. You also can obtain a combination of textures by cutting some of the meat, fat, or other garniture into 1/8- or 1/4-inch cubes and mixing them into the ground sausage farce. Stuff the sausage by hand or remove the cutting knife and grinding disk from the grinder/stuffer and proceed to stuff the casings.

Do not use saltpeter or other nitrate additives. (See Chapter 1 for an explanation and warning about saltpeter.) To help retain the pink or rosy color of sausage meat, add sweet paprika or crystalline ascorbic acid to the sausage farce. Add 1/8 teaspoon for each 2 1/2 pounds of meat.

Extenders such as soy flour and granules, skim milk, panadas, or grains are not added to a farce in order to "stretch" it or to make it cheaper, but are added for flavor, nutrition, and texture. These so-called extenders keep the sausage tender, moist, and juicy, and many also contribute additional protein as well as a distinctive taste. Add 2 tablespoons of extender for each pound of meat.

Rinse the brined or dry-salted casing under cool running water, then soak it in a bowl of tepid water mixed with 1 tablespoon vinegar or lemon juice for each cup of water. Let the casing stand in the liquid for about 30 minutes, until it feels pliable and elastic. This will remove any odor and make the casing more transparent.

Slip one end of the casing onto the faucet nozzle, and securely hold it in place. Gently run cold water through the casing. Or fit one end of the casing onto a wide-mouthed funnel and, over a sink or large bowl, pour cold water from a pitcher into the funnel and through the casing. This will rinse any salt or brine from inside the casing, as well as reveal any tears in the casing. Cut out any torn or punctured sections.

Assemble and chill the grinder/stuffer. Trim the meat of all tough connective tissue and chill. Cut the cold meat and fat into strips or cubes and sprinkle with the seasonings. Keep the mixture cold until ready to use. At the last minute, before grinding the meat, mix in one crushed ice cube made of stock or water for each pound of farce. This helps keep the meat cold enough to get a clean, sharp cut, and moist enough to blend in the seasonings. Grind the meat and fat.

After the final grinding, add any garnitures to the farce. Mix well. This will evenly distribute the seasonings and other ingredients. To test the seasonings, thoroughly sauté about 1 tablespoon of farce. Let it cool slightly, taste, and correct the seasonings if necessary. Remove the cutting knife and grinding disk from the grinder and attach the sausage stuffer. (Coarsely ground sausage meat can be ground and stuffed into casings at the same time.)

Drain the casings but do not dry them; the remaining water will keep them manageable. Oil the outside of the sausage stuffer horn or funnel. Slip the end of the casing over the sausage attachment or funnel, then carefully slide about 3 feet of casing, or as much as possible, onto the stuffer horn or funnel. Leave a 4-inch piece of casing hanging, and knot it 3 inches from the end.

Follow the manufacturer's instructions for using your sausage stuffer. To eliminate air pockets, push the sausage farce to the tip of the stuffer horn and slide the knot in the casing up to it. Hold the end of the casing slightly taut and start the grinder.

Adding small amounts of farce at a time, stuff the casing firmly and evenly, but do not pack tightly (fig. 5-1). Room must remain to twist the sausage into links without bursting the casing. If the casing breaks as you stuff it, cut it off, knot both ends, and continue. Should an air bubble form, pierce it with a pin or needle.

Remove the casing from the stuffer once all the farce is used. Twist the end as close to the sausage as possible in order to seal it. Cut off and store

5-1. Add small amounts of farce at a time, stuffing the casing firmly and evenly.

any excess casing. For link sausage, twist the sausage at about 3-inch intervals or tie each interval with 2-inch pieces of string. Or just knot the end of the sausage, coil it, and cook it as a continuous cylinder.

You may cut the sausage links into shorter sections or individual pieces for storage. Securely wrapped, sausage keeps for 2 to 5 days, refrigerated, or about 2 months if frozen. If you freeze it longer, some fats may start to turn rancid.

Venison Sausage

Most deer meat is dry and requires the addition of pork fat for moisture and texture. Make certain the meat has been properly hung and adequately aged, or it will taste unpalatably gamy.

YIELD: about 5 pounds

Marinade
1 cup red wine
½ cup red wine vinegar
1 onion, sliced
3 garlic cloves, chopped
1 carrot, thinly sliced
2 celery stalks with leaves, thinly sliced
1 bay leaf, crumbled
4 juniper berries, cracked
6 peppercorns, cracked
1 teaspoon salt

2½ pounds boneless venison, cut into strips or cubes
5 yards pork casings
1½ pounds boneless pork butt, cut into strips or cubes
1 pound bacon or fresh pork fat, cut into strips or cubes
5 crushed ice cubes (preferably made from Game Stock)
2 to 3 garlic cloves, minced or pressed
Salt to taste (not necessary if you use bacon in the recipe)
1½ teaspoons ground juniper berries
1 teaspoon black pepper
1 teaspoon hot paprika
1 teaspoon thyme

Combine the ingredients for the marinade and pour it over the pieces of venison. Marinate the meat in the refrigerator for 1 to 4 days, turning it occasionally.

Prepare the casings. Drain the venison and discard the marinade. Combine all the remaining ingredients and pass them through a medium or coarse grinding disk twice. Test the seasonings and correct if necessary. Stuff the casings and form 4-inch links. Refrigerate the sausage, uncovered, for 12 to 24 hours before cooking, in order to develop its flavor.

Securely wrapped, this sausage keeps for several days, refrigerated, or about 2 months if frozen.

Serving Suggestions
Poach the sausages for 5 minutes, then fry or broil them until crisp. Lentils with Sorrel and Red Onions make a fine accompaniment to Venison Sausage.

Pennsylvania Beef and Pork Sausage

YIELD: about 3 pounds

3 yards pork or lamb casings
2 pounds boneless beef chuck marbled with fat, cut into strips or cubes
1 pound boneless pork butt marbled with fat, cut into strips or cubes
3 crushed ice cubes (preferably made from Brown Stock)
1 to 2 tablespoons crumbled sage
1 to 1½ tablespoons ground coriander
½ tablespoon cloves
2 teaspoons salt
1½ teaspoons black pepper

Prepare the casings. Combine all the remaining ingredients and pass them through a coarse grinding disk. Test the seasonings and correct if necessary. Stuff the casings and form 3-inch links. When possible, refrigerate the sausage, uncovered, for 3 to 6 hours before cooking, in order to develop its flavor.

Securely wrapped, the sausage keeps for 2 or 3 days, refrigerated, or about 6 weeks if frozen.

Serving Suggestions
Poach the sausages, then fry or broil them until crisp. Serve them with buttery, mustard-flavored mashed potatoes and a green vegetable.

Rosemary Lamb Sausage

These lamb sausages possess a characteristic Middle Eastern flavor and aroma.

YIELD: about 3 pounds

3 yards lamb casings
3 pounds boneless lamb shoulder, cut into strips or cubes
2 egg whites
3 crushed ice cubes (preferably made from White Stock)
1 onion, minced
4 garlic cloves, minced or pressed
⅓ cup chopped fresh mint or parsley
1 teaspoon marjoram
1 teaspoon black pepper
½ teaspoon cumin
¼ teaspoon oregano
¼ teaspoon ground rosemary leaves

Prepare the casings. Combine all the remaining ingredients and pass them through a medium grinding disk. Test the seasonings and correct if necessary. Stuff the casings and form 3-inch links. When possible, refrigerate the sausage, uncovered, for 2 to 4 hours before cooking, in order to develop its flavor.

Securely wrapped, the sausage keeps for 1 to 2 days, refrigerated, or about 6 weeks if frozen.

Serving Suggestions
Fry or broil the sausages. Serve them in pita bread with shredded lettuce, diced tomatoes, and Middle Eastern Sauce.

Variations
Soak 1 cup fine bulgur in 2 cups water or stock for about 1½ hours, or until the bulgur is soft and swollen with liquid. Drain and squeeze out the excess water or stock and reserve it for another use. Thoroughly mix the bulgur into the other ingredients. Proceed as in the original recipe, but increase the length of casing required.

Milwaukee-style Sausage

YIELD: about 3 pounds

Marinade
1½ cups beer
4 peppercorns, cracked
3 garlic cloves, pressed
3 fresh sage leaves, chopped

2½ pounds boneless pork butt or loin, cut into strips or cubes
½ pound fresh pork fat, cut into strips or cubes
¼ pound bacon, cut into strips or cubes
3 yards pork casings
1½ tablespoons dill seed
4 teaspoons coarsely ground black pepper
2¼ teaspoons hot paprika
2 teaspoons dry mustard
1 teaspoon summer savory
1 teaspoon salt
1 teaspoon honey, sugar, or molasses

Combine the ingredients for the marinade and pour it over the cut-up meat, fat, and bacon. Marinate the ingredients in the refrigerator for 24 to 36 hours, stirring occasionally. Drain and discard the marinade.

Prepare the casings. Combine the meat, fat, and bacon with all the remaining ingredients and pass them through a coarse grinding disk. Test the seasonings and correct if necessary. Stuff the casings and form 5-inch links. Refrigerate the sausage, uncovered, for 2 to 4 hours (preferably overnight) before cooking, in order to develop its flavor.

Securely wrapped, the sausage keeps for 2 to 3 days, refrigerated, or about 2 months if frozen.

Serving Suggestions
Sauté, broil, or grill the sausages until thoroughly cooked. Serve them with lots of mustard, Apple Herb Sauerkraut, buns, and German potato salad.

Cheese and Basil Sausage

When frying, grilling, or broiling these sausages, take care not to overcook them or the cheese will become hard and dry.

YIELD: about 4 pounds

4 yards pork casings
2 pounds boneless pork butt, cut into strips or cubes
3/4 pound boneless beef chuck, cut into strips or cubes
1/4 pound fresh pork fat, cut into strips or cubes
3 crushed ice cubes (preferably made from Brown Stock)
1 1/2 teaspoons black pepper
1 teaspoon salt
1/2 teaspoon nutmeg
1/2 cup dry vermouth
1/4 cup chopped fresh parsley
1/4 cup chopped fresh basil
3/4 cup grated Parmesan or Romano cheese
3/4 cup 1/4-inch cubed provolone cheese

Prepare the casings. Combine all the ingredients except the parsley, basil, and cheese and pass them through a coarse grinding disk. Mix the remaining ingredients into the ground farce. Test the seasonings and correct if necessary. Stuff the casings and form 2 1/2-inch links. When possible, refrigerate the sausage, uncovered, for 3 to 6 hours before cooking, in order to develop its flavor.

Securely wrapped, the sausage keeps for about 3 days, refrigerated, or up to 2 months if frozen.

Serving Suggestions
Brown the sausages, cook them in tomato sauce, and serve with polenta. Cheese and Basil Sausage tastes just as good plainly broiled or grilled.

Sweet Pepper and Onion Pork Sausage

YIELD: about 3 pounds

3 yards pork casings
3 pounds boneless pork butt marbled with fat, cut into strips or cubes
3 crushed ice cubes (preferably made from Brown Stock)
1 onion, minced
1 bell pepper, minced
3 garlic cloves, minced or pressed
3 tablespoons chopped fresh parsley
1 tablespoon fennel seeds
2 teaspoons salt
1½ teaspoons black pepper
¼ teaspoon thyme

Prepare the casings. Combine all the remaining ingredients and pass them through a coarse grinding disk. Test the seasonings and correct if necessary. Stuff the casings and form 4½-inch links. When possible, refrigerate the sausage, uncovered, for 3 to 6 hours before cooking, in order to develop its flavor.

Securely wrapped, this sausage keeps for about 2 days, refrigerated, or 2 months if frozen.

Serving Suggestions
Poach the sausages, then fry them with julienned red and green peppers, onions, and seasonings. Sweet Pepper and Onion Pork Sausage makes a satisfying hero on whole-wheat Italian bread, or a savory frittata, quiche, or risotto.

Chili Sausage

YIELD: about 3 pounds

3 yards pork casings
1½ pounds boneless lean beef, cut into strips or cubes
¾ to 1 pound boneless pork, cut into strips or cubes
½ to ¾ pound fresh pork fat, cut into strips or cubes
3 crushed ice cubes (preferably made from Brown Stock)
1 onion, minced
1 garlic clove, minced
2 tablespoons Chili Spice
1½ teaspoons cumin
1 teaspoon salt
1 teaspoon black pepper
1 teaspoon sugar or honey
¾ teaspoon dry mustard

Prepare the casings. Combine all the remaining ingredients and pass them through a coarse grinding disk twice. Test the seasonings and correct if necessary. Stuff the casings and form 5-inch links. When possible, refrigerate the sausage, uncovered, for 3 to 6 hours before cooking, in order to develop its flavor.

Securely wrapped, Chili Sausage keeps for 2 to 3 days, refrigerated, or up to 1 month if frozen.

Serving Suggestions
These spicy, slightly hot sausages are good with a Tex-Mex meal. After cooking, bake the sausage in a shallow casserole and melt shredded Monterey Jack cheese on top. Serve with refried beans and tacos.

Variations
Curry sausage: Follow the recipe for Chili Sausage, substituting 2 tablespoons curry powder for the chili powder. You may also substitute lean lamb for the beef.

Serve the sausage with rice or bulgur pilaf.

Garlic Sausage

Garlic Sausage is fragrant but mild and makes a delicate addition to cassoulet.

YIELD: about 3¾ pounds

4 yards medium-size pork casings
3 pounds boneless lean pork (preferably from the neck or shoulder) or boneless lean pork butt, cut into strips or cubes
¾ pound fresh pork fat or unsalted fatback, cut into strips or cubes
3 crushed ice cubes (preferably made from Brown Stock)
6 garlic cloves, minced or pressed
¼ cup chilled brandy, marc, eau de vie, gin, vodka, or white wine
1½ teaspoons salt
1½ teaspoons quatre épices
¾ to 1 teaspoon black pepper

Prepare the casings. Combine all the remaining ingredients and pass them through a medium grinding disk. Test the seasonings and correct if necessary. Stuff the casings and form 4-inch links. When possible, refrigerate the sausage, uncovered, for 3 to 6 hours before cooking, in order to develop its flavor.

Securely wrapped, the sausage keeps for up to 4 days, refrigerated, or up to 3 months if frozen.

Serving Suggestions
Poach the sausages in chicken stock or water; slice them and remove the casings. Serve with a bowl of Herbed Lentils or with hot potato salad and spicy mustard. Once poached, the sausages can be baked in a brioche or bread crust and served with a mixed green salad.

Variations
For a more peppery sausage, add ¾ teaspoon cracked black pepper to the already ground mixture. Blend well.

You can vary the texture of the sausage by dicing all or part of the pork fat into ⅛- to ¼-inch cubes. Instead of passing the diced fat through the grinding disk, mix it into the meat after it has been ground.

Spicy Kielbasa

In Poland, recipes for kielbasa vary from cook to cook; it is a traditional springtime dish. Russians call this sausage *kolbasa* and serve it as part of the Easter meal.

YIELD: about 5 pounds

5 yards 2-inch-wide pork or beef casings
5 pounds boneless pork butt marbled with fat, cut into strips or cubes
5 crushed ice cubes (preferably made from Brown Stock)
5 garlic cloves, minced or pressed
1 to 2 tablespoons sweet paprika
1 tablespoon coarse or kosher salt
1 tablespoon coarsely ground black pepper
2 teaspoons marjoram
1 teaspoon summer savory
1 teaspoon allspice

Prepare the casings. Combine all the remaining ingredients and pass them through a coarse grinding disk. Test the seasonings and correct if necessary. Stuff the casings and form 18- to 24-inch links. Tie the two ends of each link together to form a ring of sausage. Refrigerate the sausage, uncovered, for 3 to 24 hours before cooking, in order to develop its flavor.

Securely wrapped, kielbasa keeps for 2 to 3 days, refrigerated, or about 1 month if frozen.

Serving Suggestions
Poach the sausage for 40 minutes or roast it in a preheated 425°F oven for about 45 minutes. Serve with caraway-seasoned sauerkraut and potatoes or with haricot beans, raw onion, and mustard.

Variations
Substitute 3½ pounds boneless pork butt and 1½ pounds boneless beef chuck for the 5 pounds pork butt.

Vary the flavor by adding 1 tablespoon mustard or caraway seeds.

Bratwurst

Bratwurst, a German specialty of Nuremberg, resemble fat frankfurters. You can make them into tiny, thin sausages for grilling or long, thick sausages (about 1½ to 2 inches in diameter) for poaching or steaming. Sliced bratwurst taste good hot or cold.

YIELD: about 3 pounds

3 yards pork casings
2 pounds boneless pork loin (with a little fat left on) or boneless pork butt marbled with fat, cut into strips or cubes
1 pound boneless lean veal, cut into strips or cubes
3 crushed ice cubes (preferably made from White Stock)
1 to 2 teaspoons salt
1 teaspoon black pepper
½ teaspoon marjoram
½ teaspoon caraway seeds
¼ teaspoon nutmeg
⅛ teaspoon allspice or mace

Prepare the casings. Combine all the ingredients and pass them through a fine grinding disk twice. Test the seasonings and correct if necessary. Stuff the casings and form 2½-inch links. When possible, refrigerate the sausage, uncovered, for 3 to 6 hours before cooking, in order to develop its flavor.

Securely wrapped, bratwurst keep for 2 to 3 days, refrigerated, or about 2 months if frozen.

Serving Suggestions
Fry or grill the bratwurst and serve them as you would frankfurters.

Variations
You may add ⅔ cup of bread crumbs soaked in milk or stock.

Vary the flavor by adding ½ teaspoon sage or coriander.

Maryland-style Sausage

Sausages made in Maryland possess a distinctive sage flavor and a fine texture. Removed from their casings and mixed with some bread or wild rice, they make a tasty stuffing for poultry or eggplant.

YIELD: about 3 pounds

3 yards 1-inch-wide pork or lamb casings
2½ pounds boneless lean pork, cut into strips or cubes
½ pound fresh pork fat, cut into strips or cubes
3 crushed ice cubes (preferably made from White Stock)
4 to 5 teaspoons crumbled sage
1½ tablespoons black pepper
1 to 2 teaspoons salt
⅛ teaspoon cayenne

Prepare the casings. Combine all the remaining ingredients and pass them through a fine grinding disk twice. Test the seasonings and correct if necessary. Stuff the casings and form 3-inch links. When possible, refrigerate the sausage, uncovered, for 3 to 6 hours before cooking, in order to develop its flavor.

Securely wrapped, this sausage keeps for 2 to 3 days, refrigerated, or about 1 month if frozen.

Serving Suggestions
Poach the sausages, then fry or broil them until crisp. They go well with poultry or with eggs for a hearty winter breakfast.

Hot Creole Sausage

In Louisiana, where these sausages are made fiery hot and spicy, they are called *chaurice*. This recipe is moderately seasoned; add more or less pepper according to your taste. Traditionally, the meat is chopped by hand, but you can grind it if you prefer.

YIELD: about 3 pounds

3 yards lamb casings
2 pounds boneless lean pork (preferably from the neck or shoulder) or boneless lean pork butt, finely diced
1 pound fresh pork belly (or fatty pork), finely diced
1 large Spanish onion, minced
2 to 3 garlic cloves, minced
1 tablespoon black pepper
1 teaspoon coarse or kosher salt
1 teaspoon sweet paprika
1 teaspoon dried red pepper flakes
½ teaspoon cayenne
3 sprigs fresh parsley, minced
2 fresh sage leaves, minced
1 fresh thyme sprig, minced
1 small bay leaf, crumbled
Pinch of allspice
Pinch of mace

Prepare the casings. Combine all the remaining ingredients and mix well. Stuff the casings and form any length links desired. When possible, refrigerate the sausage, uncovered, for 3 to 6 hours before cooking, in order to develop its flavor.

Securely wrapped, this sausage keeps for 2 to 3 days, refrigerated, or about 1 month if frozen.

Serving Suggestions
For breakfast, broil, fry, or deep fry the sausages; sprinkle with chopped parsley and serve with steaming grits. Hot Creole Sausage is a standard ingredient of jambalaya (the New Orleans version of paella) and produces a savory exchange of flavors when cooked in a pot of boiling cabbage or slowly baked with beans.

Chicken or Turkey Furters

Low in fat, these basic frankfurters can be flavored with the seasonings from your favorite recipes.

YIELD: about 3 pounds

3 yards pork or lamb casings
2 pounds cooked boneless chicken or turkey white meat, cut into strips or cubes
½ pound cooked bacon, ham, or Canadian bacon, cut into strips or cubes
½ pound cooked chicken or turkey livers, cut into strips or cubes
4 large eggs or 6 large egg whites
½ cup bread crumbs soaked in ½ cup Chicken Stock
1 teaspoon salt
1 teaspoon white pepper
½ teaspoon nutmeg
¼ teaspoon cloves
⅛ teaspoon allspice or mace

Prepare the casings. Combine all the meats and pass them through a medium or fine grinding disk. Blend the ground meat with the remaining ingredients and mix well. Stuff the casings and form 3-inch links.

Securely wrapped, these frankfurters keep for 3 days, refrigerated, or about 1 month if frozen.

Serving Suggestions
Fry, broil, grill, poach, or steam the franks and serve them with Orange Cranberry Relish or your own cranberry sauce. Sliced, they are good in a hot soup or a cold salad. Or bake them in a gratin dish with cream sauce and fresh herbs.

Variations
Eliminate the chicken livers and substitute ½ pound boneless chicken, turkey, bacon, or ham.

Deli Sausage

YIELD: about 3 pounds

3 yards pork casings
½ cup nonfat dry milk
½ to ¾ cup Chicken Stock or water
4½ slices crustless bread, crumbled, or 1 cup bread or rice stuffing, or 1 cup cooked grains (such as kasha, bulgur, or wheat berries)
3 cups diced cooked chicken or turkey
3 cups diced ham or bologna
1½ cups finely diced cheese, such as Swiss, Gouda, provolone, or Monterey Jack
2 egg whites
5 tablespoons minced fresh parsley
3 tablespoons minced scallions or chives
2 teaspoons white pepper
1 teaspoon dry mustard
½ teaspoon nutmeg
¼ teaspoon allspice
Salt to taste (not necessary if you use ham in the recipe)

Prepare the casings. In a bowl, blend the nonfat dry milk and water, then add the bread, stuffing, or cooked grains. (The bread will absorb more liquid than the rice or grains.) When most of the liquid is absorbed, combine with all the remaining ingredients and pass them through a coarse grinding disk. Test the seasonings and correct if necessary. Loosely stuff the casings and form 2½-inch links. Refrigerate the sausage for 3 to 6 hours before cooking, in order to develop its flavor.

Securely wrapped, this sausage keeps for 2 to 3 days, refrigerated, or about 1 month if frozen.

Serving Suggestions

Gently, so as not to burst the casings, simmer the sausages in stock, water, or soup. Just heat them, since the ingredients were precooked. These sausages taste good in sandwiches, casseroles, or soup. Or cut them up to serve as hors d'oeuvre with mustard.

Low-Fat Sausage

This recipe is low in fat, cholesterol, and sodium. Following these proportions, you can convert most sausage recipes.

YIELD: about 2½ pounds

3 yards pork casings
1 pound boneless lean beef or poultry, cut into strips or cubes
1 pound boneless lean pork, cut into strips or cubes
3 crushed ice cubes (preferably made from Brown Stock)
1 to 1½ cups cooked grains (such as kasha, rice, or bulgur) or crumbled firm tofu
½ onion, minced
3 egg whites
1½ teaspoons crumbled sage
1 teaspoon honey or sugar
1 teaspoon black pepper
1 teaspoon quatre épices
½ teaspoon cayenne

Prepare the casings. Combine all the remaining ingredients and pass them through a coarse grinding disk. Test the seasonings and correct if necessary. Stuff the casings and form 2½-inch links. Refrigerate the sausage, uncovered, for 12 hours before cooking, in order to develop its flavor.

Securely wrapped, this sausage keeps for 2 days, refrigerated, or about 1 month if frozen.

Serving Suggestions
Gently poach the sausage in stock, soup, or tomato sauce. Poaching helps maintain a moist textured sausage and contributes flavor. Serve as you would any other sausage.

CREPINETTES, FAGGOTS, GAYETTES, AND BOULETTES

Small patty-shaped parcels wrapped in white-veined caul fat, crépinettes taste succulent plainly baked in butter, grilled, or fried in an egg and breadcrumb coating. You can use sausage or pâté forcemeats for the stuffing. Form the patties into flat, round-edged triangles or ovals approximately a half-inch thick. Years ago, miniature crépinettes, called *pieds cendrillon,* were enclosed in layers of special paper and cooked on smoldering ashes. Today they are baked in a thin sheet of pastry.

Any sausage, terrine, or pâté farce can be made into crépinettes. Add garnitures, such as strips of meat or fish, pistachios, hazelnuts, walnuts, chopped chestnuts, cooked and drained spinach or Swiss chard leaves, or slices of truffles, to enrich the basic mixture.

When the catch is fresh, enjoy the clear, sharp taste of a seafood crépinette: silky Cotuit oysters, a julienne of radish, sorrel or spinach, and a splash of dry chablis all delicately laced in caul fat.

Small, round balls, known as faggots in the English West Country or gayettes in France, are similiar to crépinettes. A favorite picnic food and hors d'oeuvre, faggots are usually eaten while they are hot; gayettes more often are cooked, sliced, and served cold. Hot or cold, they always taste good.

Boulettes, shaped like large bullets, resemble faggots and gayettes. Often made from leftover meat or fish, boulettes are prepared and served like gayettes.

FORMING AND COOKING

Rinse the caul fat under running water, then soak it in a bowl of tepid water mixed with 1 tablespoon of vinegar or lemon juice for each cup of water. Let the fat stand in the liquid for about 30 minutes, until it feels soft and pliable.

To make crépinettes, lay the caul fat out flat; using scissors, cut it into 9-inch squares. Lay a square of caul fat on the counter or over the palm of your hand and flatten a small handful of sausage farce in the center. Wrap the fat around the filling, overlapping the edges. Gently form the patties into flat, round-edged triangles or ovals approximately ½ inch thick.

In a gratin dish with butter, bake the crépinettes for 20 to 25 minutes at 425°F, turning them after 10 or 15 minutes. Or grill or broil them for 5 to 10 minutes on each side, depending on the thickness and type of farce. Oil the crépinettes first and keep them at least 3 inches from the source of heat. You also may dip the crépinettes in beaten egg, roll them in seasoned bread crumbs, and fry.

Assemble faggots and gayettes in the same manner as crépinettes, but shape the farce into small balls, then wrap them in caul fat. Boulettes are shaped like large bullets and wrapped in caul fat.

Cotuit Oyster Crépinettes

This recipe is unusual in that it requires no additional seasoning. The radish contributes the flavor and fire typical of pepper, onion, and horseradish combined, while the lemony tang of the sorrel complements the brininess of the oyster. As a change from oysters on the half shell, serve two crépinettes (per person) as an appetizer.

YIELD: 16 crépinettes, 8 first-course servings

1/2 pound caul fat, cut into 9-inch squares
2 cups julienned red radishes
1 cup julienned sorrel or spinach (If you use spinach, add the juice of 1/2 lemon.)
48 Cotuit oysters, shucked
Splash of chablis or other dry white wine
Butter for frying or broiling

Prepare the caul fat. Blanch the julienned radish for about 1 minute, then separately blanch the sorrel (or spinach) for 5 to 10 seconds. In a bowl, toss all the ingredients except the butter until they are evenly distributed. Form each crépinette with 3 oysters and their mixture. At this point you can cover and refrigerate the patties for several hours or overnight.

Fry the crépinettes in butter or baste them with melted butter and broil.

Serving Suggestions:
Cotuit Oyster Crépinettes taste delicious served with Lemon Herb Butter Sauce.

Variations
You can substitute whatever oysters are available. Three Cotuit oysters equal about 1/4 cup. If you use smaller ones, add 1 or 2 extra oysters to each crépinette.

Liver Faggots

YIELD: about 2 1/4 pounds

1/2 pound caul fat, cut into squares
3/4 pound pork liver, 3/8-inch cubed
1/2 pound boneless lean pork, coarsely ground
2 small onions, minced
2 garlic cloves, minced
1 tablespoon crumbled sage
1 1/2 teaspoons salt
1 1/2 teaspoons black pepper
1 teaspoon quatre épices
2 eggs, beaten
1/4 pound pork liver, ground
2 to 2 1/2 cups bread crumbs
1 cup White Stock

Prepare the caul fat. Sauté the cubed liver, ground pork, fatback, onions, garlic, and seasonings for about 20 minutes over low heat. Stir occasionally to prevent sticking. Drain off the excess liquid and reserve it. Mix the sautéed meat with the eggs, ground pork liver, and bread crumbs. The mixture should hold together well; if not, add more bread crumbs. Test the seasonings and correct if necessary. Shape the faggots and wrap them in caul fat.

In a shallow baking dish greased with lard, arrange the faggots, touching, in a single layer. Add the stock and bake in a preheated 325°F to 350°F oven for 40 minutes to 1 hour. After 30 minutes, drain off the juice and combine it with the liquid reserved from the sautéed meat. Skim off all the fat, then pour the stock back over the faggots during the last 5 to 10 minutes of cooking. At this time, if the faggots are not browned, raise the temperature. You can also pass them under the broiler, at least 3 inches from the heat source, before serving them.

Faggots keep for 2 to 3 days, refrigerated, or about 1 month if frozen.

Serving Suggestions
Serve the faggots with peas and shallots (or onions) seasoned with garlic and fresh herbs and parsleyed potatoes.

Green-Leaved Gayettes

In France, charcutiers often add pork lungs and spleen to liver and sausage-meat gayettes.

YIELD: about 2½ pounds

½ pound caul fat, cut into squares
1 pound pork sausage (half lean, half fat)
¼ pound pork liver, finely diced
2 cups chopped cooked spinach
1 cup chopped cooked escarole, Swiss chard, or kale
1 small onion, minced and sautéed
1½ to 2 tablespoons lemon juice
1½ teaspoons black pepper
1½ teaspoons salt
1½ teaspoons Pâté Seasoning IV

Prepare the caul fat. Combine all the remaining ingredients. Test the seasonings and correct if necessary. Shape the gayettes and wrap them in caul fat. Cook them as you would faggots or bake them in a shallow, buttered baking dish at 425°F for about 20 minutes.

Gayettes keep for 2 to 3 days, refrigerated, or about 1 month if frozen.

Serving Suggestions
Serve the gayettes hot with mashed potatoes and salad or cold with crunchy French bread and assorted olives and pickles.

Boulettes

Boulettes contain more fat than either faggots or gayettes, and the flavor of bacon enriches their taste. Boulettes can also be made from leftover fatty pork that has been precooked.

YIELD: about 2¼ pounds

½ pound caul fat, cut into squares
1⅓ pounds boneless lean pork, cut into strips or cubes
½ pound fresh pork fat or pork belly, cut into strips or cubes
¼ pound Canadian bacon, cut into strips or cubes
3 tablespoons chopped mixed fresh herbs (such as parsley, basil, and tarragon)
2 tablespoons Madeira or sweet vermouth
1½ teaspoons black pepper
1½ teaspoons Pâté Seasoning I or II

Prepare the caul fat. Combine all the remaining ingredients and pass them through a coarse grinding disk. Test the seasonings and correct if necessary. Shape the boulettes and wrap them in caul fat. Cook and serve them as you would gayettes.

Boulettes keep for 2 to 3 days, refrigerated, or about 1 month if frozen.

BOUDINS

WHITE PUDDING SAUSAGE

Finely textured and creamy, white pudding sausages, or *boudins blancs*, possess a delicate, subtle flavor and a lightness more reminiscent of mousse than of sausage. Traditionally made from the palest pink pork, chicken, veal, rabbit, and sometimes fish or vegetables, boudins are enriched with cream, eggs, shallots (or onions), and seasonings. Garnitures folded into the pudding create an appealing mosaic of textures, tastes, and colors. Morsels of meat or fish, a jardiniere of vegetables, wild mushrooms, and truffles are but a few of the garnitures you can add.

Form boudins either into large sausages about 2 inches in diameter or into thinner links. Loosely stuff small pork or larger beef casings or wrap the filling in oiled cheesecloth, muslin, or plastic wrap. In order to ripen the flavor, refrigerate meat boudins at least 12 hours (up to 2 days) prior to cooking. Arrange the boudins on a rack or wicker tray. Slowly poach them over very gentle heat in a mixture of half milk and half stock or water. These precautions safeguard against bursting the delicate boudins while they simmer or when you remove them from the liquid. If they start to burst, quickly prick the casings in several places with a pin. Once poached, cool them on a clean, dry cloth or on several layers of paper towels. Securely wrapped meat boudins keep, refrigerated, for 3 to 4 days or about a month if frozen. Seafood boudins keep for about 2 days, refrigerated.

Serve the boudins on a bed of mashed potatoes, or on a platter accompanied with creamed spinach, peas, fried apple rings or warm apple puree, or with braised endive or fennel. In France, truffled boudins are traditionally served after Christmas midnight mass and on New Year's. Diced or thinly sliced, boudins (hot or cold) make an unusual garnish for seafood or chef salads or for tossed greens. Poached boudins can also be an innovative addition to a broth with buckwheat noodles, a fresh vegetable soup, or a heady bouillabaisse.

BLACK OR BLOOD PUDDING SAUSAGE

According to some historians, black pudding sausages, or *boudins noirs,* are Assyrian in origin. Though improved over the centuries, today they remain much the same as those of the earlier pork butchers of Tyre (Lebanon). The finest sausages are made of pig's blood and suet. Puddings made from the blood of ox, calf, sheep, fowl, rabbit, and wild game such as deer and boar are considered mediocre. The French also enjoy *boudins noirs* at Christmas and New Year's.

Achille Ozanne, a late-nineteenth-century French cook and poet, described the preparation of black pudding sausage:

Chop the onions, finely, finely,
Toss them in an equal amount of fat on a low fire,
Stirring them, until they are a beautiful golden color,
And their fragrance pervades all round . . .
Blend them with blood and season well with
Salt, pepper, nutmeg and the spices;
A glass of brandy and then you stuff the mixture
Into the pig's intestine, one end of which
Has previously been sealed. As soon as this is filled,
Tie up the other end and into simmering water
Plunge the black pudding! Once this is done,
You give them twenty minutes, and drain.

BASICS OF FORMING BOUDINS

The base of a boudin is a mousseline. Prepare the mousseline or pudding according to the individual recipe and stuff the casings as you would link sausage. Instead of using casings, you may wrap the filling in oiled cheesecloth, muslin, or plastic wrap and poach.

Grease an 18-inch length of plastic wrap for each boudin. With the 18-inch side nearest you, spoon the filling lengthwise into a 9-inch-long cylinder down the center of the plastic wrap. You may vary the length according to your preference.

Smooth one side of plastic over the mixture to remove any air bubbles, then slightly tuck it under. Pull the other side of plastic over and roll the boudin into a firm cylinder.

Twist the ends closed, and smooth the excess plastic around the cylinder. Wrap each boudin in a second layer of plastic. For cloth wrappings you will need a second layer of cheesecloth, but one layer of muslin will do. Twist the cloth ends closed and tie them with string. It may be necessary to refrigerate the boudins in order to firm them before poaching.

Dilled Pork Boudin with Chicken

YIELD: 3½ pounds

3½ yards beef casings or 4½ yards medium pork casings
¼ to ½ pound pork fat, ground
2 cups thinly sliced onions
1⅓ cups milk
1 cup bread crumbs
1½ pounds boneless lean pork from shoulder or loin, ground
2 eggs
3 egg whites
1 tablespoon Pâté Seasoning III
1 to 2 teaspoons salt
1 cup heavy whipping cream
2 tablespoons minced fresh herbs
2 teaspoons dill seeds
1 pound chicken fillets, ⅜-inch cubed
White Stock, water, or half milk/half water for poaching

Prepare the casings. Melt half the ground fat in a skillet over medium-low heat and add the sliced onions. Cover and slowly cook for 15 to 20 minutes. Cool.

Meanwhile, make a panada by bringing the milk to a boil and adding the bread crumbs. Stir constantly over medium heat until the mixture forms a thick paste and almost holds its own shape. Be careful not to burn the panada. Cool.

Mix together the remaining ground pork fat, sautéed onions, ground pork, panada, eggs, egg whites, pâté spice, and salt. Process the mixture in a food processor until it develops a velvety, thick consistency. Chill for about 15 minutes in the freezer.

Return the mixture to the food processor. With the machine running, slowly pour in the heavy cream in a steady stream. Test the seasonings and correct if necessary. Mix in the minced herbs and dill seeds and fold in the cubed chicken. Chill.

Loosely stuff the mixture into casings or form it into cylinders wrapped in greased plastic wrap. Tie the ends with string.

Bring the poaching liquid to the boiling point. Place the boudins in the pot and weight with a plate to keep them submerged; cover. Lower the heat and simmer large boudins for 30 to 40 minutes, 15 to 20 minutes on each side. Simmer thinner boudins for 7 to 10 minutes on each side. Prick the skins if necessary to prevent bursting. When cooked, the boudins expand slightly and feel firm. Remove them from the poaching liquid and allow to set and cool in their casings. Wrapped in plastic, they keep for about 3 days, refrigerated, or about 1 month if frozen.

Serving Suggestions
Remove the casings. Slice large boudins diagonally into ½-inch disks and dredge them in egg and bread crumbs. Slowly fry the crumb-coated slices in clarified butter or broil them in a buttered baking dish until browned. Serve with apple rings sautéed in clarified butter, and honey, cinnamon, and a dash of lemon juice. Allow two slices per person as an appetizer or four to five slices as a main course. Serve a proportionate amount of smaller links.

Variations
Substitute cubes of turkey or veal for the chicken fillets.

Veal or Turkey Boudin with Truffles

Like most boudins, this one can be served warm or chilled.

YIELD: about 2½ pounds

3 yards small pork casings
1⅓ pounds veal or turkey fillets, cubed
2 eggs
3 egg whites
1¼ cups heavy cream
Salt to taste
Black pepper to taste
¼ teaspoon allspice
Pinch of cayenne
Truffle juice (optional)
¼ cup duxelles (optional)
3 tablespoons black truffle, ⅛-inch diced
White Stock, water, or half water/half milk for poaching

Prepare the casings. Grind the cubed veal in a food processor with 2 eggs until the mixture develops a fine consistency. With the machine running, add 2 egg whites and, if needed, add the third egg white to make the mixture velvety and thick. Chill for about 15 minutes in the freezer.

Return the mixture to the food processor. With the machine running, slowly pour in the heavy cream in a steady stream. Add the salt, pepper, allspice, cayenne, and truffle juice. Test the seasonings and correct if necessary. Fold in the duxelles and minced truffle. Chill.

Loosely stuff the mixture into casings or form it into cylinders wrapped in greased plastic wrap. Tie the ends with string.

Bring the poaching liquid to the boiling point. Place the boudins in the pot and weight with a plate to keep them submerged; cover. Lower the heat and simmer large boudins for 30 to 40 minutes, 15 to 20 minutes on each side. Simmer thinner boudins for 7 to 10 minutes on each side. Prick the skins if necessary to prevent bursting. When cooked, the boudins expand slightly and feel firm. Remove them from the poaching liquid and allow to set and cool in their casings. Wrapped in plastic, they keep for about 3 days, refrigerated, or about 1 month if frozen.

Serving Suggestions
Remove the casings. Slice large boudins diagonally into ½-inch disks and serve them warm with light Bordelaise or devil sauce thinned with cream. Accompany with fresh vegetables and a salad. Allow two slices per person as an appetizer or four to five slices as a main course. Serve a proportionate amount of the smaller links.

Chicken Boudin with Wild Mushrooms

The mushrooms in this boudin develop a better flavor if first sautéed with a pressed garlic clove and a squeeze of lemon.

YIELD: about 2½ pounds

2 yards beef or 3 yards small pork casings
1 pound raw chicken fillets, cubed
⅓ pound smoked chicken fillets, cubed (or another ⅓ pound raw chicken fillets)
1 egg
2 egg whites
1 to 1¼ cups heavy cream
Salt to taste
White pepper to taste
Pinch of cayenne
1 tablespoon Cognac
¼ cup minced scallions
2 tablespoons minced fresh parsley
¾ to 1 cup sliced, sautéed wild mushrooms (such as chanterelles, shiitakes, oyster, or field)
Chicken Stock, water, or half milk/half water for poaching

Prepare the casings. Grind all the cubed chicken in a food processor with 1 egg until the mixture develops a fine consistency. With the machine running, add 1 egg white and, if needed, add a second egg white to make the mixture velvety and thick. Chill for about 15 minutes in the freezer.

Return the mixture to the food processor. With the machine running, slowly pour in the heavy cream in a steady stream. Add the salt, white pepper, cayenne, and Cognac. Test the seasonings and correct if necessary.

Mix in the scallions and parsley and fold in the sautéed mushrooms. Chill.

Loosely stuff the mixture into casings or form it into cylinders wrapped in greased plastic wrap. Tie the ends with string.

Bring the poaching liquid to the boiling point. Place the boudins in the pot and weight with a plate to keep them submerged; cover. Lower the heat and simmer large boudins for about 30 to 40 minutes, 15 to 20 minutes on each side. Simmer thinner boudins for 7 to 10 minutes on each side. When cooked, the boudins expand slightly and feel firm. Remove them from the poaching liquid and allow to set and cool in their casings. Wrapped in plastic, they keep for about 3 days, refrigerated, or about a month if frozen.

Serving Suggestions

Remove the casings. Slice large boudins diagonally into ½-inch disks and serve warm with Lemon Herb Butter Sauce or chilled with Watercress Sauce. Allow two slices per person as an appetizer or four to five slices as a main course. Serve a proportionate amount of the smaller links.

Variations

Instead of folding the sautéed mushrooms throughout the mixture, spread the chicken farce into a rectangle (on a greased sheet of plastic wrap) and place the mushrooms in a strip down the center before rolling up. Or sprinkle the rectangle of chicken farce with the mushrooms and roll it up, jelly-roll fashion, to form a spiral of mushrooms.

Cooked boudins may also be wrapped in brioche or bread dough and baked.

Seafood and Vegetable Boudin

You will need to process the fish in two batches if your food processor bowl is 6½ inches or less in diameter.

YIELD: about 3 pounds

2 yards beef casings
1½ pounds sole fillets, cubed
1 large shallot, minced
3 egg whites
3 tablespoons lemon juice
⅛ teaspoon nutmeg
Salt to taste
White pepper to taste
Pinch of cayenne
2½ cups heavy cream
⅓ cup baby peas, blanched until crisp tender
⅓ cup ¼-inch diced carrots, blanched until crisp tender
Court Bouillon or water for poaching

Prepare the casings. Puree the sole and minced shallot in a food processor with the egg whites and lemon juice until the mixture develops a velvety, thick consistency. Chill for about 15 minutes in the freezer.

Return the mixture to the food processor. Add the nutmeg, salt, pepper, and cayenne. With the machine running, slowly pour in the heavy cream in a steady stream. Test the seasonings and correct if necessary. Fold in the peas and carrots. Chill.

Loosely stuff the mixture into casings or form it into cylinders wrapped in greased plastic wrap. Tie the ends with string.

Bring the poaching liquid to the boiling point. Place the boudins in the pot and weight with a plate to keep them submerged; cover. Lower the heat and simmer large boudins for 30 to 40 minutes, 15 to 20 minutes on each side. Simmer thinner boudins for 7 to 10 minutes on each side. Prick the skins if necessary to prevent bursting. When cooked, the boudins expand slightly and feel firm. Remove them from the poaching liquid and allow to set and cool in their casings. Wrapped in plastic, they keep for 2 to 3 days, refrigerated, or a few weeks if frozen.

Serving Suggestions

Remove the casings. Slice large boudins diagonally into ½-inch disks and serve them warm or chilled with a watercress or herb mayonnaise. Allow two slices per person as an appetizer or four to five slices as a main course. Serve a proportionate amount of the smaller links.

Variations

Substitute scallops, salmon, pike, or other fish for the sole fillets.

Shellfish Boudin with Scallops, Shrimp, and Lobster

This boudin consists mostly of scallops, shrimp, and lobster chunks lightly bound in a fish mousseline. Its mosaic pattern is best displayed if the boudin is shaped into a large sausage about 2 to 2½ inches in diameter.

YIELD: about 2½ pounds

2 yards beef casings
¾ pound fish fillets, cubed (such as sole, salmon, or cod)
1 to 2 egg whites
¼ teaspoon nutmeg
⅛ teaspoon white pepper
3 drops Tabasco sauce
Salt to taste
1 cup heavy cream
1⅓ cups cape or sea scallops, ½-inch diced, and blanched
1⅓ cups shrimp, peeled, cleaned, ½-inch diced, and blanched
1⅓ cups lobster meat, ½-inch diced and blanched
Court Bouillon or water for poaching

Prepare the casings. Puree the cubed fish in a food processor with the egg whites until the mixture develops a velvety, thick consistency. Chill for about 15 minutes in the freezer.

Return the mixture to the food processor. Add the nutmeg, white pepper, Tabasco, and salt. With the machine running, slowly pour in the heavy cream in a steady stream. Test the seasonings and correct if necessary. Fold in the scallops, shrimp, and lobster. Chill.

Loosely stuff the mixture into casings or form it into cylinders wrapped in greased plastic wrap. Tie the ends with string.

Bring the poaching liquid to the boiling point. Place the boudins in the pot and weight with a plate to keep them submerged; cover. Lower the heat and simmer large boudins for 30 to 40 minutes, 15 to 20 minutes on each side. Simmer thinner boudins for 7 to 10 minutes on each side. Prick the skins if necessary to prevent bursting. When cooked, the boudins expand slightly and feel firm. Remove them from the poaching liquid and allow to set and cool in their casings. Wrapped in plastic, they keep for 2 to 3 days, refrigerated, or a few weeks if frozen.

Serving Suggestions

Remove the casings. Slice large boudins diagonally into ½-inch disks and serve warm with a saffron-flavored butter sauce or chilled with a saffron mayonnaise. Allow two slices per person as an appetizer or four to five slices as a main course.

Variations

Substitute crabmeat, clams, mussels, oysters, or octopus, for the scallops, shrimps, or lobster.

Bread and Onion Boudin

This sausage, based on the classic German recipe for *knepfle au torchon,* became popular during hard economic times when flour and meat were scarce and nothing could be wasted. The German Jews used leftover challah, while the Christians made theirs with stale brioche.

YIELD: 1 boudin, about 2½ pounds (4 main-course servings or 8 to 10 first-course servings)

2 onions, finely diced
2 whole leeks, cleaned and finely chopped
4 shallots, finely diced
3 garlic cloves, minced
¼ cup unsalted butter
Black pepper to taste
Salt to taste
1½ cups light cream or half-and-half
5 eggs
¼ teaspoon nutmeg
2½ cups stale challah or brioche (with crust), ½-inch cubed, toasted until golden
2 tablespoons minced fresh parsley
Diluted Chicken Stock or 2 bouillon cubes dissolved in water for poaching
⅓ cup unsalted butter, heated until browned, then cooled

Sauté the onions, leeks, shallots, and garlic in the butter over low heat. Cover and cook for about 10 minutes, until the vegetables are translucent. Season with pepper and salt, then remove from the heat.

Beat the light cream, eggs, and nutmeg together. Add the toasted bread cubes and parsley to the sautéed vegetables, then stir in the cream-egg mixture. Let the mixture sit for about 30 minutes to give the bread a chance to absorb the liquid.

Form the mixture into a cylinder and wrap in three layers of cheesecloth, 12 by 16 inches, the top layer generously brushed with oil (or use one layer of muslin). Twist the ends closed and tie them with string.

Bring the poaching liquid to the boiling point. Place the boudin in the pot and weight with a plate to keep it submerged; cover. Return to the boil, then lower the heat and simmer for about 40 minutes, 20 minutes on each side. When cooked, the boudin expands slightly and feels firm. Remove it from the poaching liquid and allow to sit until lukewarm. Remove the cloth and brush the sausage with some of the browned butter. Allow it to cool. Wrapped in plastic, the boudin keeps for 3 or 4 days, refrigerated.

Serving Suggestions
Slice the boudin diagonally into ½- to ⅔-inch disks and sauté them in the remaining browned butter until golden. Serve with a chive-flecked sour cream. You also can serve them as a side dish.

5-2. If you do not have casings for the boudin, pour the vegetable mixture into juice cans lined with buttered parchment paper. Place in a water bath and bake.

Basic Vegetable Boudin

You can make boudins from most vegetable mousselines, custards, puddings, or farce. For a garniture, fold chopped herbs, diced and sautéed mushrooms, or diced and blanched vegetables into the mixture.

The uncooked mixture may have a batterlike consistency; therefore, care must be taken when forming the boudin. Loosely stuff the mixture into casings. Do not fill the skins too tightly or they will burst when the mixture expands as it cooks. Poach vegetable boudins as you would meat boudins.

If casings are unavailable, pour the mixture into juice cans lined with buttered parchment or wax paper. If the juice cans are cardboard, wrap the bottoms and outsides in aluminum foil before baking. Bake the boudins in a water bath in a preheated 350°F oven for 35 to 45 minutes, or until cooked (fig. 5-2).

Serving Suggestions
Remove the casings or unmold from the cans. Slice large boudins diagonally into ½-inch disks. Serve chilled or steam and serve warm with sauce on the side. Allow two slices per person as an appetizer or four to five slices as a main course.

Variations
Add a sprinkling of diced cooked chicken, ham, shrimp, or tuna to the boudin mixture before forming it.

Beet Boudins

YIELD: 1 boudin, about 2½ pounds (4 main-course servings or 8 to 10 first-course servings)

2 yards beef casings
3 tablespoons unsalted butter
3 tablespoons flour
¾ cup milk
2 pounds fresh beets, cooked and pureed until smooth (or 2 1-pound cans beets, drained and pureed)
1 medium onion, minced and sautéed
½ teaspoon nutmeg
Salt to taste
Pepper to taste
3 eggs, lightly beaten
Water for poaching

Prepare the casings. In a saucepan over medium heat, melt the butter and stir in the flour. Gradually, whisk in the milk, stirring constantly until smooth and thickened. Bring to a gentle boil and stir for 1 minute. Remove from the heat and allow to cool slightly. Add the beet puree, minced onion, seasonings, and eggs. Blend well, then chill. To stuff and cook the boudins, follow the procedures in the recipe for Basic Vegetable Boudin.

Serving Suggestions
Serve chilled or steam and serve warm with hollandaise sauce.

Variations
To make cauliflower or broccoli boudins, substitute 1 to 1½ pounds cauliflower or broccoli for the beets and use 4 lightly beaten eggs instead of 3.

Add ¼ pound mushrooms, minced and sautéed in butter with a pressed garlic clove.

Frozen Berry Boudin

This summer fruit boudin is a refreshing finale to either elegant or casual fare. Unlike other boudins, it requires no cooking. Garnished, the rosiness of the strawberry and the cool, crispness of the mint accentuate the delicate pink mousseline.

YIELD: 2 boudins (about 6 servings)

2 egg whites
Pinch of salt or cream of tartar
⅔ cup superfine sugar
1 quart whole strawberries, washed, hulled, and pureed
1 teaspoon vanilla extract
1 cup heavy cream

Combine the egg whites and salt in a clean bowl and beat until foamy. Gradually add the sugar, continuing to beat the egg whites until stiff but not dry.

Combine the strawberry puree and vanilla extract. Whip the heavy cream until firm but not dry. Fold the strawberry puree into the beaten egg whites, then fold the whipped cream into the berry–egg white mixture. Chill slightly if necessary to make the mixture firm enough to handle.

Form the mixture into two cylinders and wrap each in an 18-inch-long piece of greased plastic wrap (or use juice cans lined with greased parchment or wax paper). Tie the ends with string. Freeze the boudins for at least 3 hours. They keep for 2 to 3 weeks in the freezer.

Remove the wrappings and slice the boudins with a sharp knife that first has been dipped in hot water. Serve immediately on individual chilled plates.

Serving Suggestions
Arrange two slices of boudin on a chilled plate. Garnish it with a ripe strawberry, a mint sprig, and a drizzle (about 1 tablespoon) of crème de cassis.

Variations
Substitute blackberries, raspberries, blueberries, cherries, or other fruit for the strawberries.

Tropical Fruit Boudin

YIELD: 2 boudins (6 to 8 servings)

1½ tablespoons (envelopes) unflavored gelatin
½ cup pineapple-coconut juice
3 large bananas, peeled and pureed
Juice of 1 lemon
½ cup sugar
1 teaspoon vanilla extract
1 cup heavy cream
⅔ to ¾ cup mixed fruit, ¼-inch diced, such as mango, papaya, or pomegranate kernels
1 tablespoon minced fresh mint
Toasted shredded coconut to garnish

Sprinkle the gelatin over the pineapple-coconut juice and allow it to soften for 5 minutes. Heat in a double boiler over simmering water until the gelatin dissolves.

Combine the banana puree, lemon juice, sugar, vanilla, and gelatin liquid; blend well. Chill the mixture until it just begins to set. Once it starts to set, whip the heavy cream to firm peaks. Fold the whipped cream into the banana mixture and then fold in the mixed fruit and mint. Chill slightly if necessary to make the mousseline firm enough to handle.

Form the mixture into two cylinders and wrap each in an 18-inch-long piece of greased plastic wrap (or use juice cans lined with greased parchment or wax paper). Tie the ends with string. Chill for at least 6 hours. The boudins keep for at least 3 days, refrigerated.

When ready to serve, remove the wrappings and roll the boudins in toasted shredded coconut. Slice and arrange on individual chilled plates.

Serving Suggestions
Garnish the boudin slices with a wedge of fresh fruit such as mango or papaya and a dollop of Berry Sauce.

Variations
Substitute any fruit combination for the mango, papaya, and pomegranate.

CONFITS

Confits, a beloved staple among the farmers of southwestern France, are meats or poultry that have been cooked and stored in their own fat. The word is derived from the French *confire,* meaning "to preserve." Duck, goose, pork, turkey, chicken, small game, and rabbit all lend themselves to confit making.

Originally, confits were a method of preserving meats butchered in autumn. Frugality marked the farmers' lifestyle, and they wasted nothing. Pork shoulder, hocks, ears, snouts, tongues, and rind, as well as poultry legs, gizzards, wings, and necks provided the necessary ingredients. Preserving meat was as much a part of the repertoire of the seasonal kitchen as was preserving vegetables and fruits for the long winter months.

CRAFTING AND COOKING

Traditionally, confits were cooked in earthenware crocks placed among smoldering embers. A heavy baking utensil, such as a Dutch oven, or an electric slow cooker provides a good substitute for the all but extinct kitchen hearth. Slow, even cooking, however, still remains crucial.

In order to extract the perishable juices, the meat is first lightly salted and marinated, then covered in rendered fat and cooked. Slow cooking prevents the meat from developing a stringy texture and also dissolves the fat under the skin. This process aids in preserving the confit by distributing a small amount of salt throughout the meat. Poaching in broth or cooking at higher temperatures would toughen the meat and seal in fats. Gentle simmering in fat not only tenderizes the meat but makes up for the moisture lost during the salting and marinating. Once it is cooked, allowing the confit to cool slowly in the fat will help maintain the meat's firmness and minimize shredding.

A medley of pork, goose, and duck (or any other combination of meats), cooked together in their rendered fats, develops into an intriguingly flavorful confit. Different meats cook in varying amounts of time. For instance, you might start the pork first, later add some goose drumsticks, and later still add a few duck breasts. Or you can start all the meats at the same time and remove them as they are cooked.

If you are careful not to heat the cooking fat to the smoking point, you can reuse it several times. Strain the fat and refrigerate it in a securely covered container. Duck fat keeps for about 3 months, while goose fat becomes rancid after 4 or 5 months. Frozen rendered fat keeps for a year. By adding a higher proportion of lard, the fat retains its freshness longer, ensuring a better sealed confit.

A confit can be eaten immediately or kept, refrigerated, for at least 3 months. Once opened, it spoils easily and should be used within a week. Do not freeze a confit. Freezing dries out the meat and prohibits the maturation process. Like most charcuterie, the flavor of a confit is best after it has matured for at least 7 days. If you intend to use it before that time, use the lesser amount of salt called for in the recipe.

SETTING THEM OUT

To use a sealed confit, set the crock in a warm oven or in a deep container of warm water. Once the fat softens, remove as many pieces of meat as you want and set them aside. Push the remaining confit down so that the fat covers it well, then refrigerate. Scrape the excess fat off the pieces to be cooked and heat the fat in a skillet. When sufficiently hot, add the confit and brown it on all sides for 5 to 10 minutes. Drain the pieces on a wire rack, brown paper, or paper towels. When a crisp skin is not required, steam the confit for 5 minutes over boiling water.

Confit can be served hot, cold, or at room temperature. A well-prepared confit is not salty, fatty, dry, or tough. It should possess a savory, nutlike flavor and develop a moist, tender texture. Confit is delicious served as a main dish accompanied by vegetables, as part of a pot-au-feu, in a salad, as an ingredient of a peasant soup, or with rice, lentils, or beans. After cooking a large batch of confit, the bits of meat that have fallen away may be strained out and used to make a rillette.

BASICS OF MAKING CONFIT

Trim any loose patches of skin and clumps of fat from inside and outside the cavity of poultry, including neck, back, wing tips, and gizzards. Reserve the fat for rendering. Cut each bird into eight or ten pieces. Use the wing tips and back for some other purpose, such as soup or stock. To make a confit of pork butt or shoulder, bone the meat, cut it into pieces weighing approximately ½ pound each, then individually tie them with butcher's twine to hold their shape.

Combine the ingredients for salting and rub them into the meat. If you intend to serve the confit within 5 days, use the smaller amount of salt indicated in the ingredients for the marinade. Place the salted meat in a large bowl or crock. Cover it and keep refrigerated for 12 to 24 hours (36 hours for pork).

Cut the reserved trimmed fat and skin into ½-inch pieces and place them in a deep, ovenproof casserole dish. Cook in a preheated 300°F oven for about 1 hour, or until the fat liquefies and turns clear. Pieces of golden-colored skin may float to the surface. Pour the fat through a strainer, lined with a few layers of dampened cheesecloth or muslin, into a heat-resistant container. Cool, tightly cover, and refrigerate until ready to use. The remaining bits of skin and fat, called cracklings, can be further cooked until crisp and browned. They can be seasoned with salt, pepper, or vinegar and served as a snack or sprinkled as a garnish on soups and salads.

Brush the salting mixture off the meat or quickly rinse it off under cold running water. If rinsed, briefly drain the meat. Heat the rendered fat and lard with water in an electric pot or large Dutch oven. When hot, add the meat, garlic, and whole cloves. If the melted fat does not completely cover the pieces, add more rendered fat (or lard) or cook the meat in batches.

Slowly cook the confit at about 190°F (200°F to 205°F for pork) in a partly covered electric pot or over low heat in an uncovered Dutch oven. Cook for 1 to 2½ hours (3 hours for pork), occasionally turning the pieces. The meat is cooked when it is tender enough to separate with a spoon or easy to pierce with a wooden pick. Some pieces will cook before others. Remove those with a slotted spoon or small strainer, and keep them in a covered bowl to prevent drying out. Continue cooking the other pieces until done.

If you intend to serve the confit within 5 days, shorten the meat's cooking time and use the smaller amount of salt for the marinade. Remove the meat as soon as it becomes tender and its juices run clear and golden.

When all the meat is cooked and removed from the pot, ladle the fat without the meat juices (save the juice for soup or stock) into another heavy pot to simmer. If you used a Dutch oven or something similar, continue simmering the fat in that pot. Skim off any foam as it rises to the top and simmer until all the moisture evaporates. The fat will stop sputtering after 5 or 10 minutes. At no time allow the fat to start smoking or burn. Lower the heat and simmer it longer, if necessary. Let the fat cool slightly. Strain it again.

If you plan to use the confit within a week, place the meat pieces in a crock, bowl, or jars partially filled with fat. Ladle the remaining warm, strained fat over the confit to cover the meat completely. (Straight, narrow containers require less fat to cover the meat.) When the fat solidifies, add a top layer of peanut oil, cover with foil, and refrigerate.

If you plan to keep the confit longer than a week or up to a few months, sterilize the crocks or jars in which you store the confit. Pour boiling water into the containers and let stand for 5 to 10 minutes. Pour out the water, then air dry the containers upside down on a dish rack. When they are dry and cool enough to handle, place 1/4 teaspoon salt in each. This preserves the meat juices that seep out during storage, which would otherwise sour and spoil the confit. Remove two loose bones, such as the drumsticks, and cross them on the bottom of each container. Or sterilize some small wooden sticks to be used for the same purpose, by boiling them in water for 5 to 10 minutes. Ladle in enough warm, strained fat to cover the bones. Add a layer of warm meat and cover it with fat. Add another layer of meat and cover it with fat. Arrange the meat pieces so they do not touch the sides of the container.

Continue until the last layer of meat, covered by an inch of fat, is still 1 inch below the rim of the containers. When the confit reaches room temperature, cover it and refrigerate overnight. The next day, seal the confit by pouring a 1-inch layer of melted lard over the surface to the top of the rim. When the fat solidifies, press a cover of foil onto it and cover.

COOKING CONFIT IN THE OVEN

Besides cooking confit in an electric cooking pot or on top of the stove, you can also cook it in the oven. Follow the instructions in "Basics of Making Confit" but make the following changes: Eliminate the water. Combine the melted rendered fat, the garlic stuck with a whole clove, and the pieces of meat (skin side down) in a deep baking dish or an ovenproof pot. Place the confit in a cold oven, then set the temperature to 275°F. Cook the meat for 1 to 2½ hours (3 hours for pork). After the first hour, periodically check that the fat temperature does not exceed 190°F (200°F to 205°F for pork). At the same time, test the meat for doneness. Once the meat has cooked, continue following the basic procedures.

Confit of Poultry or Rabbit

Preserve a whole goose, duck, chicken, turkey, rabbit, or small game using this recipe. If you choose to cook only certain cuts, legs are preferable; breasts require careful attention to prevent overcooking.

YIELD: 3 to 3½ quarts

Salt Marinade

3 to 7 tablespoons kosher or coarse salt
2 tablespoons chopped onion or shallots
2 tablespoons chopped fresh parsley
2 teaspoons cracked black peppercorns
1½ teaspoons chopped garlic
¼ teaspoon thyme
⅛ teaspoon allspice
⅛ teaspoon mace
1 bay leaf, crumbled

1 goose or turkey, 9 to 12 pounds; or 2 ducks or chickens, 4½ pounds each; or 9 to 12 pounds rabbit or small game
2 cups (minimum) fat rendered from the goose, turkey, ducks, chickens, rabbits, or game
4 to 7 cups (additional) rendered goose fat or lard
2 to 5 tablespoons water
5 to 8 garlic cloves, unpeeled
2 whole cloves, stuck into a piece of garlic

Follow the instructions in "Basics of Making Confit." Once the confit is cooked, you may need to remove the larger bones from the meat in order to fit the pieces into the crocks or jars.

Variations

Combine your own choice of seasonings with the salt for the marinade.

Pork Confit

You can use any cut of pork for a confit—butt, boned shoulder, hocks, tongue, ears, snout, fresh ham, or loin (although loin tends to become dry).

YIELD: 3 to 3½ quarts

Salt Marinade
2 to 5 tablespoons kosher or coarse salt
1 tablespoon crumbled sage
1½ teaspoons cracked black peppercorns
1 teaspoon chopped garlic
¼ teaspoon thyme
¼ teaspoon crumbled rosemary

3½ pounds pork butt or boned pork shoulder
4 to 7 cups rendered lard, goose, or duck fat (or a combination)
3 to 4 tablespoons water
5 garlic cloves, unpeeled
1 whole clove, stuck into a piece of garlic

Follow the instructions in "Basics of Making Confit," but make the following changes: After cooking, allow the pork to cool in the fat, undisturbed, for 1 hour. Then place the pork pieces in a bowl and allow the meat to firm up and cool slightly. While the pork is still warm, remove the strings. The confit is ready to be stored.

Pork confit tastes best when allowed to ripen for at least 2 weeks before serving. It keeps for about 4 months, refrigerated.

Onion-Shallot Confit

The sweet-and-tart flavor of this unorthodox confit holds its own as an hors d'oeuvre served with crackers or as a condiment to pâté.

YIELD: about 3 cups

½ cup currants or raisins
½ cup crème de cassis
½ cup unsalted butter
1 pound onions, thinly sliced
½ to ¾ pound shallots, thinly sliced
1 garlic clove, minced
½ cup sugar or ¼ to ⅓ cup honey
1¾ teaspoons black pepper
1 small bay leaf
1 teaspoon coarse or kosher salt
¼ teaspoon nutmeg
1 cup dry white wine
¼ cup red wine vinegar

Marinate the currants in the crème de cassis until ready to use. In a large heavy skillet over medium heat, melt the butter and stir in the onions, shallots, garlic, sugar, pepper, bay leaf, salt, and nutmeg. Cover and reduce the heat to low. Cook for about 30 minutes, stirring occasionally, or until the onions and shallots are very soft.

Drain the currants; add the crème de cassis, wine, and vinegar to the skillet and increase the heat to medium high. Cook the mixture, uncovered, for about 10 minutes, stirring occasionally, until the liquids reduce and thicken.

Stir the currants into the onion-shallot mixture and continue to cook about 10 minutes more, until the confit resembles the consistency of marmalade.

Serve the confit at room temperature. Covered, it keeps for about 3 days, refrigerated.

Variations

Eliminate the shallots and use more onions instead.

Add ½ teaspoon caraway seeds to the onions while cooking.

RILLETTES AND RILLONS

Rillettes—or potted meats, as the English call them—consist of small pieces of well-seasoned, cooked meats or fish that have been pounded or shredded into fibers, mixed with rendered fat or butter, then preserved in little stoneware, porcelain, or glass crocks. Instead of pounding the flesh, you can drop 1-inch cubes onto the whirling metal blade of a food processor. Using a pulsing action, finely mince the meat or fish but avoid pureeing. Either method works well, but do not pass the meat through a food grinder before or after cooking it. The resulting texture is not suitable for a rillette. Popular meats for making rillettes are goose, duck, pork, rabbit, pheasant, or any leftover meats such as chicken or smoked turkey. Haddock, smoked fish such as trout and salmon, shrimp, crab, lobster, and carp roe all produce particularly tasty seafood rillettes. Rillettes also can be made of cheeses, vegetables, or nuts.

Rillons, tiny cubes of browned meats, are prepared in the same manner as rillettes, but they are not shredded.

Potted like confits, rillettes and rillons keep for 6 months to a year. Because of their high fat content, they also freeze well. Serve them cold for a midday snack, or as an hors d'oeuvre with crackers or a crusty chunk of bread. Stuffed into cherry tomatoes, pearl onions, or celery stalks, rillettes make good appetizers. Heated, rillons are used to garnish mashed potatoes (or other pureed vegetables) and are especially flavorful when grilled with a thin slice of cheese.

Pheasant Rillette

Pheasant Rillette is like a basic black dress. Dress it up with puff pastry for a hot canapé, or dress it down in a crock for an autumn picnic in the woods.

YIELD: about 2 cups

3/4 pound boneless pheasant, 1/2-inch diced
1/2 pound boneless pork, 1/2-inch diced
3/4 pound fresh pork fat, 1/2-inch diced
1/2 cup water
1/4 cup Madeira
1 bay leaf
Salt to taste
Black pepper to taste
Grated nutmeg
Rendered fat to seal (optional)

Bring all the ingredients except the salt, pepper, nutmeg, and rendered fat to a boil in a stainless steel or enameled saucepan. Reduce the heat, cover, and simmer for 2 to 3 hours, stirring occasionally. When the meat starts falling apart, remove the bay leaf and drain the meat, reserving the fat. Cool it overnight.

Shred the meat with two forks, or mince it in a food processor using a pulsing action. Do not puree it. Mix in the salt, pepper, nutmeg, and as much of the reserved fat as you like.

Pack the rillette into a 2-cup crock and serve at nearly room temperature. The rillette tastes better after being refrigerated for 24 hours. Covered with a 1/2-inch layer of rendered fat and foil, it keeps, refrigerated, for several months. After opening, use within a week.

Serving Suggestions
Serve the rillette with Melba toast, crackers, or bread. For hot canapés, spread the rillette between two strips of puff pastry dough and cut the filled dough into small sticks or diamonds. Brush the tops with egg wash and bake until puffed and golden.

Variations
Substitute duck, goose, partridge, or quail for the pheasant.

Rabbit Rillette

YIELD: about 2½ cups

1 pound boneless rabbit meat, ½-inch diced
⅔ pound boneless pork loin or butt, ½-inch diced
½ pound fresh pork fat, ½-inch diced
½ cup water
½ cup white wine
2 garlic cloves, peeled
1 tablespoon Pâté Seasoning V
Salt to taste
Black pepper to taste
Rendered fat to seal (optional)

Bring all the ingredients except the salt, pepper, and rendered fat to a boil in a stainless steel or enameled saucepan. Reduce the heat, cover, and simmer for about 3 hours, stirring occasionally. When the meat starts falling apart, remove it from the heat. Drain the meat, reserving the fat. Cool the mixture overnight.

Shred the meat with two forks or mince it in a food processor using a pulsing action. Do not puree it. Mix in the salt and pepper to taste and as much of the reserved fat as you like.

Pack the rillette into a 3-cup crock and serve it at nearly room temperature. The rillette tastes better after being refrigerated for 24 hours. Covered with a ½-inch layer of rendered fat and foil, it keeps, refrigerated, for several months. After opening, use within a week.

Serving Suggestions
Serve as you would any rillette.

Variations
Mix ¼ cup sautéed, minced shallots or onions into the cooked rillette before packing it in a crock.

Add ¼ teaspoon sage to the seasonings.

Pork Rillette

You also can make this recipe using a combination of pork and beef.

YIELD: about 2 cups

Seasoning Sachet
1 small carrot, cut into 4 pieces
2 garlic cloves, peeled
1 small onion, quartered
1 fresh thyme sprig
3 fresh sage leaves
1 bay leaf
5 black peppercorns, cracked

1 pound boneless pork shoulder, 1-inch cubed
1/2 pound fresh pork belly, without rind, 1-inch cubed
1 cup dry white wine
1/4 cup water
Salt to taste
Black pepper to taste
Rendered fat to seal (optional)

Wrap the seasoning sachet ingredients in a cheesecloth bag and tie with string.

In a heavy casserole fitted with a lid, combine all the ingredients for the rillette except the salt, pepper, and rendered fat. Add the seasoning sachet and bake the mixture, covered, in a 300°F oven for 4 to 5 hours, until the meat falls apart. Remove the seasoning sachet and drain the meat, reserving the fat. Let the rillette cool overnight.

Shred the meat with two forks or mince it in a food processor using a pulsing action. Do not puree it. Mix in the salt and pepper and as much of the reserved fat as you like.

Pack the rillette into a 2-cup crock and serve it at nearly room temperature. The rillette tastes better after being refrigerated for 24 hours. Covered with a 1/2-inch layer of rendered fat and foil, it keeps, refrigerated, for several months. After opening, use within a week.

Serving Suggestions
Serve as you would any other rillette.

Smoked Chicken Rillette

YIELD: about 1 1/2 cups

10 to 12 ounces smoked chicken fillets, diced
2 garlic cloves, pressed
1/2 cup unsalted butter
1 tablespoon Madeira
1/2 teaspoon Dijon-style mustard
1/8 to 1/4 teaspoon white pepper
Pinch of thyme
Pinch of nutmeg
Salt to taste

Coarsely grind the smoked chicken in a food processor. Add the garlic and butter and blend. Add the remaining ingredients and process until the mixture develops a coarse consistency.

Spoon the rillette into a 2-cup serving bowl and serve slightly chilled. Covered with plastic wrap, this rillette keeps for 5 to 7 days, refrigerated.

Serving Suggestions
Garnish with a bay leaf or fresh herb sprigs. Serve the rillette on crackers or crusty French bread accompanied by cornichons and other pickled vegetables. Smoked Chicken Rillette tastes especially good stuffed into precooked artichoke hearts and served either hot or cold. Serve this rillette as you would any other.

Variations
Substitute smoked turkey, unsmoked but cooked chicken or turkey, or ham with chicken or turkey for the smoked chicken in the recipe.

Add 1 or 2 drained and mashed anchovies.

Omit the mustard and add 1 or 2 tablespoons tomato puree or sauce.

Add 1 or 2 tablespoons duxelles.

Beef Rillon

YIELD: about 2 cups

Seasoning Sachet
1 bay leaf
5 black peppercorns, cracked
5 coriander seeds, cracked

1 pound boneless beef rump, 2-inch cubed
½ pound slab bacon, 1-inch cubed
½ cup red wine or water
1 tablespoon Pâté Seasoning I
2 garlic cloves
Salt to taste (optional, the bacon usually has enough salt)
Black pepper to taste
Rendered fat to seal (optional)

Wrap the seasoning sachet ingredients in a cheesecloth bag and tie with string.

In a heavy casserole fitted with a lid, combine all the ingredients for the rillon except the salt and pepper. Add the seasoning sachet and bake the mixture, covered, in a 250°F oven for 4 hours. Uncover the casserole and continue to bake at 350°F, until the meat is browned and crisp. If you prefer, instead of baking, you can simmer the beef cubes in a covered pot on top of the stove for 4 hours. Raise the heat, uncover the pot, and cook until browned and crisp.

Drain the rillon, sprinkle with salt and pepper, and serve at room temperature or slightly chilled. It keeps for about 3 days, refrigerated.

Note: To store longer (up to several months), pot the rillon as you would a confit. Pour a layer of lard into a sterilized 3-cup crock and chill until firm. Add the drained rillon to within ½ inch of the top, and cover with a ½-inch layer of lard. The next day, seal the filled crock with aluminum foil or a tightly fitting lid. Store in a cool place.

Serving Suggestions

To serve the rillon, melt the fat enough to remove the meat cubes. Heat them quickly in an open pan, drain, and serve. Skewer the meat cubes with toothpicks and set them out with mustard, mayonnaise, horseradish-cheddar spread, or another dip.

Pork Rillon

YIELD: about 3 cups

Seasoning Sachet
2 bay leaves
¼-inch slice fresh ginger
2 fresh thyme sprigs
10 black peppercorns, cracked
2 whole cloves

1 pound fresh leaf lard, 1-inch cubed
2 pounds boneless pork shoulder, 2-inch cubed
½ cup white wine or water
⅛ teaspoon nutmeg
Salt to taste
Black pepper to taste
Rendered fat to seal (optional)

Wrap the seasoning sachet ingredients in a cheesecloth bag and tie with string.

Melt the lard in a heavy casserole. Add all the ingredients for the rillon except the salt and pepper. Add the seasoning sachet and bake the mixture, covered, in a 250°F oven for at least 4 hours. Uncover the casserole and continue to bake at 350°F, until the meat is browned and crisp. If you prefer, instead of baking, you can simmer the pork cubes in a covered pot on top of the stove for about 4 hours. Raise the heat, uncover the pot, and cook until browned and crisp.

Drain the rillon, sprinkle with salt and pepper, and serve at room temperature or slightly chilled. It keeps for about 3 days, refrigerated.

Note: To store longer (up to several months), pot the rillon as you would a confit. Pour a layer of lard into a sterilized 3½-cup crock and chill until firm. Add the drained rillon to within ½ inch of the top and cover with a ½-inch layer of lard. The next day, seal the crock with aluminum foil or a tightly fitting lid. Store in a cool place.

Serving Suggestions
To serve the rillon, melt the fat enough to remove the meat cubes. Heat them quickly in an open pan, drain, and serve. Skewer the meat cubes with toothpicks and set them out with mustard, sweet-and-sour sauce, mayonnaise, Chinese duck sauce, or another dip. Pork Rillon also makes a delicious ingredient in a quiche.

Salmon Rillette

Make this recipe using your favorite variety of smoked salmon. Smoked Scotch salmon enhances the reddish-orange color of the rillette and gives it a pleasantly gamy flavor. Norwegian salmon, delicately streaked with ribbons of fat, produces a paler orange rillette with a light, creamy taste. Atlantic or Nova Scotia salmon makes a mildly smoked, soft rillette, while Pacific smoked salmon (sometimes labeled Pacific Nova Scotia) is fattier, less smoky in flavor, and tastes fishier.

YIELD: about 3½ cups

¾ pound smoked salmon, diced
1 cup unsalted butter
Pinch of cayenne
Pinch of nutmeg
1 teaspoon coriander seeds, dill seeds, or fennel seeds, coarsely ground
1 to 2 tablespoons dry white wine
1 tablespoon lime juice
½ pound poached salmon, flaked (or ¾ pound fresh salmon to be poached in court bouillon)
2 teaspoons finely chopped chives or scallions

Blend the diced smoked salmon, butter, cayenne, nutmeg, coriander, wine, and lime juice in a food processor until smooth. Add the flaked poached salmon and chopped chives. Blend by frequently turning the machine on and off until the mixture attains a coarse texture.

Spoon the rillette into a 3½- to 4-cup decorative bowl and serve at room temperature. Covered with plastic wrap, the rillette keeps for 2 to 4 days, refrigerated.

Serving Suggestions
Serve the rillette with French bread, crackers, or toast and a crock of sour cream, softened cream cheese, or crème fraîche mixed with fresh herbs such as chives, parsley, dill, or coriander. Or spread the mixture onto thin slices of smoked salmon, roll up, and chill. Slice into 3/8-inch pinwheels when ready to serve.

Variations
Add elegance to the rillette by folding in 4 ounces of black or red caviar. In addition to the crock of sour cream, serve a small side dish of grated, hard-cooked eggs.

Smoked Trout Rillette

YIELD: about 3 cups

1½ pounds smoked trout, flaked
1 cup unsalted butter, cut into small pieces
Pinch of nutmeg
1 tablespoon dry sherry
1 tablespoon lemon juice
2 to 4 tablespoons freshly grated horseradish

Blend the smoked trout, butter, and nutmeg in a food processor. Add the sherry and lemon juice and process again. Transfer the trout mixture to a bowl and fold in the horseradish.

Spoon the rillette into a 3-cup decorative bowl and serve slightly chilled. Covered with plastic wrap and refrigerated, this rillette keeps for 3 to 5 days.

Serving Suggestions
Garnish with capers and serve like the Salmon Rillette.

Variations
For a crab or shrimp rillette, substitute 2 cups diced, cooked crab or small shrimp for the smoked trout. Substitute ½ cup whipped heavy cream or crème fraîche for the butter.

Tuna and Watercress Rillette

YIELD: about 2 cups

7 ounces chunk white tuna in oil, drained
1¼ cups mayonnaise
6 ounces cream cheese, softened
2 tablespoons lemon juice
1 teaspoon Dijon-style mustard
¼ to ½ teaspoon black pepper
2 cups watercress leaves
4 scallions, finely chopped
2 tablespoons finely chopped fresh mint
1 to 2 tablespoons capers

Puree the tuna, mayonnaise, cream cheese, lemon juice, mustard, and black pepper in a food processor until smooth. Add the watercress, scallions, mint, and capers. Process by frequently turning the machine on and off and scraping the mixture from the sides of the bowl. Process until the ingredients are well mixed but retain some texture. Spoon the rillette into a 2-cup crock and chill for at least 2 hours before serving. Sealed in plastic wrap and refrigerated, it keeps for about 1 week.

Serving Suggestions
Serve the rillette on an hors d'oeuvre platter or as you would any other rillette.

Shrimp and Scallop Rillon

YIELD: 2½ to 3 cups

¾ cup unsalted butter
½ pound small shrimp, peeled and deveined (20 to 25 shrimp)
½ pound cape scallops
1 to 2 tablespoons lemon juice
Pinch of mace
Pinch of nutmeg
Pinch of cayenne
2 tablespoons chopped fresh dill
Salt to taste
White pepper to taste
Clarified butter to seal (optional)

Slowly melt the butter in a saucepan and add the shrimp, scallops, lemon juice, mace, nutmeg, and cayenne. Stirring occasionally over low heat, allow the shrimp and scallops to cook through. Do not permit the mixture to bubble or the shellfish will toughen. Cool slightly and add the dill, salt, and pepper.

Spoon the rillon into a crock. Sealed with a layer of clarified butter and plastic wrap, it keeps for about 1 week, refrigerated. After opening, use within 2 or 3 days.

Serving Suggestions
Melt the butter in the crock; remove and drain the shrimp and scallops. Serve the shellfish skewered with toothpicks as an hors d'oeuvre. Shrimp

and Scallop Rillon also makes an appetizing garnish for salads, plainly broiled fish fillets, or pasta.

Basic Cheese Rillette

You can make a rillette from any of your favorite cheeses or a combination of them.

YIELD: about 3 cups

1 pound any cheese (soft to hard), diced or crumbled
1/4 to 1/2 cup unsalted butter
2 to 4 tablespoons wine, brandy, or liqueur
Dijon-style mustard
Spices and seasonings to taste
Fresh herbs, chopped

Blend the cheese and butter in a food processor. Use the smaller amount of butter for soft or semi-soft cheeses and the larger amount for hard cheeses. Add more butter if the spread needs to be softer. Add the wine, brandy, or liqueur, a bit of mustard, and the seasonings. Transfer the cheese mixture to a bowl and fold in any fresh herbs.

Spoon the rillette into a 3-cup decorative bowl and serve at room temperature. Most cheese rillettes keep for 1 to 3 weeks, refrigerated.

Serving Suggestions
Cheese Rillette, like most other rillettes, goes well with assorted breads and crackers or can be a dip for crudités or sliced fruit. It makes an inviting spread for a grilled sandwich topped with sliced tomato, zucchini, asparagus, apples and raisins, fish, or meat. Use it to form a crispy crust for casseroles or in place of hard sauce served with apple pie. You might even want to place a dollop of Cheese Rillette and some bread crumbs on clams on a half shell and bake them. Form the rillette in a butter mold to add a fancy touch to a dinner table or buffet.

Variations
For added richness and flavor, substitute a triple crème cheese such as Le Roi and L'Explorateur, or substitute crème fraîche, cream cheese, or Mascarpone for the butter.

Marinate the cheese in wine or cider for 3 to 12 hours before blending it. Add some of the marinade to the mixture.

Lemon zest, freshly grated horseradish, garlic, onion, green peppercorns, caraway, dill, or fennel seeds, capers, nuts, Worcestershire sauce, and anchovy paste are a few of the seasonings you can use.

Gorgonzola Rillette

YIELD: about 3 cups

1 pound Gorgonzola cheese, diced
6 to 8 ounces Mascarpone cheese
½ teaspoon anchovy paste (optional)
4 tablespoons finely julienned fresh basil
4 tablespoons finely julienned scallions
2 to 4 tablespoons chopped, toasted pignoli nuts

Blend the Gorgonzola, Mascarpone, and anchovy paste in a food processor. Transfer the cheese mixture to a bowl and mix in the basil, scallions, and pignoli.

Spoon the rillette into a 3-cup decorative bowl and serve at room temperature. Covered with plastic wrap and refrigerated, this rillette keeps for 7 to 10 days.

Serving Suggestions
Sprinkle the top with a combination of finely chopped pignoli nuts and parsley mixed together.

Cheddar and Walnut Rillette

YIELD: about 3 cups

1 poundCheddar cheese, shredded
½ cup unsalted butter or cream cheese
1 teaspoon mustard
Dash of Worcestershire sauce
4 tablespoons port, Madeira, or cider
¼ to ⅓ cup chopped walnuts

Blend theCheddar, butter, and mustard in a food processor. Add the Worcestershire sauce and wine and blend again. Transfer the cheese mixture to a bowl and fold in the walnuts.

Spoon the rillette into a 3-cup decorative bowl and serve at room temperature. Covered with plastic wrap and refrigerated, this rillette keeps for about 3 weeks (2 weeks if made with cream cheese).

Serving Suggestions
Serve as you would any cheese rillette.

Nutty Rillette

Make a nutty rillette from a single kind of nut or a combination of various nuts.

YIELD: 3⁄4 to 1 cup

1⁄2 pound unsalted nuts (such as almonds, pecans, hazelnuts, cashews, macadamias, or walnuts)
1⁄2 teaspoon molasses
1⁄4 teaspoon tamari soy sauce
1⁄8 cup unsalted butter, cut into small pieces

Roast the skinless nuts on a baking sheet for 10 to 15 minutes in a 400°F oven, shaking them midway. Remove the nuts from the oven and let them cool.

Grind the nuts in a food processor until they form a paste, occasionally scraping them from the sides of the bowl. Add the molasses and soy sauce and process again. Add the butter and blend by frequently turning the machine on and off until all the butter gets mixed in. If necessary, add more butter to form a spreadable paste.

Spoon the rillette into a 1-cup crock and serve at room temperature. Covered with plastic wrap and refrigerated, it keeps for about 1 month. Allow it to reach room temperature before serving, or it will be too hard to spread.

Serving Suggestions
Serve the rillette on crackers topped with a bit of cheese or spread it onto bread with cream cheese or preserves. The rillette also tastes good on sliced smoked turkey, chicken, or ham sandwiches.

Variations
Blend a fruit butter, jam, or preserve into the rillette for added sweetness. Nutty Rillette also makes an appetizing addition to pureed ham, tongue, cooked chicken, or turkey.

Eggplant Tahini Rillette

YIELD: 3½ to 4 cups

2 pounds eggplant (about 2 medium)
½ cup tahini
Juice of 1 lemon
¼ cup unprocessed bran
3 garlic cloves, pressed
2 to 3 tablespoons nutritional yeast (or 1 tablespoon brewers' or torula yeast)
½ to 1 tablespoon cumin
Cayenne to taste
⅓ cup chopped fresh parsley
2 tablespoons chopped fresh coriander
½ medium red onion, minced
3 plum tomatoes, minced

Prick the skins of the eggplants in several places and roast them on a baking sheet at 375°F for about 45 minutes, turning once. The eggplants will be soft and their skins wrinkled when cooked. Allow them to cool until they are easy to handle (about 1 hour).

Scoop the eggplant pulp from the skins and mash it in a bowl with a fork. Mix in the remaining ingredients and blend well.

Spoon the rillette into a 1-quart decorative bowl and serve at room temperature or slightly chilled. Covered with plastic wrap and refrigerated, the rillette keeps for about 1 week.

Serving Suggestions
Serve the rillette with wedges of whole wheat pita, rye, pumpernickel, or French bread or crackers. The rillette makes a tasty stuffing for cherry tomatoes, mushroom caps, celery, and other vegetables. It also makes a flavorful dip for crudités. Garnish the rillette with chopped parsley and slivers of black olives.

Avocado Rillette

YIELD: about 3 cups

2 ripe avocados, mashed
¼ cup sour cream
Juice of 1 lemon
2 tablespoons Vinaigrette Dressing
2 plum tomatoes, minced
1 small red onion, minced
2 tablespoons unprocessed bran
2 tablespoons chopped fresh coriander
2 garlic cloves, pressed
1 fresh or canned serrano chili, seeded and minced (or 1 tablespoon Chili Spice)
1 teaspoon mustard
Black pepper to taste
Salt to taste

Combine the mashed avocados, sour cream, lemon juice, and vinaigrette. Add the remaining ingredients and mix well.

Spoon the rillette into a 3-cup decorative bowl and serve slightly chilled. To retard discoloration, place the avocado pits on the rillette until ready to serve. Covered with plastic and refrigerated, the rillette keeps for 3 to 4 days.

Serving Suggestions
Avocado Rillette tastes especially good served with tortilla or corn chips. It makes an excellent sandwich—stuffed into pita bread with lettuce, alfalfa sprouts, and sliced tomatoes. Serve it as you would Eggplant Tahini Rillette. Sprinkle it with a garnish of chopped coriander leaves and minced tomatoes and red onions.

Variations
Substitute mayonnaise, yogurt, crème fraîche, or Mascarpone for the sour cream.

Avocado blends well with seafood. Add 1/4 cup smoked salmon or trout bits (1/4-inch diced) or shellfish such as cooked titi shrimp.

Dessert Rillette

YIELD: 3 to 3½ cups

2/3 cup honey
1 cup peanut butter
2 teaspoons molasses
1 teaspoon vanilla extract
1/2 cup wheat germ
1/2 cup dry milk
1/4 cup unprocessed bran
1/4 cup ground sunflower seeds
2 tablespoons carob powder (unsweetened)
2 tablespoons unsweetened shredded coconut

Blend the honey, peanut butter, molasses, and vanilla together in a bowl. Add the remaining ingredients and mix well. If the consistency is too firm, add equal amounts of honey and peanut butter, starting with a tablespoon of each until the mixture is thick but spreadable.

Spoon the rillette into a 3½-cup decorative bowl and serve at room temperature. Covered with plastic wrap, this rillette keeps for about 2 weeks without refrigeration, longer if refrigerated. Allow it to reach room temperature before serving, or it will be too hard to spread.

Serving Suggestions
Garnish the rillette with a sprinkling of coconut and serve it with sweet crackers, cookies, or sliced fruits such as pears or apples. You can even

sandwich the rillette between two cookies, Oreo style. Form the rillette into small balls (about the size of a marble or walnut) and roll them in shredded coconut or carob powder to serve as a dessert, or crumble it to make an unusual topping for cheesecake, ice cream, or fruit salad.

CHAPTER SIX

Condiments and Accompaniments

This chapter contains many of the recipes for sauces, relishes, chutneys, and dressings suggested throughout the book, as well as some recipes not previously mentioned.

VEGETABLE RELISHES AND SAUCES

Apple Herb Sauerkraut

YIELD: about 1⅔ quarts

2 tablespoons bacon fat
½ pound onions, sliced
½ pound unpeeled apples, cored and sliced
2 pounds sauerkraut
½ cup white wine
½ cup Chicken Stock
1½ teaspoons caraway seeds
4 juniper berries
1 bay leaf
1 whole clove
Black pepper to taste

Sauté the onions and apples in hot bacon fat. Add the remaining ingredients and simmer until most of the liquid evaporates. Remove the juniper berries, bay leaf, and clove. Serve warm or chilled.

Cabbage Pear Relish

YIELD: about 5 cups

2/3 pound white cabbage, shredded
1 unpeeled firm pear, cored, 3/16-inch julienned
1/3 cup chopped unsalted pistachios, cashews, walnuts, or pecans
1/2 to 3/4 cup heavy cream
2 tablespoons Dijon-style mustard
Cayenne to taste
Salt to taste

Combine all the ingredients and toss well. Chill.

Braised Red-Cabbage Relish

Serve this relish with pork dishes.

YIELD: about 1 quart

Marinade
5 cups red cabbage, shredded
3 tablespoons red wine
1 1/2 teaspoons sugar
Pinch of salt

1 tablespoon bacon fat or vegetable oil
1/4 pound onions, thinly sliced
1/4 pound unpeeled apples, cored and julienned
1/8 teaspoon thyme
1 bay leaf
1 cup Chicken Stock
Salt to taste
Black pepper to taste

Combine the ingredients for the marinade and marinate the cabbage overnight. Sauté the onions, apples, thyme, and bay leaf in bacon fat. When tender, add the marinated cabbage and stock. Simmer for 20 to 30 minutes, until tender, then season with salt and pepper. Serve warm or chilled.

Dal

YIELD: about 3 cups

1 1/8 cups red lentils (masoor), hulled and split
3 3/4 cups water
2 garlic cloves, chopped
1 1/2 slices fresh ginger (1/8-inch thick)
2 1/4 teaspoons turmeric
1/8 to 1/4 teaspoon cayenne
1 1/8 teaspoons salt
1 1/8 teaspoons lemon juice
2 teaspoons chopped fresh coriander
1 teaspoon chopped fresh parsley
2 1/4 tablespoons clarified butter or olive oil
3/4 teaspoon cumin seeds
Pinch of asafoetida (an Indian spice) (optional)

Wash the lentils and remove any grit. Bring them to a boil in 3 3/4 cups water. Remove the scum that accumulates on the surface. Add the garlic, ginger, turmeric, and cayenne. Reduce the heat and simmer the dal, partially covered, for about 1 hour, stirring occasionally. The dal is cooked when it is thicker than pea soup but thinner than oatmeal. Add the salt, lemon juice, coriander, and parsley.

Heat the clarified butter or oil. Add the cumin seeds and asafoetida powder. In a few seconds, when the asafoetida sizzles and the cumin seeds darken, pour them over the lentils. Serve the dal warm.

Herbed Lentils

Toss cooked but firm, warm lentils in Vinaigrette Dressing with lots of fresh chopped herbs such as parsley, scallions, dill, basil, and tarragon.

Lentils with Sorrel and Red Onions

Toss cooked but firm, warm lentils with Vinaigrette Dressing, lots of finely diced red onions, and fresh chopped sorrel.

Artichoke Dip

YIELD: about 2 cups

9 ounces (1½ jars) marinated artichokes
2 tablespoons minced onion
2 garlic cloves
1 teaspoon lemon juice
Pinch of Chili Seasoning
Dash of cayenne
1 cup sour cream, yogurt, or crème fraîche

Puree all the ingredients except the sour cream in a food processor. Stir in the sour cream. Chill.

Middle Eastern Sauce

This sauce goes well with fresh vegetables and with lamb.

YIELD: about 3½ cups

1 tablespoon tahini
2 garlic cloves, minced or pressed
⅓ teaspoon white pepper
¼ teaspoon sweet paprika
1½ teaspoons white or cider vinegar
¼ cup vegetable oil
½ teaspoon salt
2 cucumbers, peeled, seeded, grated, and drained
1 pound thick yogurt

Using a mixer on medium speed, blend all the ingredients except the yogurt. Beat in the yogurt until the sauce is creamy. When possible, refrigerate the sauce overnight in order to develop its flavor. Securely covered and refrigerated, it keeps for about 5 days.

Carrot Tahini Dressing

YIELD: about 2½ cups

4 to 5 carrots, finely shredded or grated
1 small onion, julienned
2 to 3 garlic cloves
3 tablespoons vinegar
2 tablespoons tahini
1⅓ tablespoons honey
½ teaspoon grated fresh ginger
¼ teaspoon soy sauce
½ cup vegetable oil
2 tablespoons chopped fresh parsley or basil
Black pepper to taste

Puree the carrots, onion, and garlic in a food processor. Add the vinegar, tahini, honey, ginger, and soy sauce. With the machine running, gradually pour in the oil. Mix in the parsley and pepper. Chill.

Creole Sauce with Okra

Creole Sauce tastes good with poultry, pork, fish, and even vegetable preparations.

YIELD: about 1 quart

1 tablespoon bacon fat
1 cup finely diced onions
½ cup finely diced green bell pepper
½ cup thinly sliced okra
½ cup thinly sliced celery
2 garlic cloves, minced
¾ to 1 teaspoon chopped, seeded jalapeño pepper, fresh or canned
1 bay leaf
¼ teaspoon thyme
1 25-ounce can peeled plum tomatoes with juice, roughly chopped
Salt to taste
Black pepper to taste
2 tablespoons brown roux (optional)

Sauté the onions in hot bacon fat. When translucent, add the green pepper, okra, celery, garlic, jalapeño, bay leaf, and thyme. Sauté until crisply cooked, then add the tomatoes, salt, and pepper. Simmer 10 minutes. Whisk in the roux to thicken the sauce slightly.

Tomato Chutney

YIELD: about 3 cups

8 garlic cloves
½ cup finely chopped crystallized ginger
1½ cups red wine vinegar
1 35-ounce can plum tomatoes, with juice
1 small onion, finely diced
1½ cups packed brown sugar
1 teaspoon salt
¼ teaspoon red pepper flakes
¼ teaspoon cinnamon
½ cup toasted pignoli nuts
½ cup golden raisins

Puree the garlic, ginger, and ½ cup vinegar in a food processor. Over medium heat, bring the pureed mixture, remaining vinegar, tomatoes with their juice, onion, brown sugar, salt, red pepper flakes, and cinnamon to a boil. Reduce the heat and simmer for about 2 hours, until the chutney thickens. Stir in the nuts and raisins and simmer for another 5 minutes. Chill.

Tomato Concasse

Ripe tomatoes, peeled and seeded
Olive oil
Salt
Black pepper

Finely dice the tomatoes. Mix them with the smallest amount of olive oil, just enough to barely coat. Season with salt and pepper.

Tomato Coriander Sauce

This sauce has a refreshing, perky flavor and makes a good accompaniment to fish or vegetable dishes.

YIELD: 2½ cups

1½ cups peeled, seeded, and chopped ripe tomatoes with their juice
½ Spanish onion, finely chopped
¼ to ½ cucumber, seeded and finely chopped
1 garlic clove, minced
¼ fresh or canned jalapeño pepper, seeded and minced
2 tablespoons red wine vinegar
1 tablespoon chopped fresh basil
¾ teaspoon oregano
1 tablespoon olive oil
Salt to taste
Black pepper to taste

Combine all the ingredients and mix well. Serve chilled.

Tomato Herb Coulis

This tangy sauce, fragrant with herbs, goes well with hot and cold vegetable or seafood preparations.

YIELD: about 2 cups

1 1-pound can crushed tomatoes
2 tablespoons red wine vinegar
1 tablespoon olive oil
1 garlic clove, minced or pressed
⅓ teaspoon salt
⅓ teaspoon vegetable salt (Spike brand)
2 tablespoons chopped fresh basil
2 tablespoons chopped fresh coriander
1 tablespoon chopped fresh parsley
1 tablespoon chopped fresh dill
Freshly grated black pepper
Pinch of cayenne

Combine all the ingredients and mix well. Adjust the seasonings to taste.

Tomato Dill Sauce

For variation, substitute basil for dill. This recipe makes a good sauce for poultry, fish, and vegetable pâtés and terrines.

YIELD: about 2 cups

1¼ cups peeled, seeded, and chopped ripe tomatoes with their juice
3 tablespoons red wine vinegar
3 tablespoons olive oil
1 teaspoon tomato puree
1 garlic clove, pressed
½ bunch fresh dill, chopped
Salt to taste
Black pepper to taste

Mix all the ingredients together. Serve chilled.

Watercress Sauce

YIELD: about 2½ cups

1 cup tightly packed watercress leaves
3 anchovy fillets, rinsed and dried
⅓ cup chopped scallions or chives
1 tablespoon chopped fresh parsley
3 tablespoons lemon juice
2 tablespoons olive oil
½ teaspoon salt
¼ teaspoon black pepper
¼ teaspoon nutmeg
1 cup mayonnaise
½ cup sour cream or yogurt

Puree all the ingredients in a food processor except the mayonnaise and sour cream. Stir in the remaining ingredients. Chill.

FRUIT AND SWEET SAUCES

Chestnut Sauce

Good with venison and other game dishes.

YIELD: about 3 cups

1½ cups chestnut puree
⅓ cup Chicken or Vegetable Stock
1 tablespoon Frangelico or amaretto liqueur
1 to 2 teaspoons honey
Pinch of pepper
Pinch of salt
¾ to 1 cup heavy cream

Blend all the ingredients except the heavy cream in a food processor. With the machine running, slowly pour in half the heavy cream. Stir in the remaining cream until the mixture reaches a smooth, thick consistency. Serve the puree warm or at room temperature.

Apple Mint Sauce

Serve this sauce with lamb, pork, or poultry.

YIELD: about 3 cups

1 pound unpeeled Granny Smith apples, cored and thinly sliced
1/4 cup water
2 tablespoons lemon juice
Pinch of cinnamon
Honey to taste
2 tablespoons chopped fresh mint

Simmer the apples, water, lemon juice, and cinnamon over low heat for 15 minutes, until the apples become tender. Puree the apple mixture and honey in a food processor. Stir in the chopped mint. Serve warm or chilled.

Apple Chutney

You can substitute quince for the apples.

YIELD: about 1 quart

1 pound unpeeled cooking apples, cored and sliced
1 Spanish onion, sliced
1 1/2 cups raisins
2 2/3 cups cider vinegar
2 cups honey
2 2/3 tablespoons minced fresh ginger
2 tablespoons lemon juice
1 large garlic clove, minced
2 teaspoons sweet paprika
3/4 teaspoon salt
1/2 teaspoon cinnamon
1/4 teaspoon mace
1/8 teaspoon cloves
1/8 teaspoon cayenne
1/2 pound unpeeled cooking apples, cored and sliced

Combine all the ingredients except the last 1/2 pound of apples and bring to a boil. Simmer for 40 to 45 minutes. Add the remaining apples and simmer for another 15 minutes, or until quite thick. Chill.

No-Cook Apple Chutney

YIELD: about 5½ cups

1 pound cooking apples, cored and grated with peel
2 tablespoons lemon juice mixed with 2 tablespoons water
½ pound white onions, grated
¾ cup golden raisins
1 green bell pepper, finely diced
2 tablespoons finely diced pimiento
⅓ cup finely diced pitted dates
3 tablespoons finely chopped crystallized ginger
2 tablespoons cider vinegar
1 teaspoon honey
1 teaspoon salt
¼ teaspoon cardamom

Toss the grated apples in the lemon water. Drain and discard the liquid. Combine the apples with the remaining ingredients and mix well. Chill. Marinate the chutney at least overnight.

Dried-Fruit Compote

This compote goes well with duck.

YIELD: about 1 quart

1 pound mixed dried fruits (such as apricots, prunes, figs, peaches, pears, apples, raisins)
Zest of 1 lemon, julienned
1 tablespoon lemon juice
1 cinnamon stick
2 whole cloves
2 cups water

Combine all the ingredients and soak overnight. Bring the compote to a boil and simmer for about 20 minutes, or until the fruit becomes tender. Add more water if necessary. Serve warm or cold.

Orange Poached Plums

YIELD: about 2 cups

Juice of 1 orange
½ orange, peeled and diced
Zest of ¼ orange, julienned
½ pound Victoria plums, halved and pitted
2 tablespoons honey
1 cinnamon stick
2 cloves

Combine all the ingredients in a casserole dish. Bake in a 350°F oven for about 15 minutes, or until the plums become tender. Serve warm or chilled.

Orange Cranberry Relish

YIELD: about 1 quart

1 large orange
1 pound fresh cranberries
1⅛ cups sugar
3¼ ounces frozen orange juice concentrate
3¼ ounces water

Julienne and blanch the zest from the orange. Remove and discard the rind and dice the flesh. In a saucepan combine the zest and diced orange with the remaining ingredients. Simmer for 15 to 30 minutes, stirring occasionally, until the cranberries burst. Chill.

Spicy Orange Relish

This relish goes well with shrimp.

YIELD: about 3 cups

3 cups orange marmalade
2 ounces prepared horseradish
1⅓ ounces dry sherry

Puree all the ingredients in a food processor. Chill.

Peach Chutney

Peach chutney tastes good with tongue, ham, and poultry.

YIELD: about 2 cups

1½ cups dried peaches, softened and plumped in water
1 small onion, diced
1 garlic clove, minced
2 tablespoons orange juice
¼ cup cider vinegar
¼ cup water
⅔ cup sugar
⅛ teaspoon cinnamon
⅛ teaspoon allspice
Pinch of cloves

Bring the peaches, onion, garlic, orange juice, vinegar, and water to a boil. Reduce the heat and simmer for 10 to 15 minutes, stirring occasionally. Add the remaining ingredients and simmer until thickened, stirring continuously for about 15 minutes. Serve warm or cold.

Peach Brandy Sauce

YIELD: about 1½ cups

⅔ cup peach brandy
¼ cup strained lemon juice
½ to ¾ teaspoon ginger
½ to ⅔ cup honey
2 tablespoons chopped fresh mint

Combine all the ingredients and blend well.

Variations
Substitute cherry or apricot brandy for the peach brandy and rename the sauce appropriately.

Spiced Brandied Peaches

YIELD: About 2½ cups

Juice of 2 oranges
Zest of 1 orange, julienned
2 tablespoons red-currant jelly
1 cinnamon stick
2 whole cloves
¼ cup peach brandy
Pinch of allspice
4 large peaches, peeled, pitted, and cut into ¼-inch-thick wedges

Gently over low heat, bring the orange juice and zest, the jelly, cinnamon, cloves, brandy, and allspice to a boil. Place the peach wedges in a casserole dish and pour the heated ingredients over them. Bake in a preheated 350°F oven for about 10 minutes, basting occasionally.

Raspberries and Peaches in Wine

YIELD: about 1 quart

1 pound raspberries, hulled
2 peaches, peeled, pitted, and thinly sliced
1 cup white wine
Honey to taste
Pinch of cinnamon

Mix all the ingredients together and chill for at least 2 hours. Puree ½ cup of the fruit and stir it back into the mixture.

Cumberland Sauce

This is a typically British sauce that goes well with meats.

YIELD: about 2 cups

3/4 cup port wine
1 1/2 tablespoons mixed orange and lemon zest, julienned and blanched
3/4 cup red-currant jelly
Juice of 1/2 orange and 1/2 lemon
1 1/2 teaspoons chopped shallots, blanched
1 1/2 teaspoons Dijon-style mustard
3/4 teaspoon grated fresh ginger
1/8 teaspoon cayenne

Bring the port wine to a boil, then reduce the heat. Add the remaining ingredients and simmer until the jelly completely dissolves. Serve the sauce warm or chilled.

Brandied Lemon Sauce

For desserts, serve this sauce at room temperature or slightly warmed.

YIELD: about 1 2/3 cups

2/3 cup Cognac
2/3 cup honey
1/3 cup fresh lemon juice
1/2 to 1 teaspoon ginger
Pinch of allspice

Combine the ingredients and blend well.

Spiced Raisins in Wine

Serve this raisin sauce with pork, ham, or game.

YIELD: about 2 cups

3/4 cup mixed dark and golden raisins
1 cup red wine
1/2 cup water
2 whole cloves
1 cinnamon stick
1/8 teaspoon allspice
2 tablespoons lemon juice
2 tablespoons brown sugar
2 teaspoons cornstarch

In a saucepan, bring to a boil the raisins, wine, water, cloves, cinnamon, and allspice. Cover and gently simmer for 10 minutes. Remove the cloves and cinnamon stick.

Separately blend the lemon juice, brown sugar, and cornstarch. Return the raisin sauce to a boil and stir in the sugar mixture until the liquid thickens. Serve warm or chilled.

Pickled Cherries

YIELD: 1 quart

2/3 cup red wine vinegar
2/3 cup packed brown sugar
1 1/3 cups hot water
1 1/2 pounds sour cherries, pitted, stems removed
1 cinnamon stick
2 whole cloves

Over medium heat, bring the vinegar and sugar to a boil. Cook for about 10 minutes, or until the sugar starts to carmelize. Carefully, avoiding splatters, stir the hot water into the sugar syrup. Return to the boil and add the cherries, cinnamon, and cloves. Boil for 30 seconds, then remove from the heat. Serve warm or at room temperature.

Black Bing Cherry Sauce

YIELD: about 2 1/2 cups

1 17-ounce can pitted black bing cherries
1/4 cup red wine
3 tablespoons minced shallots
1 1/2 cups brown gravy or Bordelaise sauce
Pinch of sugar, if necessary
Salt to taste
Black pepper to taste

Strain the juice from the cherries into a saucepan with the red wine and shallots. Reduce the liquid by about a third. Add the brown gravy and bring to a boil. Stir in the cherries and season. Serve warm.

Berry Sauce

This sauce goes well with hot or cold desserts, as well as with some meat dishes such as duck terrine. You can use most any berry or a combination of berries in this recipe. Because blueberries tend to recongeal after pureed, add a bit more lemon juice if you use them.

YIELD: about 3 cups

1 quart whole berries, rinsed, stemmed and pureed
Honey to taste
Juice of 1/2 lemon or lime
1 teaspoon grated lemon or lime zest

Combine all the ingredients and blend well. Chill before serving.

Variations
Add a dash of liqueur.

For a sweet-and-sour flavor substitute 2 tablespoons vinegar in place of the lemon juice.

Fruit Sauce

YIELD: about 2 cups

1 cup pomegranate juice
1 1/4 teaspoons red-currant jelly
3/4 cup sliced strawberries
3/4 cup diced cantaloupe
3/4 cup diced pineapple
8 teaspoons Grand Marnier
Juice of 1/2 lemon
Cinnamon to taste

Heat the pomegranate juice and currant jelly until boiling. Quickly blanch the fruit in the boiling liquid. Remove the fruit and reduce the juice by about half. Puree the fruit and reduced juice in a food processor. Stir in the Grand Marnier, lemon juice, and cinnamon. Chill.

Gooseberry Almond Sauce

This is a good sauce to serve with duck, goose, pork, or oily fish such as mackerel, trout, or eel.

YIELD: about 1 1/2 cups

1/2 pound gooseberries, hulled
1 cup water
2 tablespoons butter
2 ounces blanched almonds, chopped
1 tablespoon flour
1/8 teaspoon allspice
Salt to taste
White pepper to taste

Bring gooseberries and water to a boil. Reduce the heat and simmer for 5 minutes, until the berries are tender. Puree the gooseberries, then press them through a sieve.

Sauté the almonds in butter until they turn golden brown. Stir in the flour and simmer for 2 or 3 minutes. Add the puree, stirring constantly until the sauce boils and thickens. Simmer for 2 more minutes. Season with allspice, salt, and pepper. Serve hot or cold.

Persimmon Sauce

YIELD: about 2 cups

2 cups persimmon puree
Juice of 1/2 lemon (or less, according to taste)
2 tablespoons honey
1 to 2 tablespoons chopped fresh mint
1/2 teaspoon cinnamon
1/4 teaspoon vanilla extract

Combine all the ingredients. Gently heat and serve warm or at room temperature.

Four-Pepper Mignonette Sauce

This sauce develops its best flavor after 2 to 3 days.

YIELD: about 1 1/2 cups

1 cup malt vinegar
1/4 cup chopped shallots
2 tablespoons white wine
1/4 cup mixed cracked peppercorns, such as green, black, white, and red
1/4 teaspoon allspice
1/2 teaspoon salt
1/2 teaspoon honey or sugar

Combine all the ingredients and mix well.

Curried Fruit Sauce

YIELD: about 1¾ cups

1¼ cups Chicken or White Stock
4 teaspoons mango chutney, chopped
1 garlic clove, pressed
¾ to 1 tablespoon curry powder
⅛ teaspoon cumin
⅛ teaspoon turmeric
⅛ teaspoon white pepper
Pinch of cloves
2 tablespoons white wine
½ cup dried fruit (raisins, chopped apples, or apricots)
1 tablespoon cornstarch mixed with 2 tablespoons cold water

Bring the stock to a boil. Add the chutney, spices, wine, and dried fruit. Return to a boil. Stir in the cornstarch paste to thicken. Serve warm.

HERB SAUCES

Pesto Sauce

YIELD: about 2¼ cups

2½ garlic cloves, peeled
2½ cups fresh young basil leaves
1¼ tablespoons pignoli nuts, toasted
Pinch of coarse salt
1¼ to 1⅔ tablespoons grated Parmesan cheese
1¼ to 1⅔ tablespoons grated Pecorino cheese
1 cup olive oil

Grind the garlic, basil, nuts, and salt in a food processor until they reach the consistency of a coarse paste. Gradually add the cheese. Stir in the olive oil. Serve at room temperature.

Variations
Substitute ¾ cup fresh parsley leaves for ¾ cup of basil leaves.

Creamy Basil Sauce

This recipe perks up any vegetable preparation.

YIELD: about 2½ cups

1½ cups vegetable oil
½ to ¾ cup chopped fresh basil
¼ cup red wine vinegar
¼ cup sour cream, yogurt, or mayonnaise
2 shallots, minced
½ teaspoon black pepper
Salt to taste

Puree the oil, basil, and vinegar in a food processor. With the machine running, add the sour cream and shallots. Season with pepper and salt. Chill.

Variations
Substitute parsley for the basil and rename the sauce appropriately.

Caper Dill Sauce

This dressing makes a good accompaniment to steak tartare or even seafood, and it stores well in the refrigerator.

YIELD: about 3¾ cups

1½ cups vegetable oil
¾ to 1 cup cider vinegar
1 cup drained capers, chopped
¼ cup minced shallots
¼ cup chopped fresh parsley
¼ cup chopped fresh dill
Pinch of sugar

Mix all the ingredients well. Stir before serving.

Chive Sauce

This sauce accentuates the taste of fish or vegetable dishes. It must be served warm.

YIELD: about 2 cups

1/4 cup dry white wine
2 tablespoons minced shallots
1 1/2 cups heavy cream
4 teaspoons Chicken Stock
1 tablespoon pureed watercress
3 tablespoons cold water
2 tablespoons finely chopped fresh chives
6 tablespoons unsalted butter
1 tablespoon lemon juice
1/8 teaspoon allspice
Salt to taste
White pepper to taste

Reduce the white wine and shallots over high heat until all the wine evaporates and the shallots are just moist. Add the heavy cream and stock. Boil, uncovered, until the liquid thickens and is reduced by a third.

Puree the watercress, water, chives, and butter in a food processor. Add the shallot-cream mixture, lemon juice, and allspice. Season with salt and pepper and serve warm.

Variations
Substitute scallions, dill, fennel tops, or tarragon for the chives and rename the sauce appropriately.

Sherry Herb Sauce

This creamy sauce combines the freshness of lemon and dill with a hint of sherry.

YIELD: about 2 1/2 cups

2 cups mayonnaise
2 to 3 tablespoons lemon juice
3 tablespoons chopped fresh parsley
3 tablespoons chopped fresh dill
3 to 4 tablespoons cream sherry

Mix all the ingredients together except the sherry. Depending on the consistency and flavor you desire, add 3 or 4 tablespoons sherry to the sauce.

MAYONNAISE, MUSTARD, AND OTHER SAUCES

Lemon Mayonnaise

Although classic mayonnaise recipes call for egg yolks, you may use whole eggs when preparing it in a food processor or electric mixer. I prefer this method because the addition of the egg white makes a lighter-textured mayonnaise with more nutritional value.

YIELD: about 2 cups

1 whole egg
1½ teaspoons Dijon-style mustard
¾ teaspoon salt
¼ teaspoon white pepper
½ teaspoon Aromat (if unavailable, increase salt to 1 teaspoon)
1 tablespoon cider vinegar
1½ cups oil (half vegetable/half olive oil)
2 tablespoons lemon juice

Blend the eggs and mustard in a food processor until the mixture thickens and turns pale yellow. Quickly add the salt, pepper,Aromat, and vinegar. With the machine running, slowly pour in the oil in a thin, steady stream. As the mayonnaise emulsifies, add the lemon juice. Adjust the seasonings to taste. This mayonnaise keeps for about a week, refrigerated in a covered container.

Rustic Sauce

YIELD: about 1¼ cups

1 garlic clove
2 hard-cooked egg yolks
2 anchovy fillets
1½ teaspoons tomato paste
1 cup mayonnaise
1½ tablespoons lemon juice
¼ to ½ teaspoon Tabasco sauce
Pinch of saffron

Puree the garlic, egg yolks, anchovies, and tomato paste in a food processor. Add the mayonnaise. Combine the lemon juice, Tabasco, and saffron and add to the sauce. Blend well. Chill.

Remoulade Sauce

YIELD: about 1¼ cups

1 cup mayonnaise or Lemon Mayonnaise
1½ teaspoons Dijon-style mustard
1½ teaspoons finely diced gherkin pickles
1½ teaspoons chopped capers
1½ teaspoons chopped fresh herbs (parsley, chervil, and tarragon)
1 teaspoon chopped fresh dill
½ teaspoon anchovy paste

Combine all the ingredients and mix well.

Radish Remoulade

YIELD: about 2 cups

1 pound radishes, finely julienned or grated
½ cup white wine vinegar
1½ tablespoons Dijon-style mustard
1 teaspoon caraway seeds
Pinch of salt
½ cup Remoulade Sauce

Marinate the radishes in the vinegar, mustard, caraway seeds, and salt for 2 hours, refrigerated. Drain the radishes and discard the liquid. Toss the radishes with the Remoulade Sauce. Serve chilled.

Horseradish Sauce

YIELD: about 2 cups

1 cup heavy cream, whipped to soft peaks
4 tablespoons fresh bread crumbs
2 to 4 tablespoons grated fresh horseradish or drained prepared horseradish
1⅓ tablespoons Dijon-style mustard
1 tablespoon minced fresh chives
¼ teaspoon nutmeg
Dash cayenne
White pepper to taste
Salt to taste

Mix the ingredients together. Cover and chill for at least 1 hour before serving. Serve chilled.

Mustard Horseradish Sauce

YIELD: about 1¼ cups

1 cup mayonnaise
¼ cup Dijon-style mustard
2 tablespoons grated fresh horseradish
Black pepper to taste

Combine all the ingredients and mix well. Serve chilled.

Mustard Sauce

YIELD: 1½ cups

¼ cup Dijon-style mustard
¼ cup dry English mustard
1 cup Vinaigrette Dressing

Make a paste of the mustards. Slowly whisk in the vinaigrette dressing to form an emulsion. Chill.

Creamy Mustard Sauce

YIELD: about 3 cups

1 cup heavy cream, whipped
½ cup mayonnaise
¼ to ⅓ cup Dijon-style mustard
1 tablespoon prepared horseradish
1 tablespoon chopped capers
1 tablespoon lemon juice
¼ teaspoon salt
¼ teaspoon white pepper

Mix the whipped cream and mayonnaise together. Add the mustard, horseradish, capers, and lemon juice. Season with salt and pepper. Chill.

Mustard Herb Sauce

A good accompaniment for hot or cold poultry and beef dishes.

YIELD: about 3 cups

5 hard-cooked egg yolks, mashed
½ cup Dijon-style mustard
6 tablespoons red wine vinegar
1¼ to 1½ cups vegetable oil
White pepper to taste
5 hard-cooked egg whites, sieved or finely minced
2 tablespoons minced shallots
1 tablespoon chopped fresh dill
1 tablespoon chopped fresh basil
1 tablespoon chopped fresh coriander

Completely blend the egg yolks, mustard, and vinegar in a bowl. In a slow, steady stream, pour in the oil, constantly whipping it as you would in making mayonnaise. When the mixture emulsifies, add the remaining ingredients. Chill.

Piquant Mustard Dill

This sauce, which is traditionally served with *gravad lax,* also goes well with other fish.

YIELD: about 1 cup

1 small garlic clove, minced or pressed
4 tablespoons Dijon-style mustard
2 tablespoons sugar or 1 tablespoon honey
¼ to ½ teaspoon white pepper
Pinch of salt
2½ tablespoons red wine vinegar
6 tablespoons vegetable oil
5 tablespoons finely chopped fresh dill

Blend all the ingredients together except the oil and dill. Slowly whip in the oil as you would for mayonnaise. Stir in the dill. Chill.

Vinaigrette Dressing

YIELD: about 1 cup

½ cup olive oil
¼ cup cider vinegar
2 shallots, minced
1 small garlic clove, pressed
½ teaspoon Dijon-style mustard
1 tablespoon chopped fresh parsley
1 tablespoon finely chopped dill pickles
1 teaspoon finely chopped capers
Black pepper to taste

Whisk all the ingredients together. Chill.

Variations
Substitute ⅓ cup lime juice for the vinegar to make a Lime Vinaigrette Dressing.

Velouté Sauce

For a fish velouté, substitute fish stock for the meat stock.

YIELD: about 2 cups

2 tablespoons unsalted butter
2 tablespoons all-purpose flour
2 cups gelatinous Chicken or White Stock
Pinch of nutmeg
Salt to taste
White pepper to taste

Melt the butter and stir in the flour to make a roux. When it stops foaming, pour in all the stock. Whisk the sauce until it comes to a boil. With the pan half off the burner, slowly simmer the sauce for 20 to 30 minutes. Season to taste. Serve hot.

Lemon Herb Butter Sauce

This delicate sauce, which is perfect for fish, must be served warm.

YIELD: about 1 cup

1 cup dry white wine
1½ tablespoons minced shallots
1 tablespoon finely chopped fresh parsley
1 teaspoon finely chopped fresh tarragon
1 teaspoon fennel seeds, crushed
¼ teaspoon fresh thyme leaves
3 fresh basil leaves, chopped
½ teaspoon drained green peppercorns, crushed
Pinch of salt
1¼ cups unsalted butter, cut into walnut-size pieces
Juice of 1 lemon

Combine and heat all the ingredients except the butter and lemon juice. Reduce the liquid until almost all the wine evaporates and the ingredients form a paste. Press the paste through a fine sieve to extract about 2 tablespoons of juice.

Over low heat, combine the extracted juice with four pieces of butter. Slowly, whisk the remaining butter, piece by piece, into the sauce, adding a few drops of lemon juice each time until all the ingredients are used. The sauce will be a little thicker than heavy cream.

GLOSSARY

ACIDULATED WATER: Cold water with vinegar, lemon, or lime juice added in a small quantity. Dip fruits and vegetables into this water to keep them from discoloring.

ASPIC: Meat, fish, vegetable, or fruit jelly.

BALLOTINES: Traditionally consisted of meat, boned, stuffed, and rolled into a "ballot" or bundle. Ballotines usually are braised and served hot, although they also may be served cold.

BOUCHÉES: Miniature puff pastry shells—originally, small enough to be consumed in one bite.

BOUDIN: Finely textured, creamy pudding sausage.

BOULETTES: Bullet-shaped faggots or gayettes, usually made from leftover meat or fish.

CAUL FAT: A lacy fat membrane surrounding the paunch and intestines of an animal. Used as a casing for meats and fish.

CHARCUTERIE: Traditionally, cooked meat products, particularly pork. In this book the word represents a method of cooking and a manner of serving food. Also a store that sells charcuterie.

CHARCUTIER: A person who prepares charcuterie.

CHAUD-FROID: From the French *chaud,* meaning warm, and *froid,* meaning cold. A sauce or dish prepared warm and eaten cold.

CONFIT: Traditionally consisted of meat slowly cooked in rendered fat and potted in a fat-sealed crock to preserve it.

CRÉPINETTE: Small patty-shaped parcels of meat or fish, wrapped in caul fat and baked, grilled, or fried.

DARIOLE MOLDS: Smooth-sided cylindrical molds usually holding 4 to 8 ounces.

DUXELLES: A sauté of minced mushrooms, shallots, and seasonings.

FAGGOT: The English word describing small, round crépinettes, usually eaten hot.

FARCE: Ground, chopped, or pureed stuffing with which to fill pâtés, terrines, sausages, galantines, ballotines, or other meat or fish. Synonym for *forcemeat.*

FATBACK: Thick, solid strips of white fat from the back of a pig. Thinly slice fatback to line pâtés and terrines.

FINE HERBS: A mixture of parsley, chervil, tarragon, and chives.

FORCEMEAT: Ground, chopped, or pureed stuffing with which to fill pâtés, terrines, sausages, galantines, ballotines, or other meat or fish. Synonym for *farce.*

GALANTINE: Traditionally, a cold dish made of boned, stuffed, and poached chicken. Today it includes other meats, fish, vegetables, and fruits.

GARDE MANGER: A chef specializing in preparation of cold dishes, especially pâtés, buffet items, and decorations such as ice carvings.

GARNITURE: In this book it refers to the whole or diced food garnish mixed into a farce or other preparation. For example, pistachios and mushrooms may be used as garnitures mixed into a pâté.

GAYETTES: The French word describing faggots—small, round crépinettes, usually sliced and eaten cold.

GLAZE: A stock or gravy reduced to a syrupy-thick consistency. Or, to coat a food, for instance, to glaze a terrine with aspic.

HERB BOUQUET (*bouquet garni*): A bunch of herbs and spices often tied in cheesecloth or muslin so that they are easily removed. The exact contents of the bouquet vary.

MOUSSE: A pâté, terrine, or mold made of smooth, pureed farce to which gelatin, whipped cream, and/or egg is added. A mousse can be sweet or savory and served hot or cold.

MOUSSELINE: A smooth, pureed farce usually containing cream and/or aspic.

PANADA: An egg, bread, flour, potato, or rice mixture used to lighten and bind ingredients together.

PÂTÉ: A farce encased in pastry, baked, and usually served cold.

PEEWEE EGG: A category of eggs (in their shells) weighing 15 ounces per dozen.

RAFT: The crust of ingredients that floats to the top of a stock during clarification.

RILLETTE: Classically defined as seasoned meat mixed with fat, shredded or pounded into a paste, and potted in a crock. Today rillette also is made of fish, vegetables, cheeses, or nuts.

RILLONS: Small cubes of seasoned cooked meat sealed with fat in a crock; they sometimes are made of fish.

SALPICON: Finely diced meat, fish, or vegetables bound with a gravy or sauce. Commonly used as a filling for puff pastry or timbales.
TERRINE: A crustless pâté cooked in an earthenware, china, or metal mold lined with fat. Usually served cold. Also the name of the mold.
TIMBALE: A small pâté or terrine cooked in a dariole or timbale mold.
TITI SHRIMP: A category of tiny shrimp with a count of 75 to 120 shrimp to the pound. They are available frozen or canned.
TORTE: A savory filling encased in a round pastry crust.
VOL-AU-VENT: A large puff pastry shell or patty usually encasing a sauced filling.

INDEX